The iMac Book

Don Rittner

Foreword by Guy Kawasaki

Publisher
Keith Weiskamp

Acquisitions Editor
Stephanie Wall

Marketing Specialist
Diane Enger

Project Editor
Dan Young

Technical Reviewer
Nancy Benz

Production Coordinator
Wendy Littley

Layout Design
April Nielsen

Cover Design
Jody Winkler

The iMac Book

Limits Of Liability And Disclaimer Of Warranty

The author and publisher of this book have used their best efforts in preparing the book and the programs contained in it. These efforts include the development, research, and testing of the theories and programs to determine their effectiveness. The author and publisher make no warranty of any kind, expressed or implied, with regard to these programs or the documentation contained in this book.

The author and publisher shall not be liable in the event of incidental or consequential damages in connection with, or arising out of, the furnishing, performance, or use of the programs, associated instructions, and/or claims of productivity gains.

Trademarks

Trademarked names appear throughout this book. Rather than list the names and entities that own the trademarks or insert a trademark symbol with each mention of the trademarked name, the publisher states that it is using the names for editorial purposes only and to the benefit of the trademark owner, with no intention of infringing upon that trademark.

The Coriolis Group, LLC.
14455 N. Hayden Road, Suite 220
Scottsdale, Arizona 85260

602/483-0192
FAX 602/483-0193
http://www.coriolis.com

Library of Congress Cataloging-in-Publication Data
Rittner, Don.
The iMac Book/by Don Rittner.
p. cm.
Includes index.
ISBN 1-57610-429-X
1. iMac (Computer). I. Title.
QA76.8.I52R58 1999
004.165--dc21 98-53324
CIP

Printed in the United States of America
10 9 8 7 6 5 4 3 2 1

Look For These Other Books From The Coriolis Group

Mac OS 8.5 Black Book

Mark Bell

The Mac OS 8.6 Book

Mark Bell

Adobe PageMill 3 f/x And Design

Daniel Gray

Dedicated to
My Very Own InnerNet

Nancy, Christopher, Kevin, Jackson,
Jennifer & Jason.

❧

About The Author

Don Rittner ordered his first Macintosh in January 1984. After receiving his Macintosh, he started the Macintosh Enthusiasts Club of the Capital Area (MECCA—Albany, New York). Today, MECCA is one of the oldest operating Mac user groups in the country.

In 1985, he became a columnist and user group editor for *Macazine*, an early national Mac magazine for Apple user groups. In 1988, he was the user group editor for *Mac Horizons*, another national Mac magazine. Over the years, Don has contributed articles for numerous national magazines, such as *MacWeek*, *Online Access*, and *MacUser*, among others. In 1988, he created MUG News Service, a computer news service that reaches half a million Mac users worldwide.

Don has published more than 12 books in areas of history, science, computers, and the Internet. He wrote his first book, *Pine Bush—Albany's Last Frontier*, in 1975, while attending the University at Albany as an undergraduate. In 1985, Don received his graduate degree from the Rensselaer Polytechnic Institute in Troy, New York. Don's eco-writing efforts and his concern for the environment are credited with helping to save more than 2,000 acres of Albany's endangered Pine Bush wilderness from development. He was also presented with the Nature Conservancy's Oak Leaf Award in 1977.

In 1992, Don wrote the first Internet book for the general public, *EcoLinking—Everyone's Guide to Online Environmental Information* (Peachpit Press), followed by *Whole Earth Online Almanac* (Brady) and *MacArcade* (Ventana). He publishes a monthly Internet magazine called *The MESH—Inside Cyberspace* (visit **www.themesh.com** for the Web version). Don currently produces and hosts a weekly radio show called *Inside The Net,* which broadcasts live in the Capital District region of New York State, and is simulcast on the Internet at **www.wrow.com**.

Don is also the president of The Learning Factory, a unique education center in Albany, New York.

Acknowledgments

I have been a Macintosh user for 15 years. To this day, I am still amazed at how helpful the Mac community is to new beginners and old-timers. Many people unselfishly share their talents and spend hours of time giving out advice and sharing their experiences so that others avoid the pitfalls of computing. Many people have shared their knowledge and helped me in the preparation of this book. I thank the following people for their contributions:

Aron Suzuk, Andrew Welch, Bill Kane, Brenda Tupper, Brian Breslin, Brock Kyle, Cabel Sasser, Chris Kidwell, Chris Silverberg, Darren Seay, David Tiberio, Erik J. Barzeski, Eric Dahlinger, Gareth Anderson, Gideon Greenspan, Greg Nye, J. Zack, Jason Pierce, Jayme Curtis, Jeff Mangels, Jeremiah L. Glodoveza, Joe Ryan, John A. Vink, John Allsopp, John C. Mozena, John Stiles, Joseph C. Lee, Joseph M. Saul, Kelly Crowe, Laini Nance, Lucas Roebuck, Matthew M. Linton, Michael Yee, Mike Fahrion, Mike Kubovcik, Peter Li, Phil Shapiro, Rolf Braun, Ron Lichty, Scott J. Kleper, Scott William, Sean McBride, Shawn King, Stephanie Da Silva, Steve Chamberlin, Sue Nail, Thorsten Lemke, and to those I inadvertently left out, my apologies.

Special thanks to Joe Lee for letting me use his photo (Figure 1.1) of the inside panel of the iMac. Joe's iMac button is the little plastic reset button to the right of the picture.

To Roger Gibbs and Franklin Tessler for being there every Saturday.

To Christopher, Kevin, and Jackson for putting up with those long nights and still having a hug for me when I needed it.

To the wonderful people at The Coriolis Group. I especially thank Stephanie Wall for accepting this book proposal and having such a great attitude. To Ann Waggoner Aken, a brief but pleasant stint as editor, and to Kristine Simmons, who tried to make sense of what I was typing. To Diane Enger, for ensuring that everyone knows that the book is available. To Wendy Littley, for making sure that the text was laid out perfectly. To April Nielsen for the iMac Book's brilliant design. To Jody Winkler for the hard work on the creative cover design. Special thanks to Paula Kmetz for keeping an eye on the big picture.

Special thanks to my project editor Dan Young, who besides being a great guy, continues to help save wildlife in Arizona.

To Margot Maley for finding The Coriolis Group for me, and to Nancy M. Benz for making sure all those URLs had a place to go!

Last, but certainly not least, to my friend Guy Kawasaki, for convincing so many developers in the early 1980s to write software for this computer we all have come to love.

Foreword

When Don asked me to write the foreword for The iMac Book, I was thrilled. If you know me, you know I love the Mac! Much of my earlier life was spent evangelizing about the Mac, then a new computer, and letting others know about the great benefits of this easy-to-use personal computer. The only computers on the streets in those days were not user-friendly at all. You had to read massive manuals, refer to instructions and passwords, and know secret codes and handshakes on a daily basis. Office assistants had notes written all over their hands so that they wouldn't forget what to do next.

The Mac became the answer for a lot of people, especially those with a creative bent—and those who wanted to get a job done without worrying about C: prompts. Fellow Mac users have told me time and time again that they never cracked their Mac tutorials because the desktop and menus were so user-friendly.

In 1988, I met Don, a young, creative individual with a lot of talent. He was a fellow Mac evangelist at a national Apple user group conference. The Mac was perfect for him—an environmentalist, archaeologist, educator, and researcher.

He had started the first Mac users group in Albany, New York, and asked me if I would talk to his user group about a software company that I was running at the time. That was also the year Don created MUG News Service, a computer news service just for Mac User Group editors.

It was a great service for software developers (like me), and user group editors loved it because they received lots of great articles for their newsletter and special offers by a sponsoring company. I was Don's first sponsor of MUG News!

Don went on to write his first Net book, *EcoLinking- Everyone's Guide to Online Information* (Peachpit Press 1992). He wanted to link the worldwide environmental community via the Internet. That same year I wrote *Selling the Dream - How to Promote Your Product, Company, or Ideas - And Make a Difference - Using Everyday Evangelism* (HarperCollins Publishers, 1992). We both wanted to change the world.

Now (and how appropriate, just before the upcoming millennium), we have the iMac!

The iMac is revolutionary. It's cool. It's fast. And using Sherlock, you can search the entire Internet from your desktop. These and many more incredible features are built into its sleek design, and it is available in a multitude of colors, too. But most importantly, fifteen years after the release of the first Mac, the iMac is still very easy to use, sporting the same smiling operating system that Mac users have come to love!

Don's book shows you how to use the iMac for fun and as a research tool. It directs you to thousands of software programs and hundreds of Web sites that will give you the latest and greatest goodies for your iMac. It uncovers Web sites for technical support and shows you how to connect and communicate with fellow iMac users from around the world. There is a wealth of information packed in this book for you and your kids!

This book is like the iMac itself: it's easy to use. It's written in a nontechnical style especially for new computer users. If this is your first computer, welcome to the Macintosh Revolution!

Happy reading, and "Think Different"!

Guy Kawasaki
CEO, garage.com
Author of *Rules for Revolutionaries*

Contents At A Glance

Table Of Contents

Introduction

Rittner's Computer Law: The Macintosh is not a computer. It's a way of life.

A Computer Or A Change In Lifestyle?

Congratulations on owning the most powerful and coolest-looking personal computer of all time—the Apple iMac.

You are now a member of the growing Macintosh community, which consists of artists, scientists, teachers, homemakers, students, musicians, writers, and any other professional you can name. The Macintosh is an equal opportunity computing platform. It's truly the computer for the "rest of us" who "Think Different."

Apple's new iMac is an innovative and powerful personal computer. It's part of the same "Macintosh Revolution" that turned the computer industry on its head in 1984 and now repeats that feat as we enter the new millennium. The iMac is faster, less expensive, and technologically superior to earlier Macs, but the familiar, legendary easy-to-use operating system—the one that smiles at you when it starts—is still there.

With your new iMac, this book, and an inexpensive Internet connection, you have a powerful education and research tool, or you can simply play games and have a great time. Beneath the sleek design of the iMac lies a specially designed computer to help you become part of the Net generation—to become an integral part of the ever-growing Internet, a worldwide network of people and information that is available 24 hours a day, 7 days a week. This book will show you how to get on the Internet and how to explore its full potential.

It's true that there are more Windows-based personal computers than Macintosh computers—no question—but there are also more people driving Ford cars than Mercedes Benz cars. No one argues which ride is the best! The measure of how well a computer performs is whether it gets the work done, it doesn't need repairs every other week, it is easy to learn to use, and it has the right software to do the job. The iMac performs in the top of its class in all areas. Twenty-five million Mac users can't be wrong.

What's In The Book?

This book is not a technical treatment on the inner workings of the iMac microprocessor, although you are directed to Internet sites that have all the technical information you could ever desire. This book is written in nontechnical language for the beginning computer user.

I have not written everything there is about your iMac or the Internet. That would require thousands of pages and a heftier price tag. After all, much of the excitement of owning a new computer is the adventure in learning how to use it. Apple has done a great job in supplying tutorials and help files that will answer many of your questions. This book is meant to supplement that information, not rewrite or replace it.

I assume you have unpacked your iMac and already spent time familiarizing yourself with some of the basic features and operations of the iMac. I also assume you are brand-new to computers or you are coming over from the Windows PC world for the first time.

To give you a solid foundation on the operation of the iMac and the Internet, the 10 chapters of this book will cover the following areas.

Chapter 1—The iMac And You

Chapter 1 presents an overview of your iMac hardware and system. It discusses various options on adding peripherals such as removable media, printers, scanners, and other hardware support. You will learn how the iMac operating system works, how to increase memory, how the software works, and how to expand the iMac's capabilities in the future.

Chapter 2—Getting Online

Chapter 2 will introduce you to the Internet, the global network that connects more than 100 million people around the world. You will learn how to get your iMac ready to "surf" the Net and what hardware and software you need to get online. Internet tools such as email, FTP, Telnet, and Web browsers are explained. Find out whether you need a local or national Internet provider. When you are done with this chapter, you will know how to navigate the Net and find information on any subject that interests you.

Chapter 3—Usenet: The News Network

The Internet is not the only computer network that connects to the world citizenry. Usenet is a global distributed news network that rides over the Internet. It connects you to millions of people who discuss thousands of topics on a daily basis. If you are looking for dialog with like-minded people on any topic from aspirin to zoology, Usenet is the place to be. This chapter explains the proper use of Usenet and how it differs from the Internet.

Chapter 4— Netiquette: How To Communicate On The Internet

The Internet is multi-cultural. It reaches people in more than 170 countries, and it's easy to offend someone if you don't know the rules. A code of civil behavior has developed on the Net, and this chapter explains the proper use of this online etiquette. This is an importance chapter. You might want to read it twice.

Chapter 5—iMac Resources: Internet Mailing Lists

Once you are online, you will find that your email account is a ticket to subscribe to thousands of electronic newsletters and mailing lists—online discussions with millions of people on more than 80,000 topics. This chapter explains what a mailing list is, how to subscribe to one, and how to create your own for free.

Chapter 6—iMac Resources: Ezines, Web Sites, News, and Chat

Along with newsletters and mailing lists are hundreds of online magazines that you can read monthly or even have delivered to your virtual mailbox. Find iMac-specific Web sites for keeping up on the latest developments or support. Learn how to chat live with friends, family, or total strangers from around the world using online chat rooms or special chat software programs.

Chapter 7—Using Your iMac For Research

The iMac and the Internet are a powerful combination for gathering information. Learn how to use Net search engines and Apple's Sherlock and get access to specialized databases, online libraries, and much more.

Chapter 8—Feed Your iMac: How To Get Tons Of Free, Not So Free, And Commercial Software

Thousands of software programs that will run on your iMac are available for free or low cost. This chapter will show you how to find those Web sites where you can download software directly to your iMac. Need to purchase a commercial program? Want to read a review before you buy it? Find out where to download a demo or purchase from the best Mac mail-order companies online. Learn how to protect yourself from computer viruses.

Chapter 9—Technical Support And Maintenance For Your iMac

Learn the most common problems associated with your iMac and how to correct them. This chapter will point you to many online tech support Web sites that will help you if you get into trouble. Learn how to troubleshoot your iMac and the best maintenance tips for keeping your iMac healthy and sound.

Chapter 10—Having Fun With Your iMac

The iMac is designed for fun and entertainment too! Hundreds of games are available to you for downloading from the Net and playing online. This chapter will show you where they are and how to keep informed about the latest release or upgrade of your favorite game.

I have done my best to make this book a non-technical introduction to the iMac and the Internet and avoid computer jargon whenever possible. I give you the basic facts about the iMac: how to use it and how to get on the Internet with a minimum amount of fuss. This book is for those who may feel intimidated by computers or the Internet or people who have a working knowledge of computers and chose the iMac as their first computer purchase. This book is not the final or complete source of information on the iMac. It will not cover every technical issue, troubleshoot every problem, or teach you how to use every inch of the iMac or its software.

Once you are up and running on the Net, you will have the ability to get answers to any questions you have. You will have access to some of the best Macintosh minds and tools on the Internet. If you are an old-time Mac user, you can simply skip Chapter 1. The rest of the book will provide you with a great deal of reference material, however.

Throughout this book, I direct you to a variety of resources on the Internet for making your computing experience a pleasant and productive one. I also have created an area on my Web site, The MESH—Inside Cyberspace (**www.themesh.com/imac**), that links many of these resources. Feel free to use it, and let me know how it can be improved. You can reach me at drittner@wizvax.net or themesh@global2000.net.

On A Personal Note

During March 1976, I was busy preparing plans for the upcoming summer "dig." As the city archeologist for Albany, New York, I decided to continue work on two 17th and 18th century tavern sites that we had begun excavating located along a 300-year-old colonial road. The road bisected the famous Albany Pine Barrens, or "Pine Bush," a unique natural area of endangered plants and animals. A number of us environmental "activists" were trying to save the Pine Bush from becoming pavement from shopping malls and building lots.

On the other side of the continent, Steve Wozniak and Steve Jobs were finishing work on a computer circuit board that they called the Apple I computer. I had never heard of Jobs or Wozniak, nor did I know that what they started would have a profound effect on how I would work and think almost a decade later.

Early one morning in late January 1984, I had pulled an all-nighter, reconstructing on paper one of my colonial tavern sites, brick by brick. I decided to go to the local plaza for breakfast and then take a walk, during which I encountered a small computer store. In the window was a squarish beige box with a row of bricks across the front screen. I wondered out loud how I could draw that brick wall because I had been up all night attempting to make one look half as good. You probably guessed by now that I was looking at a Macintosh computer—the first Macintosh computer. The computer store had just received it. I entered the store, and without the assistance of anyone (some things never change), I reconstructed one of my colonial tavern sites within minutes. I ordered my first Mac 10 minutes later. I had to wait a month to get it. Each store was allotted only one per month.

Every original Mac user has a similar story about his or her first Mac. I suppose it's similar to remembering the first time you heard a Beatles song if you're a baby boomer. Some things just have that kind of effect on you.

Life was certainly fine before I owned a Mac, but there is no doubt that owning a Macintosh over the last 15 years has made my life a whole lot more interesting, productive, and positive. It certainly made my environmental work and research easier during the 1980s. I'm not trying to be religious about it, but to many people who saw the personal computer as an empowerment tool, it sure was an exciting time. Remember, this was the *beginning* of the personal computer revolution!

Today, it seems anyone under the age of 20 considers a personal computer nothing more than a large Walkman or a place to check movie reviews. Even to my seven-year-old son, it's just another "thing" for playing games and sending email to his friends around the world. Even revolutions can lose their edge of excitement, I suppose.

When you realize that a good refrigerator costs more than an iMac, it's safe to say that personal computers are here to stay, regardless of whether you think they have changed the world. I know Steve Jobs and company have changed the world. I also know that some of us Mac users saved a few thousand acres of endangered wilderness. Mac folks not only *Think Different*, but also they *act different*.

I don't know why you bought your iMac, but I do know that someday, you will say it was one of the wisest things you ever did.

Don Rittner
Schenectady, N.Y.
January 1, 1999

1 The iMac And You

Rittner's Computer Law: Digital wisdom is made of recycled electrons that are meaningful until you pull the plug.

iMac—The Computer

The iMac was released in August 1998, and this innovative, 21st century, multi-colored, translucent computer was a hit right from the start. Apple Computer sold 800,000 iMacs in its first 16 weeks. It's not surprising, considering the iMac is easy to set up (less than 20 minutes) and inexpensive, and contains the latest computer technology all in one integrated unit. It also comes fully loaded with a nice assortment of software.

Apple has released three models of the iMac. They all look identical. The original model, M6709LL/A, was released in August 1998. The second model, M6709LL/B, was released shortly after to address some initial shortcomings of the first. Apple released 5 new models in January 1999 which had a larger hard drive, lower cost, faster processor, and a choice of five colors. These models **M7389LL/A iMac—Strawberry**, **M7392LL/A iMac—Lime**, **M7391LL/A iMac—Tangerine**, **M7390LL/A iMac—Grape**, **M7345LL/A iMac—Blueberry**, are all identical in features, the only difference being the color.

The first two models of iMac have a lightning-fast PowerPC G3 microprocessor running at 233MHz. The newer 1999 models have a PowerPC G3 microprocessor running at 266MHz. In plain English, you have a pretty snappy computer. It's fast!

The iMac is also the first Mac to have a Universal Serial Bus (USB), a high-speed connection that lets you easily attach peripherals without powering down the computer. You can attach many third-party printers, scanners, digital cameras, graphic pads, game pads, joysticks, and storage devices such as Superdisks or Zip drives on the USB. Simply plug

Megahertz

Megahertz is a measure of a computer microprocessor's clock speed. The higher the number, the faster your computer performs its tasks. Computer companies like to use clock speed the way auto companies promote the top speed of their cars. It's nice to have the speed, but if you're only driving to church on Sundays, well....

Stop Looking (For Old Mac Users)

USB replaced Apple's Serial, ADB, and SCSI ports. These three ports are not on the iMac.

them in. There are currently over 100 USB devices being advertised for the iMac.

If you have two iMacs or another PowerMac model at home or work, connect them quickly into your own network with built-in Ethernet networking. No hubs required. All you need is a special crossover cable that costs less than $20. On each computer, plug each end of the crossover cable into the Ethernet ports, access the AppleTalk control panel from the Apple menu, and select Ethernet Built-in.

Belkin Products (**www.belkin.com**) has several lengths of crossover cables:

- A3X126-08-5 Crossover Cable, 8' UPC: 7-22868-15114-3
- A3X126-10-5 Crossover Cable, 10' UPC: 7-22868-14174-8
- A3X126-15-5 Crossover Cable, 15' UPC: 7-22868-15064-1

If you are a student, jack into the Net from your dorm room.

Your iMac has a speedy internal modem for dial-up connections and can connect at a rate of 56,000 bits per second. However, the built-in high-speed Ethernet is ready to put you on the Net even faster when the emerging ADSL (Asymmetric Digital Subscriber Line) or cable modem reaches your area. FAXstf software allows you to send and receive faxes with your internal modem.

Bits And Bytes

- 1 bit (b) = A binary 1 or 0
- 1 kilobit per second (Kbps) = 1,024 bits per second
- 1 megabit per second (Mbps) = 1,048,576 bits per second
- 1 gigabit per second (Gbps) = 1,073,741,824 bits per second
- 8 bits = 1 byte (B)
- 1,024 bytes = 1 kilobyte
- 1,024 kilobytes (KB) = 1 megabyte
- 1,024 megabytes (MB) = 1 gigabyte
- 1,024 gigabytes (GB) = 1 terabyte

That Ain't Music I Hear

If you hear a high-speed whirl when you put in a certain CD, check the top of the CD. If it features a lot of artwork, the extra weight of the CD makes the drive work harder. Apple has a CD update that will deal with this. Be sure to install it. To download the update, go to Apple's Web site (**http://asu.info.apple.com**).

The CD Is A Snap

Make sure you snap down the CD when you put it in the CD-ROM drive until you hear a click. If you haven't already, install the CD-ROM firmware update available from Apple's support page (**www.apple.com/imac**).

Bits (little b's) refer to the speed of data communications transferred in seconds across two communication points. Bytes (big B's) refer to the amount of memory in a computer or storage capacity such as on a hard drive.

The built-in high-resolution monitor and 2D/3D graphic acceleration deliver superb resolution for crystal-clear graphics. You can control the height, width, and orientation of your screen display using software controls.

ADJUSTABLE SCREEN SIZE: *If you don't like that black border around the monitor, you can increase the width and height of your screen by accessing the Monitors and Sound control panel, selecting geometry, and then using the icons to the right and bottom of the screen icon.*

A 24x-speed CD-ROM drive located in the front of the iMac gives you quick access to software, games, and information.

The original iMac, Model A, came bundled with Mac OS 8.1 and several software programs for productivity and Internet connectivity. Model B and older models of the iMac include Mac OS 8.5, Adobe PageMill for Web design, and some hardware improvements in graphic handling. The newer 1999 iMacs include *World Book* and *EdView Internet Safety Kit, Family Edition*, as shown in Tables 1.1 and 1.2.

Your software package should include:

- A trial version of EarthLink TotalAccess, a national Internet Service Provider.
- ClarisWorks 5.0, an integrated program that includes a word processor, a spreadsheet, communications, painting and drawing accessories, and a database.
- FAXstf for turning your modem into a fax machine.
- Kai's Photo Soap SE for cleaning up your digital photos.
- Outlook Express, an email and Usenet newsreader application.
- Quicken Deluxe 98 to take care of personal finance.
- Two Internet browsers, Microsoft Internet Explorer and Netscape Navigator.

- The Williams-Sonoma Guide to Good Cooking, giving you a good reason to put the iMac in the kitchen.
- Two games, Nanosaur and MDK, for some shoot-`em-up entertainment.

Table 1.1 1998 Models A and B iMac configurations.

Configuration of the iMac	M6709LL/A	M6709LL/B
System software	OS 8.1	OS 8.5
OS updates	Install 8.5 or 8.51	Install 8.51
Display	15" CRT (13.8" viewable)	15" CRT (13.8" viewable)
PowerPC G3 processor	233MHz	233MHz
Backside cache	512K, Level 2	512K, Level 2
System bus speed	66MHz	66MHz
4GB IDE hard drive	Yes	Yes
24X CD-ROM drive	Yes	Yes
Internal modem	56K (v.90)	56K (v.90)
Modem firmware*	1.0	1.0 or 1.0.2
Video		
SGRAM	2MB	6MB **
Resolution		
640x480 at 117Hz	24 bits	24 bits
800x600 at 95Hz	24 bits	24 bits
1024x768 at 85Hz	16 bits	24 bits
System Memory		
32MB SODIMM SDRAM (expandable to 128MB or more by third-party manufacturers)	Yes	Yes
Graphics		
Graphics controller	ATI Rage IIc	ATI Rage ProTurbo
Networking		
Ethernet (10/100 base-T)	Yes	Yes
Universal Serial Bus (USB) ports (12Mbps)	2 ports	2 ports
Infrared technology (IrDA) port (4Mbps)	Yes	Yes
Audio		
Built-in Stereo Speakers with SRS sound	Yes	Yes

(continued)

Table 1.1 1998 Models A and B iMac configurations (continued).

Configuration of the iMac	M6709LL/A	M6709LL/B
Microphone	Yes	Yes
2 Headphone jacks	Yes	Yes
1 Line-in mini-jack	Yes	Yes
1 Line-out mini-jack	Yes	Yes
Peripherals		
Apple USB keyboard	Yes	Yes
Mouse	Yes	Yes
Floppy drive	No	No

**Note: If modem irregularities are reported, make sure modem version 1.0.2 is installed. The modem updater is located in the CD Extras folder on the Mac OS system software CD.*

***4MB SGRAM DIMM is installed on the logic board. Video memory is not upgradable.*

In January 1999, Apple released a new model of the iMac in five designer colors with the following specifications as shown in Table 1.2.

Table 1.2 1999 iMac configurations.

Configuration of the iMac. (Different model numbers represent different colors. All of the machines are configured identically.)	M7389LL/A iMac—Strawberry, M7392LL/A iMac—Lime, M7391LL/A iMac—Tangerine, M7390LL/A iMac—Grape, M7345LL/A iMac—Blueberry
System software	OS 8.5
Display	15" CRT (13.8" viewable)
PowerPC G3 processor	266MHz
Backside cache	512K, Level 2
System bus speed	66MHz
6GB IDE hard drive	Yes
24X CD-ROM drive	Yes
Internal modem	56K (v.90)
SGRAM (up to 128MB)	6MB
Resolution	
640x480 at 117Hz	24 bits
800x600 at 95Hz	24 bits
1024x768 at 85Hz	24 bits

(continued)

Table 1.2 1999 iMac configurations (continued).

Configuration of the iMac. (Different model numbers represent different colors. All of the machines are configured identically.)	M7389LL/A iMac—Strawberry, M7392LL/A iMac—Lime, M7391LL/A iMac—Tangerine, M7390LL/A iMac—Grape, M7345LL/A iMac—Blueberry
System Memory	
32MB SODIMM SDRAM (expandable to 128MB or more by third-party manufacturers)	Yes
Graphics	
Graphics controller	ATI Rage Pro Turbo
Networking	
Ethernet (10/100 base-T)	Yes
Universal Serial Bus (USB) ports (12Mbps)	2 ports
Infrared technology (IrDA) port (4Mbps)	No
Audio	
Built-in Stereo Speakers with SRS sound	Yes
Microphone	Yes
2 Headphone jacks	Yes
1 Line-in mini-jack	Yes
1 Line-out mini-jack	Yes
Peripherals	
Apple USB keyboard	Yes
Mouse	Yes
Floppy drive	No

Software includes: AppleWorks, Microsoft Internet Explorer, Microsoft Outlook Express, Netscape Navigator, Adobe PageMill, TotalAccess, EdView Internet Safety Kit, Family Edition, FAXstf, Quicken for Macintosh Deluxe 98, Photo Soap SE, World Book Macintosh Edition, Nanosaur, Williams-Sonoma Guide to Good Cooking.

Making The Right Connections

Hooking up your iMac couldn't be easier. Connect the keyboard to the iMac, the mouse to the keyword, and a power cord to the wall. How's that for simplicity?

You make the connections to other peripherals in a recessed area through the hinged door on the right side of your iMac. It has a large circular hole. You put your forefinger through the hole. Your thumb rests on top of the iMac exterior, above the finger, for resistance. Pull the door down and away. Do not pull too hard as you can pull the door right off the iMac (yes, I did it).

A common mistake people make is running their phone lines or USB cables through the hole. Nope, that's for your fingers. Look at the bottom of the door. There are cutout areas on both sides of the door for your cords to come through.

This panel is the control center to the outside, as shown in Figure 1.1.

Turn your iMac to the side so you can look directly into the recessed area that contains all your connections to networking, the Internet, and audio:

- Sound in and out for microphone or external speakers.
- Type A ports for USB connections. One is already filled by your keyboard.

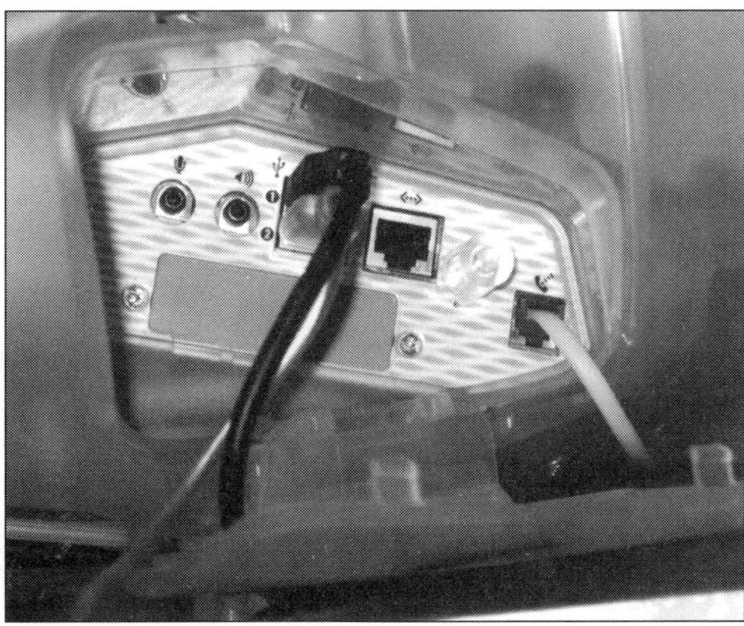

Figure 1.1
This diagram from Joseph Lee shows the iMac connection ports.

- 10/100 base-T Ethernet. If you have access to faster Net service that requires Ethernet (such as Time Warner's Road Runner service), you will plug it in here.
- The reset button. If you have the Model A iMac, the reset key combination does not work, so you can use a straightened-out paper clip to restart your iMac by pushing one end here. You can also purchase an innovative reset button from iMacButton (**www.imacbutton.com**) for around $10, as shown in Figure 1.1. If you have Model B or a later model of the iMac, the button on your monitor will act as a reset switch.
- The programmers button. Leave it alone unless you're a programmer.
- Modem port. This is where you connect your telephone line into the internal iMac modem so you can get on the Internet.
- The rectangular box on the bottom was rumored to be for future expansion by Apple. Apple, however, denied it and with the newer models of iMac, the slot is gone.

Beam Me Up, Scotty

You will notice on the front of your iMac (Models A and B), to the right of the left speaker (the Bondi blue perforated oblong), is an egg-shaped dark piece of plastic. This is your infrared transmitter and receiver. What do you do with it? If you have another device such as a PowerBook that has a compatible infrared protocol, you can beam files back and forth without plugging in anything.

This infrared unit transmits infrared light in a 30-degree radius, broad-casting away from the computer. Apple recommends a minimum distance between beaming devices of three feet for proper connectivity. That's not good enough for the *Enterprise*! According to Apple, the iMac sends files using the IrDA (Infrared Data Association) protocol. This protocol transmits data up to 4MB per second and can use AppleTalk and TCP/IP protocols. The iMac infrared port is compatible with several of Apple's PowerBook computers, including the PowerBook 2400, 3400, and G3 and PowerBook G3 Series computers, but not my trusty old PowerBook 5300 or the PowerBook 190 and 1400. Apple says other infrared-capable Apple products are not compatible because they use a different infrared lens and transmitter.

Quite frankly, I don't see a big need for this technology at the present time, unless you do a lot of traveling and you carry a PowerBook that is IrDA-compatible. On the other hand, with real time video just around the corner, maybe I can use my TV remote to channel surf, as I do with my regular TV.

Based on the success of USB, Apple has decided that for desktop computers, it will focus on USB as the way devices connect and has removed the infrared device from the new iMacs released after Model B.

Music To My Ears?

In front of your iMac are two Bondi blue stereo speakers: one on the left with the infrared receiver, and one on the right with two jacks for headphones. The stereo-realistic sound from SRS (Sound Retrieval System) Labs can be disabled in the Memory and Sounds control panel, but why would you do that? SRS produces a nice stereo effect.

You can add an external Plaintalk microphone by plugging it in the sound-in jack located in the panel on the right side of the iMac. It has a picture of a microphone. The built-in microphone on the top of the iMac (the small vertical slit in the middle) may be too far away for dictation software when it becomes available for the iMac.

You can hook up external speakers using the sound-out port next to the sound-in port. I have a nice set of LabTec's (**www.labtec.com**) LC 1030 speakers.

Updaters

Since the release of the iMac, Apple has released a few software updaters primarily for Models A and B of the iMac, as shown in Table 1.3. You should download them and update your iMac to ensure it will work properly. All of these updates can be downloaded from Apple's support page (**http://asu.info.apple.com**). Read each README file that comes with an update to see if it is for your model of iMac.

Table 1.3 iMac updates.

Release Name	Version	Release Date
iMac Update	1.0	09/02/98
iMac Firmware Update	1.0	12/17/98
iMac Update	1.1	12/17/98
iMac CD Update	1.0	09/11/98
iMac Internal 56k Modem Script	1.0	08/25/98
Apple System Profiler	2.1.2	10/21/98
Apple Spec Database	8/98	08/19/98
Apple Spec Database	8/98	08/19/98
Apple Modem Updater U.S.	1.2.1	10/16/98
Mac OS Update	8.1	03/02/98

Periodically check Apple's Updates page (**http://asu.info.apple.com**) for new software updates for your iMac.

That Little Green Light

The little green light on your iMac next to the right speaker lets you know that your iMac is on and working. If the light is amber, it means:

1. You just started your iMac. The light will remain amber until the screen appears (gray at first).
2. Your iMac is sleeping.
3. You just woke it up.
4. There is a video hardware problem. Not good!

If you have Model B or a later version of the iMac, it does even more.

- If the system is off, it will turn on.
- If the system is asleep, it will wake up and present the Shutdown dialog box.
- If the system is on and running, it will present the Shutdown dialog box.
- If the system is in a hung (frozen) state, it will power down the system automatically. This may take up to 7 seconds to complete.

What Can I Attach To My iMac?

You can literally connect hundreds of devices to your iMac thanks to the new Universal Serial Bus. However, don't throw away those old serial or SCSI devices just yet.

Universal Serial Bus

USB, or Universal Serial Bus, is a new iMac solution for attaching peripherals to your computer. You can quickly connect scanners; digital cameras; printers; modems; keyboards; mice; joysticks; graphics tablets; floppy and hard drives; removable storage drives such as Zip, Iomega, and the new Superdisks; and a host of other devices directly to your iMac. You can do this without turning off your computer, configuring IDs, sticking in cards, cussing, or other nuisances. As soon as you plug in a device, the iMac recognizes the device's software driver and loads it.

USB also has a faster data transfer rate, up to 12 megabits per second, than previous peripheral connections. Bit rate is explained in the next chapter, but briefly, it is the speed at which data is transferred between peripherals in a second, over a network or through a modem to the Net. Apple's two earlier ports, Serial and the Apple Desktop Bus (ADB), had slower data transfer rates: Serial transferred 230 kilobits per second, and the ADB poked along at 10 kilobits per second. Also gone with the iMac is the SCSI (Small Computer Serial Interface) connection that was used to plug devices such as external hard drives, scanners, and the like, to your Mac. Each of these connections had different speeds and requirements, and although it wasn't difficult to connect devices, it could take a little time, and if you really screwed up, you could fry your motherboard. You were also limited to how many devices you could attach to your Mac. SCSI, for example, maxed out at seven devices.

USB allows you to attach up to 127 devices to your iMac without turning it off. You install the driver software for each device. Take one end of the inexpensive USB cable and plug it in (called hot swapping) to your iMac or a USB hub. It's that simple. The device is automatically configured when your iMac recognizes it has been attached.

Several third-party peripherals use the USB and are ready for the iMac. Ric Ford (**www.macintouch.com/imacusb.html**) has a list of USB devices ready for the iMac.

Connecting More Than Two USB Devices

Connect your iMac to hundreds of inexpensive devices using simple plug-and-play USB.

Hubs

Although USB can support up to 127 devices at once, you obviously don't have that many USB ports on your iMac. You have four USB ports. After you plug in your keyboard and mouse, you have one free USB port left on the keyboard and one on your iMac.

To daisy chain USB devices, you have to connect to a device that is classified as a hub—your iMac or keyboard is a hub—or an actual standalone hub, a device that has four or more USB ports. Hubs can then be cascaded (connected) to each other. Hubs can draw from the power of the USB itself or a separate power supply. There are a number of hubs available for the iMac from third-party companies.

The USB Quad Hub Kit From Peracom

This four-port hub can be connected to four more hubs, giving you 20 connections. It is powered by the bus or a separate power supply, and each port is individually controlled and powered. The kit retails for around $80. Visit Peracom's Web site (**www.peracom.com**) for more information.

Entrega Technologies USB Hubs

Entrega has a 4-port and 7-port hub for $79.95 and $129.95. The hub is color matched to the iMac and can be connected to more than one. Entrega's Web site is **www.entrega.com**.

See Apple's Web site at **http://www.apple.com/usb/usbproducts.html** for a listing of over 100 USB devices of the iMac.

High-Speed Peripherals

As of this writing, rumor has it that there is a hidden port called the Mezzanine in the underbelly of the iMac motherboard that might support Firewire-compatible peripherals. However, Apple removed it in Model B and later versions of the iMac. Apple's official word on it is this: "The Mezzanine connector was used during the development and manufacture of iMac. It is no longer needed and therefore has been removed from the iMac 266 logic board. Apple has never spoken of any product plans in conjunction with this connector and discouraged any developer planning to take advantage of it."

Firewire is a hot-swappable, fast serial data bus. Firewire allows the quick transfer of huge amounts of realtime digital data, up to 50MB per second, into a computer from devices such as video camcorders, music systems, digital video disks, and so on. It is designed to replace SCSI, the previous standard that was used to connect external hard drives, CD-ROM drives, and the like.

Firewire was developed at Apple Computer, and in 1997, the Mac OS was the first operating system to adopt it, but now, it is an industry-accepted technology, and that means any computer platform can use it.

If the rumors are true that the Model A iMac can use this port, it opens all kinds of expansion capabilities for the iMac. Some third-party companies have advertised making products for use with this port. You can read about these developments if you visit the many iMac-specific Web sites or subscribe to Mac mailing lists and electronic magazines. You will learn about these resources later in this book.

Take Me To The Mezzanine

If you're in a hurry, here are some Web sites that have stories about the Mezzanine. (You will learn about these Web addresses in the next chapter.)

- *MacWeek* article—**http://205.181.112.131/1232/mezzanine.html**
- *MacNews Network*—**www.macnn.com/imac/mezzanine/shtml**
- *Mactimes*—**www.mactimes.com/features/staff1998.html**
- CERN technical Information—**wwwinfo.cern.ch/ce/ms/mezzanines/pmc-top.html**

Remember, if you have Model B or later versions of the iMac, forget it. Apple took the Mezzanine slot out!

No Floppy?

Apple was criticized at first for having no floppy drive with the iMac. It was pure genius, in my opinion. With the popularity of removable media such as Iomega's Zip and Jazz drives or Syquest's removable drives, the floppy's days are numbered. It did have a great run, though. The first floppy was built in 1968 by IBM.

An enterprising person came up with a workaround for the no-floppy-to-copy problem and created a Web site that gives anyone a free 3MB virtual floppy on the Net. It's advertising supported, and you must give a credit card number. If you decide not to buy an alternative, visit the Web site **http://iMacFloppy.com** and use the service.

Reformatting A PC Superdisk

You might want to reformat a PC-formatted Superdisk to a Mac. Open your Control Panel folder and select File Exchange. Remove the mount at startup selection at the bottom of the panel by clicking it. Then, access your File Sharing control panel and turn off file sharing. Insert your PC-formatted Superdisk and open the Special menu, select Erase Disk, and choose your option. Be sure to reverse these steps when you are done.

Floppy Drive Replacement!

I have several thousand floppies of information that I have collected over the last 20 years or so. I still need access to that data once in a while. There is a solution for the no-floppy iMac.

Imation And Winstation Superdisk

Imation Corp, a spinoff of 3M's data and storage business division and Panasonic, was the first company to produce an alternative to the floppy, the Superdisk. Winstation Systems Corp, a Washington-based company, also produces a USB Superdisk for the iMac (and was the first to offer a SCSI Superdisk as well), as shown in Figure 1.2.

The Superdisk drive connects to your USB port and reads and writes PC- and Mac-formatted 1.4MB floppies and a new 120MB Superdisk, which holds the equivalent of 85 floppies. A Superdisk retails for around $15. The drive retails for around $150. Now, you know why the floppy drive will soon become an addition to the computer museum.

Imation's Web site is **www.imation.com**. Winstation's Web site is **www.winstation.com**.

Attaching A Printer To Your iMac

You certainly want to print from your iMac. If you already have a printer from an older Mac or PC, you might still be able to use it on your iMac.

Figure 1.2
The Winstation Superdisk holds the equivalent of 85 floppies.

Keyspan's USB Serial Adapter

Keyspan's adapter plugs directly into a USB port on your iMac and provides two old-style serial ports (RS-422 mini-DIN8 ports) for connecting to Mac serial devices. It supports data rates up to 115.2Kbps per port and draws its power from the USB connection, so you don't need a separate power adapter. It emulates the printer port on one of the two ports.

Keyspan's adapter is compatible with many serial devices, but it does not support MIDI, Geoport or LocalTalk, or any device that requires "external clocking of the baud rate (e.g., Connectix QuickCam camera or the Visioneer Paperport)." It is reported to disable your infrared features as well, but developers are working on a fix.

Keyspan's adapter supports certain Apple StyleWriters, Epson Stylus Color printers (300 and 500 only), and HP DeskWriters (540C, 600 Series and 800 Series). It does not support Apple StyleWriters 1500,

2200, 2400, or 2500. Other compatible devices include Wacom Tablets, Palm Pilot, Epson, Olympus, Apple, Kodak and Agfa Cameras, CoStar LabelWriters, and modems. The adapter retails for around $80. Keyspan's Web site is **www.keyspan.com**.

PowerPrint 4.5 By Infowave

PowerPrint may be the printing solution for your iMac. If you have access to any PC printer, or you want the option to purchase a wider variety of printers not currently available on the Mac side, PowerPrint is a solution.

PowerPrint is a product of Infowave Software Inc., a specialized software company with an imaging and wireless division.

PowerPrint makes it possible to print to almost any PC-compatible printer, which includes laser printers, inkjets, specialty printers, and multifunctional peripherals. PowerPrint supports more than 1,500 PC printers at the time of this writing. You can check the compatibility chart on the Web site (**http://technology.infowave.com/printer_database.html**).

PowerPrint USB actually is a suite of Macintosh printer drivers and a special USB-to-parallel cable for connecting your iMac to parallel port printers, as shown in Figure 1.3. The retail price is $99. Infowave's Web site is at **www.infowave.com**.

USB-Ready Printers

Several USB-ready printers or adapters are available from Epson and Hewlett-Packard. Ethernet-to-LocalTalk bridge adapters by Asante and Farallon allow you to use a LocalTalk printer with your iMac. Visit your local computer retailer to see them or visit their web sites:

- Epson—**http://prographics.epson.com**
- HP—**http://www.hp.com**

USB Scanners

UMAX was out the door with a USB-equipped scanner, the UMAX Astra 1220U, which retails for $179. It is a 36-bit, single-pass device with

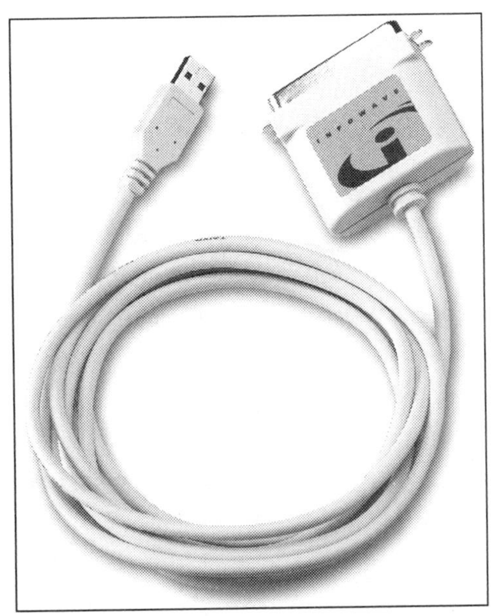

Figure 1.3
PowerPrint can connect you to more than 1,500 PC printers.

an optical resolution of 600 by 1,200 pixels and a maximum scanning area of 8.5 by 11.7 inches. You can check out the specs at the Web page (**www.umax.com/graphsite/umaxen/scanner/consumer/a1220u.cfm?scanners+Astra+1220u**).

Microtek (**www.microtek.com**) has the Microtek SlimScan C3 for around $80 and features a standard resolution of 300 x 600 pixels per inch (4,800 dpi interpolated), whereas Agfa (**www.agfahome.com**) has the 1212u for around $130 and features 600 x 1200 pixels per inch (9,600 dpi interpolated).

Besides scanning graphics, you can use your scanner to take printed documents and turn them into editable text. This is called Optical Character Reading (OCR) and most scanners bundle Caere's Omiscan (**www.caere.com**) software which is an excellent OCR program. There are others on the market like TextBridge from XEROX (**www.xerox.com**), or Olduvai's Read-It O.C.R. (**www.olduvai.com/products.html**).

Adding More Memory

Memory in your computer is called Random Access Memory (RAM). It's also temporary. When you shut off your iMac, whatever was in the RAM goes to digital heaven. Poof!

Your hard drive, floppy, Zip, or Superdisk is where your software programs reside. Your iMac accesses the software program and puts chunks of it in the RAM to work with. The more memory in your iMac, the better—the more software it can put there. Imagine RAM as a balloon. The larger the balloon, the more air it holds. Some programs require a lot of RAM to work properly; if you don't have enough RAM, you definitely will have problems. It's like trying to pour 16 ounces of water into an 8-ounce glass.

RAM is put in your iMac on little electronic cards, called modules, or DIMMs (Dual Inline Memory Module). There are many different kinds of RAM modules, and not all of them work on the iMac. The iMac works with a specific kind of RAM—SDRAM SODIMMs. SDRAM stands for Synchronized Dynamic Random Access Memory. SODIMM stands for Small Outline Dual Inline Memory Module. SDRAM describes the characteristics of the RAM, and SODIMM is the actual physical device, the little card you snap into your iMac. At the present time, SDRAM SODIMM is the only kind of RAM card you can put in your iMac. Trying to put other kinds of RAM into your iMac is asking for big trouble, not to mention voiding that one-year warranty.

There are two ways you can add memory to your iMac. You can do it yourself or have a certified Apple technician do it for you. Obviously, the latter option will cost you extra. On the other hand, if you do it yourself and fry your motherboard, you're out the cost of the iMac.

The iMac has two RAM slots, one above and one below the processor card. Each accepts SODIMMs, but the upper slot only accepts modules that are 2 inches in size, and the lower slot accepts smaller 1.5-inch modules.

Apple originally advertised that the maximum amount of memory you could have was 128MB—64MB in the upper slot and 64MB in the lower slot. However, third-party RAM makers have produced a 128MB SODIMM that will fit in the upper and lower slots, giving you a potential 384MB of RAM (256MB is a reality now). That is more than you will ever need...well, maybe.

It isn't hard to add memory to your iMac, and some iMac Web sites show you how to do it step by step. You need to justify doing it yourself. If you are relatively handy with a screwdriver, understand what static electricity is, and can afford to buy another iMac if you screw it up, then go ahead and put the memory in yourself. If you're the type of person who lifts up the hood of your car and can only locate the battery (like me), then perhaps you should spend the extra money and let a qualified technician do it. The additional cost of $30 to $50 to install more RAM is worth the knowledge that if the technician blows it, you get another iMac.

If you add memory to the upper slot by yourself, you are not voiding Apple's warranty. However, if you add memory to the bottom slot by yourself, you are voiding your warranty.

Video RAM Expansion

Your iMac also uses RAM for video display. If you own the Model A iMac, it includes 2MB of SGRAM (Synchronous Graphic RAM) for video on the main logic board. It can be expanded up to 6MB with an additional 2MB or 4MB of SGRAM on a 144-pin SODIMM. The Model B and newer iMacs have the maximum 6MB Video RAM already installed.

Increasing the size of the installed video RAM from 2MB to 4MB or 6MB increases the maximum color depth available at the highest monitor resolutions. At 6MB, you will be able to display millions of colors if your monitor is set to display 640 x 480 or even 1,024 x 768 resolution.

According to Apple, any additional video RAM that isn't used for the current display mode is made available to QuickDraw 3D applications for more data storage, such as textures, which results in faster 3D graphics performance.

Watch That Video Switching!

For owners of the Model A iMac: If you have not increased your video RAM to 6MB, do not try to change the resolution of your monitor on the fly using the control strip to the higher 1,024 x 768 number. Your screen will go blank, and you must restart your iMac to bring it back to the original resolution.

The price of memory at the present time is low, so regardless of how you install it, you should increase both computer and video RAM by as much as you can afford.

If you do want to upgrade yourself, a couple of good iMac Web sites provide step-by-step instructions, including photographs. iMac Info (**http://imac.macguys.com/ram.html#wizard**) has a great RAM guide that gives you a way to determine how much total RAM you will need. Just answer some questions, and the guide will indicate the amount of RAM you need to buy.

IMac2Day (**www.imac2day.com/tech/visualRAM.shtml**) has great visual step-by-step instructions on upgrading RAM, including video RAM if you have the Model A iMac.

Where can you get the best prices on RAM? I personally buy my RAM from The Chip Merchant, a mail-order firm in California: (800) 426-6375 Extension 3 or **www.thechipmerchant.com**. It often has the lowest prices, but I like its guarantee the best. As long as you have your receipt, you can replace any module that becomes defective—any time. I have had excellent service from them for years.

You can also check out RAM prices by consulting RamSeeker (**www.ramseeker.com**), a Web site that lists the prices of RAM offered by several online retailers.

iMac Model A Or B?

Look at the box your iMac shipped in. A sticker on it has the model number. If you purchased it new, the Model A shipped with Mac OS 8.1, and the Model B shipped with OS 8.5.

Increasing Your RAM Via Software

You can also increase your RAM without installing SODIMMs. RAM Doubler, by Connectix Corporation (**www.connectix.com**), is a software program that lets you get the most out of your physically installed RAM.

RAM Doubler handles memory more efficiently than the Apple system does, and you can actually adjust the memory increase from zero up to triple the amount you already have. Connectix and RAM Doubler have been around for a long time. The company has always produced excellent, quality software (and the famous Quickcam). If you want to increase your memory but don't feel like adding the actual real memory modules, RAM Doubler is the solution, and it is available for around $50.

Your iMac's Engine

Imagine your iMac is a Lamborghini. Your system folder is the engine. Without an engine, you can't start your car (no matter how cool it is). Without a system folder, you can't start your iMac (no matter how cool it is). It's that simple.

The operating system of the iMac, the Mac OS, as it's called, is a collection of files that work in harmony with each other to allow you to perform your creative tasks and to allow the computer to work properly. You periodically take your car to the shop and tune it up. Apple helps you do the same. Apple upgrades the system software but lets you tune it up yourself through software updates.

Instead of discussing the virtues of a particular version of the OS (8.5.1 is the most recent one as of this writing), I will talk about the operating system in general terms. There are whole books written about each version of the Mac OS. You can read all about the iMac's current System 8.5 in *The Mac OS 8.5 Black Book* by Mark Bell (The Coriolis Group), a perfect companion to this book.

As each new upgrade of the system software occurs, you should peruse the Mac tech support Web sites to see what initial problems people have and then install the upgrade if it applies to your model. Some updates may apply only to a certain problem or feature in a particular model. You can learn about the new features of any upgrade from the Mac support community or from Apple's own Web site (**www.apple.com**). As you can imagine, each new version of the Mac OS fixes bugs from previous versions and adds new functionality to your iMac.

Your system folder resides on your startup disk, your hard drive. It's the one with the smiling icon on the folder. If you double-click the folder you will see several folders and files inside. Most of them came with the iMac, but some of them you create as you install new software programs or do your work. The system folder is also where other applications store files and access them when needed. You normally should not open your system folder unless you have a problem.

Let's look at some of the more important files in the system folder, shown in Figure 1.4.

System And Finder

The System and Finder files work as a team like Batman and Robin and are the most important two files in the system folder. One cannot operate very well without the other. The Finder controls what you see on the desktop, floppies, Zip disks, and so on. The System, on the other hand, controls things such as memory, font handling, icons, sounds, starting your iMac, and other tasks. Both files must exist if your iMac is going to work. There is no need to bother them. Leave them alone, and let them do their work in peace.

Control Panels Folder

Control panels give *you* control of how you want your Mac to look. Control panels change the background color or design of your desktop,

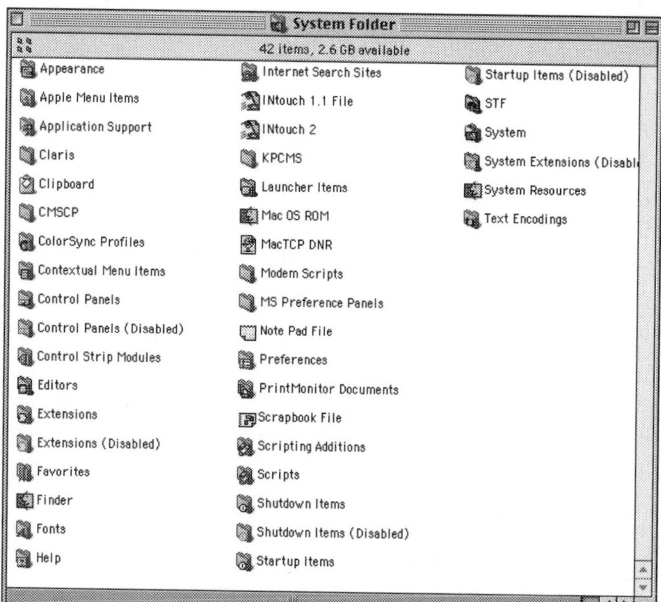

Figure 1.4
Under the "hood" of your iMac: the system folder.

make your mouse faster or slower, change the date and time, and so on. Control panels let you customize the look and feel that is right for you. You can access control panels by opening the Apple menu and selecting the control panels folder. Often, a new software program or piece of hardware comes with its own control panel to modify for working with existing programs.

Extensions Folder

Extensions, called inits (short for initialization file), are little files—software hooks—that increase the function of your system in some way, usually when you add a software program or piece of hardware. An init may contain special instructions that allow your iMac to interact with a UMAX USB Astra scanner or Casio digital camera, for example. Many software programs install inits automatically, and one of the more common problems associated with the Mac is init conflicts, in which one init may fight with another for the same space. You can turn extensions on or off using the Extensions Manager (a control panel) or holding down the spacebar when restarting your iMac. For example, if you use your scanner only occasionally, turn off the init associated with it by moving it to the disabled extensions folder or use the Extensions Manager (remember to put it back when you want to use the scanner again). Although inits are normally not big files, each one does take up memory.

Fonts Folder

Fonts represent the way humans communicate with words and numbers. The fonts folder contains several fonts from Apple, but you can add more. There are thousands of fonts available, although you are limited to how many you can use at once. If you are not going to start a new career in desktop publishing or graphic design, you don't need a lot of fonts. Fonts take up memory.

The Preferences Folder

If you use certain programs over and over, you may create certain templates or preferences. When you create custom settings, they are stored in the preferences folder. Many of your software programs store preferences automatically. The preferences folder is also a common place for problems to occur. Sometimes, preference files get corrupted and will not let you open a program or crash your computer. Often, a fix is as simple as tossing the preference file into the trash can and letting the program create a new one. You'll read more on this in Chapter 9.

The Way It Works—Desktop 101

Sit back, relax, and take a look at the iMac monitor. The area you're looking at is called the desktop. The part of the Mac OS that lets you work with the desktop and all its components is called the Finder, as I said previously, and you know it's located in the system folder. Assuming you have not altered the desktop in a major way after unpacking your iMac, you have an icon on the top-right corner called Macintosh HD, a trash can on the bottom right of the screen, and one or two more icons below the first icon.

Your desktop is your workspace. This is where you do your creative thing—write your novel, keep track of your finances, create a newsletter, or simply play games. The desktop is your creative space.

You most likely have a trash can somewhere around your desk. Your iMac's trash can serves the same purpose. During those times when your creative juices don't seem to be flowing or you're in the mood to tidy up, you throw things in the garbage. On your iMac, you grab the "garbage" and move it to the trash can. Once in a while, you empty the garbage.

Under my desk, I have a file cabinet with a lot of file folders. To keep organized, I put all my work in manila file folders, give them a name, and arrange them in my file cabinet in some order, alphabetically, categorically, or whatever I choose. Some things I don't put in folders at all. When I need access to a particular document, I open my file drawer, look for the folder, open it, and extract the document. This is the same scenario played out on your iMac. The icon in the top-right area of your screen, the one called Macintosh HD (hard drive), is where you keep all your work. It is a large electronic file drawer, or repository, where you keep all your software applications and the products they make.

You open your "file cabinet" by double-clicking your hard drive icon. It opens a window and displays the contents, arranged as icons or buttons or as a list. You will see either folders or separate file icons. These are the programs and files that came with your iMac. You can create your own folders, name them, put stuff in them, and arrange them. When you open a file folder, you have access to its contents. Those contents are files created either by you or your software programs.

You access information, open folders, start software programs, and move things around your iMac by using your mouse. You probably noticed that there is only one button on the mouse. You only need to click it once or twice. Unlike other computers and operating systems, you perform all tasks on the iMac with a simple single or double click of the mouse. Why cramp your finger from dancing around a mouse with three or more buttons?

You click once on a file or folder if you want to move it around (hold the button down to drag), get information about the file or folder, or rename it. You double-click a file or folder if you want it to do something such as open (a folder) or start an application such as a word processor, spreadsheet, game, or any other program. You double-click the application (such as ClarisWorks) or a file that was created by it (a book report written in ClarisWorks). It will launch the file either way. You launch the software program to begin a new file. You double-click an existing file if you want to modify it. It will open its parent application automatically.

Across the top of the desktop is a set of menus. The five menus on the desktop are File, Edit, View, Special, and Help. The Apple menu, to the far left of these five menus, is a special menu. It's always there, no matter what software program you use. The other menus to the right of the Apple menu will change according to the software program you use. Each Mac software program has its own bells and whistles. You access their features through menus.

The first two menus, File and Edit, appear for every iMac program, although some of the things you can do within the menus will change. It depends on the type of software program you're using (word processor, spreadsheet, or paint program). The five menus are the basic tools to help you organize your iMac and the stuff on it. Take a look at them in more detail.

The File Menu

Figure 1.5
The File menu.

The File menu, shown in Figure 1.5, gives you control over actions on individual files. You can open or close a file, print, or make copies, including making an alias (a copy that links the original no matter where you put it). Add a file to your favorites folder (located under the Apple menu). You can give a file a label (color code) and set up your printing criteria.

Sherlock, the search engine, is located on the File menu under the Find option. More on Sherlock, the information detective, later in Chapter 7.

You will notice that most items have keyboard shortcuts. For example, if you press the Command key (with the cloverleaf or Apple icon) with the letter O, you will open a file. Most keyboard equivalents are common sense: O for open, P for print, and F for find. However, when you get into some of the robust software programs, especially from Microsoft, you have to become a hand contortionist to use many of the keyboard equivalents.

The Edit Menu

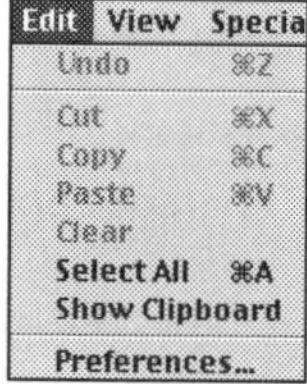

Figure 1.6
The Edit menu.

The Edit functions, as shown in Figure 1.6, appear in every software program on the iMac, including the desktop. You have the ability to cut, copy, or paste information, select all information, and show the clipboard, the area of your iMac memory where the information is temporarily stored. On the desktop, you are limited to performing these functions on the names of files or folders. Once you start using applications such as a word processor, you will love these functions.

The Preferences option under the Edit menu gives you the ability to arrange the spacing, size, and order of files on your desktop, to spring-load your folders (time them to pop open), and change the color and titles of your labels.

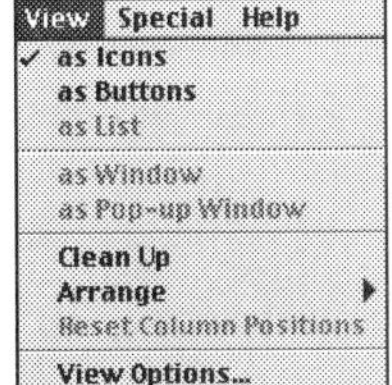

Figure 1.7
The View menu.

The View Menu

The View menu, as shown in Figure 1.7, allows you to change the way your windows display files and folders as icons or buttons or as a list. You can change the amount of information displayed as a list by using the Edit menu (the Preferences section). The View options allow you to arrange the display and size of icons.

You can also change the way a window looks when opened, either as a regular window or a pop-up window, one that has a labeled tag on it. You will appreciate this feature if you have a lot of windows open while you work. You can clean up and rearrange your files and folders and clean up your desktop.

Figure 1.8
The Special menu.

The Special Menu

The Special menu, as shown in Figure 1.8, lets you empty the trash, eject a floppy, Superdisk, or Zip cartridge, and erase and format a blank disk. You can put your iMac to sleep (temporarily), restart your iMac (after you install a new software program), or shut down to end your iMac experience for the day.

Figure 1.9
The Help menu.

The Help Menu

The iMac has a good built-in help section, shown in Figure 1.9, and that's why I don't plan on rewriting it. Type a keyword, and you see the section of the Help menu that will answer your questions. If you select Show Balloons, everywhere you place your cursor, a little cartoon-like balloon will pop up and tell you what the selected item does. Balloons drive me nuts and will annoy you, too, but they are helpful for first-time users.

You can choose to watch a small interactive tutorial that explains how to type a simple letter and how to move files around. Mac OS help is part of the Help Center and has 15 sections on the most commonly asked questions.

The Apple Menu

The Apple menu, as shown in Figure 1.10, is like an extra workspace, a side desk, so to speak. It gives you access to additional tools that you can use or shortcuts to other tools residing somewhere on your iMac. There are

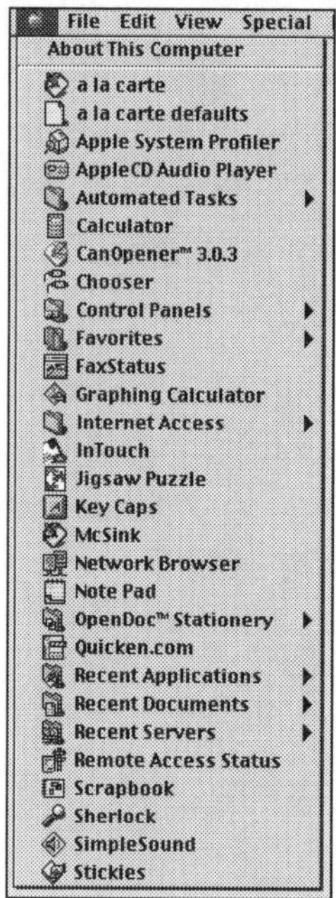

Figure 1.10
The Apple menu.

mini applications such as a calculator; note pad; stickie notes; folders that contain links to the most recent programs, documents, or servers you were using; control panels; Net connectivity tools; and so on.

You can drop anything you want into the Apple menu folder. I even drop in small reminder notes to myself. Open your system folder, locate the Apple menu folder, and drop in the item. You can also make an alias of the file with the Command key+M on your keyboard.

The Apple menu is one of the best features of the desktop. It allows you to prepare your workspace for a specific task. If you are a desktop designer, you might have tools and links in the Apple menu that will help you in your design. A writer can have a dictionary, thesaurus, and other writing tools. A scientist can have special calculators or math programs, and so on.

The Apple menu also contains some important items, such as the Chooser, which lets you select various printers; Sherlock (System 8.5), the premier Internet search tool from Apple; the Scrapbook for collecting art, sound, and text files for easy access; and a shortcut to your control panels.

A Bundle Of Goodies

You iMac came with a nice assortment of software programs. Perhaps the most important program is AppleWorks, formerly ClarisWorks (and still called that).

ClarisWorks is an integrated software package that gives you a word processor, spreadsheet, paint, draw, database, and communications program—six programs in one package.

ClarisWorks has a large installed base of users. A number of individuals, user groups, and Web sites cater to ClarisWorks and offer templates, tutorials, and advice. Rather than write a ClarisWorks manual here, I will point you to the Web sites that will give you all the tutorials and templates you need to get up and running.

ClarisWorks Tutorials

Several versions of The ClarisWorks Tutorials are available for your use.

ClarisWorks Tutorials By Cindy O'Hora

http://users.desupernet.net/ohora/Clarisworkstutorials.html

Cindy has many tutorials that cover word processing, drawing, database, and spreadsheet functions. She uses version 4.0, but most tutorials are applicable to the 5.0 version that came with your iMac.

South Dakota Computer-Using Educators

www.cue.dsu.edu/CWTut.htm

This Web site has a number of online tutorials for ClarisWorks. Although many of them are done in previous versions of ClarisWorks, they should work with the newer version you have for the most part. Here are the names of the tutorials: Word Processing Features, Word Processing Icons, Stationery, Slide Shows Made Simple, Creating a Database, Frames, Mail Merges, Mailing Labels, Importing and Exporting, Setting Preferences, Shortcuts, Making It Click, Outlines, Applying Bullets, Libraries, Creating a Business Card, Charts and Graphs, and Headers and Footers.

The ClarisWorks User Group

www.cwug.org

Formed in 1991, CWUG has more than 15,000 members in the United States and 51 other countries all dedicated to helping ClarisWorks users. It publishes a great newsletter filled with tutorials, tips, and information about ClarisWorks. It offers a huge library of public domain software for downloading as well as special discounts on commercial software, including ClarisWorks. The membership costs $39 a year.

Tutorials From The Education Center

www.bev.net/education/ntia/ClarisWorks/

This site offers a set of five tutorials on word processing, database, painting, drawing, and spreadsheets.

I Want To Be...

When you bought your iMac, you had a reason other than just being cool. You want to get on the Internet like everyone else, or you think that it can help you fulfill a dream, start a new business, write that prize-winning novel, or design the school newsletter.

The following sections recommend sets of software titles or Web sites in a few of those want-to-be categories. These recommended software programs are the most popular or perform the best in their fields.

Additional hardware you may need for many of these pursuits includes a scanner (UMAX Astra 1220u is a fine one), printer, graphics drawing pad, digital camera, or camcorder.

Accountant/Finance/Run Your Own Business

Ready to start that new business from home? Quicken and Quickbooks are both excellent accounting programs by Intuit, Inc. (**www.intuit.com**). Quickbooks is geared toward the small business. Quicken 98 comes with your iMac and is more suited for the family, although I still use the original Quicken for my business (about 10 years old), and it works fine.

If you need to do real heavy number crunching, Excel is the premier spreadsheet program from Microsoft (**www.microsoft.com**).

Rutger's Accounting Resources Web page (**www.rutgers.edu/Accounting/raw/internet/internet.htm**) contains hundreds of links to accounting resources, including software reviews.

You can't start a business without a good business plan. PaloAlto Software (**www.palo-alto.com**) has great marketing and business plan software products for the Mac.

Desktop Design/Publishing/Graphic Art

The following tools will let you create simple one-page flyers or entire catalogs and books. QuarkXPress (**www.quark.com**) and Adobe PageMaker (**www.adobe.com**) are the two leading programs for desktop publishing.

Canvas by Deneba Software (**http://ww2.deneba.com**) is a fully integrated desktop and design program.

Adobe Photoshop (**www.adobe.com**) is the premier image manipulation program.

Adobe Illustrator (**www.adobe.com**) or Fractal Design Painter (**www.fractal.com**) let you design in freehand. They are great for logo development.

Check out the Web site desktopPublishing.com (**http://desktoppublishing.com/ezine.html**) for a list of several online desktop magazines that you can access for free.

Programming

Perhaps you want to create the next hottest software program for the iMac and be adored by millions. Here are some programming languages you can obtain.

Visual MacStandardBasic by Zcurve Software (**www.zcurve.com**) retails for $99. FutureBASIC II by Staz Software (**www.stazsoftware.com/staz.html**) retails around $229. A complete set of tutorials and samples get you up and running quickly.

CodeWarrior Professional by Metrowerks (**www.metrowerks.com**) is an integrated development tool for multiple-language and cross-platform development. With CodeWarrior Professional, you can develop in C/C++, Java, and Pascal. CodeWarrior is priced at $499.

COBOL Programming for The Web (**www.infogoal.com/cbd/cbdweb.htm**) lists many Web sites that deal with this language. Cobol is in big demand due to the Year 2000 (Y2K) bug problem.

Pro Fortran for the Macintosh by Absoft Corporation (**www.absoft.com/pro.fortran.html**) retails for around $900. Fortran is used in the science industry.

Apple Computer is supporting the MKLinux project to port Linux, a freely distributed Unix-like operating system. You can obtain the free software at **www.mklinux.apple.com**.

The Mac Programming list at **http://apocalypse.org/pub/u/wildboar/MacintoshPages/Programming.html** is a list of Web links to sites that deal with a variety of programming types.

Macintosh Programming Languages (**http://felix.unife.it/Root/d-Bigsurf/28-Mac_Programming**) lists just about every freeware and shareware programming language you can run on the Mac and links to the sites so you can get the software.

Music

Looking to be the next MTV star? Do songs like "I Want to Hold Your iMac" or "Rock Around the iMac," dance in your head? Maybe music is your gig.

Moore Music (**www.mooremusic.com.au**) in Australia is one of the biggest online providers of music software and hardware. It has a great list of most Mac MIDI software and hardware. You can also visit Mark of the Unicorn's home page (**www.motu.com**), where you can get the specs on Mac MIDI software.

Video Editing/Photo

Take those home movies and make them Academy Award-winning productions. Adobe Premiere (**www.adobe.com/prodindex/premiere/main.html**) is a pricey $895 video-editing program for the professional.

With Avid Cinema (**www.avidcinema.com/products/index.htm**), you can create new movies or modify your existing collection of videotapes by using editing techniques, music, voiceovers, titles, and special effects. Then, publish the final video to tape, CD-ROM, or as a QuickTime movie. Avid Cinema's software is designed especially for people with no prior video-editing experience, making it as easy as following four steps. The software retails for about $120.

Photoshop, listed earlier, is a must since it is used for special effects. Apple's QuickTime Pro (**www.apple.com**) can create, edit, and publish video for a mere $30.

Web Developer

Do you have an eye for design and you love the Net? Perhaps you would like to design Web sites for a living. The following editors create Web pages:

- Adobe PageMill (**www.adobe.com**)
- FrontPage (**www.microsoft.com**)
- GoLive CyberStudio (**www.golive.com**)
- GraphicConverter is a shareware program that lets you convert many different graphic image file formats. It is a great program to convert images to GIF or JPEG for the Web. You can download this program from most shareware software sites on the Net (see Chapter 8) or from the Web site of the program's author **www.lemkesoft.de**.
- HTML Markup and Markdown, a $15 shareware program (**http://printerport.com/klephacks/markup.html**)
- PageSpinner (**www.optima-system.com/pagespinner/**)
- Photoshop (**www.adobe.com**) is used to create Web designs and special effects.
- WorldWide Weaver (**www.miracleinc.com**)

Writer/Playwright/Author

Are you the next Stephen King or Tom Clancy? Obviously, you can use any text editor for simply writing, but if you want to write screenplays, TV scripts, or other professional writing projects, the following programs will help: Collaborator III, Comedy Writer, Dramatica Pro, Dramatica Writer's Dreamkit, Plots Unlimited, StoryBuilder, StoryCraft, Final Draft, Movie Magic Screenwriter, ScriptThing, Scriptware, MovieBuff, Hollywood Connection Kit, ScriptReader, Three by Five, Movie Magic Budgeting, Movie Magic Scheduling, Production Manager, Storyboard Artist, and Storyboard Quick.

For a good summary of features and the ability to purchase online, visit MasterFreeLancers (**www.masterfreelancer.com**) and The FreeLancer's Online Store (**www.screenwriterstore.co.uk**)

I Can Run What On My iMac?

Your iMac is not confined to running only the Mac operating system, contrary to what you may have heard. You can run Windows on your iMac with the purchase of an inexpensive PC emulator program called

Virtual PC from Connectix Corporation (**www.connectix.com**) or SoftWindows from Insignia Design (**www.insignia.com**). Both cost around $150. These two programs are PCs on a disk. They emulate the Windows 95 or 98 operating system. This lets you run any PC software, increasing the number of software programs you can run on the iMac by thousands.

Both products are a complete Windows 98 Pentium MMX PC in software. Virtual PC can be purchased in DOS and Windows 95 as well, as shown in Figure 1.11. If you have a copy of Windows 3.1 around (why?), you can install that on top of the DOS version of Virtual PC. You can actually run dozens of different operating systems on your iMac from Nintendo 64 to the old CP/M. Chapter 8 explains in more detail. There are versions of Linux and Unix available for the iMac as well.

Caring For And Cleaning Your iMac

Your iMac has a built-in handle at the top like the original Mac of 1984. When you use it to move your iMac, be sure to place your other hand under the iMac. Do not rely on the handle by itself. Also, do not use the movable bar on the bottom of the iMac for a handle. It's a tilt bar to

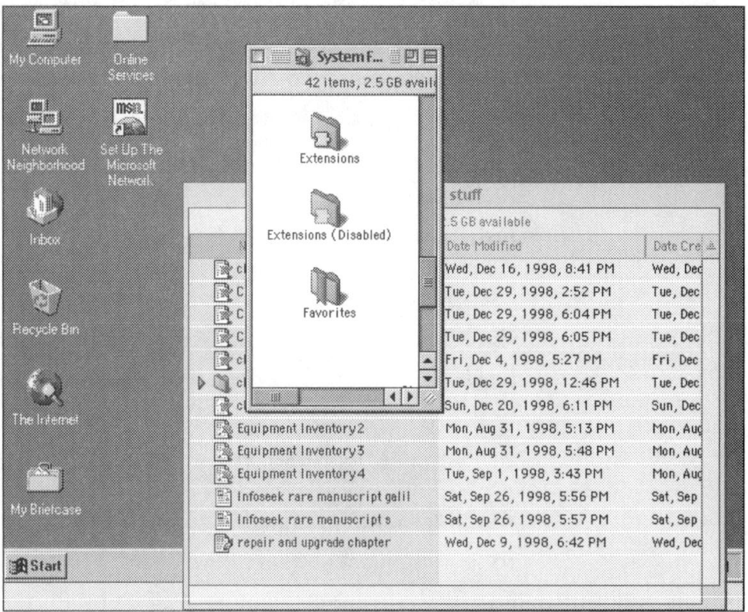

Figure 1.11
Just try to do this on a PC—Windows 95 and the Mac desktop available at the same time!

Forget The Period!

When typing an email address or URL (Web address) from this book, be sure NOT to include the period or comma that may appear after a URL. This inclusion of a period or comma is for publishing conventions and is NOT part of the Net address.

adjust your viewing angle, and it is not designed as a handle. It will snap, your iMac will drop to the ground, and you will be thoroughly depressed.

Apple strongly recommends that you do not ever use any alcohol-based cleaners or powder-based cleaning agents. Using these on your iMac will discolor and scratch the plastics, which will not be covered under warranty. I use a lint-free cloth with warm water and no solvent. Unless you have your iMac under a service bay at a local garage, why do you need to use such harsh chemicals? Baby your iMac. Keep it clean by wiping it down every other day.

Take The iMac 101 Class

Apple offers a free, self-paced, online tutorial that covers many of the details about your iMac. There is a test at the end of the tutorial to gauge your skills. Visit the online class at **www.info.apple.com/info.apple.com/te/training/overviewimac/index.html**. When you are through with the tutorial and test, print it out and save it as a reference along with this book.

2 Getting Online

Rittner's Computer Law: Civility is only a passenger—not a driver—on the information superhighway.

The Internet

The Internet, a.k.a. the Net, is a worldwide electronic mesh of people and information—a digital repository of human knowledge. The genesis of the Internet occurred as early as 1957 when Russia launched Sputnik, the first man-made satellite. As a reaction, the United States government created the Advanced Research Projects Agency (ARPA). Located in the Department of Defense, ARPA's purpose was to jump ahead of the Russians in science and technology. Almost 10 years later, MIT's Larry Roberts published the first plan for a computer network. It was called ARPANET, a blueprint that later became the present Internet. The first four computers of ARPANET, Nodes 1 through 4, were commissioned in 1969.

Thirty years later, there are more than 36 million host computers on the Internet, spanning more than 170 countries. The Internet is a computer network of computer networks. What started as a project of the Cold War is fast becoming the tool that brings people together.

What's All The Hype?

According to MediaMart Research Inc., 72 million American adults (and more than 100 million people worldwide) have access to the Internet. You are about to increase that number by one with this book and your iMac. After all, the "i" in iMac stands for Internet.

It seems that every time you turn on a TV or radio or pick up a newspaper, you see a discussion about the Internet. I remember only a short time ago, you couldn't get a reporter interested in the subject. Today, the Net is pervasive. Even plumbers have their own Web pages. Everyone, it seems, wants to be on the Net.

Why did it reach this level of acceptance? It's pretty simple. People want to connect to the Net because they will have access to those 100 million people and more than 100 million documents. Talk about empowerment! The Internet is becoming the communication and information hub of the world, and you don't have to be a Fortune 500 company to have access. The Internet doesn't care whether you're Stephen Hawkin or Joe Blow. Everyone has equal access.

What Can You Do On The Internet?

I often hear the same questions from diehard anti-technology folks: What good is the Internet? What can you do with it? Why should I be on it? Isn't it just for techies?

Here are a few things you can do with your iMac and a Net connection:

- Correspond with friends and family—even make new friends—using electronic mail. You won't need the frustration of missed phone calls or garbled answering machine messages. There's no reason to lose touch with loved ones. Electronic mail operates 24 hours a day, 7 days a week. It waits in your mailbox until you want to read it.
- Chat with friends, family, or even strangers in realtime in thousands of public or private chat rooms. If you have an inexpensive camera, you can also see whom you are talking to.
- Use your iMac to view Niagara Falls, Tokyo's skyline, or traffic moving into Russia at Finland's Vaalimaa border crossing. View live weather satellite images of your region. You can even look under a woman's bed and see whether you can find the ghosts keeping her awake, view the icebergs live from Mawson Station in Antarctica, and experience other sights you couldn't possibly see without physically going there.
- Visit online exhibits at museums and collection centers around the world. Have you always wanted to visit the Guggenheim? The London Museum of Natural History? The Vatican? You can—on the Net.
- By using your email account, you can join in global discussions with people around the world and talk about your similar interests. Join a mailing list; there are more than 80,000 topics. Can't find a list that

interests you? Create your own for free. You won't need once-a-month meetings at 7 P.M. at the local library. Mailing list discussions continue 24 hours a day, 7 days a week, regardless of the weather or holidays.

- Thumb through a card catalog at a library in Germany, Australia, or the United Kingdom, or in thousands of other libraries around the world, as though you were standing in the lobby. These libraries never close.
- Search thousands of databases from NASA star catalogs, movies and TV listings, business listings, and even food recipes when you need them, anytime, any day.
- Book your vacation, including airline tickets and hotel reservations (with cheaper prices, too). Find the best hotel rates, bed and breakfast inns, places to visit, customs, and other things you need to know—all online.
- Download thousands of freeware, shareware, and even commercial software programs to your computer. Grab complete texts of books and other manuscripts, artwork, music, video clips, and even maps.
- Learn, learn, learn! Take thousands of free or low-cost distance-learning classes from academic institutions around the world. Learn from some of the best minds—and you don't have to dress up for class.
- Read the daily news from the *New York Times* and other major newspapers around the world. Listen to interactive radio such as NPR or CBS News. Would you rather watch the news instead of listen to it? No problem! Watch CNN Interactive, Fox News Live, and even the BBC using Realmedia software (which is free). Like to read *Newsweek*, *Scientific American*, or *Time*? Yup, they're online, too.
- Ready to buy a new car or house? Check the latest mortgage rates. Find out what problems are associated with that model of car or van you want from people who already own them.

Did I mention that you can do all this for about $25 a month?

Net Or Web?

Net or Web? People want to differentiate the two, but they're the same. The Internet is a global computer network of computer networks, with millions of computers all speaking the same language to each other. The World Wide Web, on the other hand, is a multimedia interface for the Internet. It allows you to view text, graphics, animation and video and even hear sound, all from one central starting point, a Web page. It's a nice way to organize information in all forms on the Internet. For the purposes of this book, the Net and Web are the same.

The Tools

In this chapter, you will learn the basics of using your iMac to get on to the Net. You already have everything you need except for an inexpensive Internet connection. Here is what you need to get online:

- A computer with a communication port (your iMac)
- A modem (it's in your iMac)
- A standard phone line or cell phone (got it, right?)
- An Internet Service Provider
- Software to connect to the Net (you have it)

If you are brand-new to computers and exploring the Internet, you will find that both are easy to learn, especially compared to learning them a few years ago. Most, but not all, personal computers from the start had the ability to communicate with one or more computers. Before today's Internet became widespread and popular, you connected to computer bulletin boards or university computers, but it wasn't always easy. You had to manually set up special communications software. It didn't always work. If you didn't know what communication settings the other computer needed, you were out of luck. Compounding the problem was the fact that certain brands of modems didn't work with other brands, and so on. It was often a chore and not always a pleasant experience to get online. However, when you finally did connect to a computer bulletin board, you knew that you were about to do something special. Using your computer to communicate with someone else in the world is exciting and empowering.

Today, my five-year-old son doesn't bat an eye! "What's all the fuss?" he tells me as he sends email to his friends in other countries.

What's A Modem?

Your iMac is ready to surf (a term that means using the Internet, not making a trip to the beach). Your iMac is Internet-ready. Your iMac has a built-in modem. A modem is an electronic device that connects your iMac to a telephone line and converts the digital data from your computer to analog (sound) frequencies. The modem sends these sounds through the phone line to a receiving computer's modem.

A modem on the other end of the line takes the sounds it receives and converts them back to digital form, which is processed and displayed on the receiving computer's monitor screen. It can be in the form of text, pictures, sound, or video. This two-way process is called modulation/demodulation, and the word modem comes from the contraction of the device's real name, MOdulator/DEModulator. Now, you know how the name modem originated!

Modems send data in both directions simultaneously and are called "duplex" modems. Duplex modems are used for communicating on the Net, bulletin boards, other computers, and generally any kind of connection you want to make.

The speed at which modems transmit data over the phone line is measured as bits per second (bps), also known as the bit rate. The higher the number (for example, 33,000 and 56,000), the faster the transmission of data over the phone line. Speed does not mean quality or reliability, however.

When I was first introduced to online communications in the late 1970s, 300 bps was the only speed possible for telecommunications. I could eat lunch and read the newspaper before a page of text scrolled off my monitor. I still thought it was cool. Today, 56,000 bps (56K) is the most popular speed; your iMac modem transmits at 56,000 bps or lower speeds. Soon, with the distribution of ADSL (Asynchronous Digital Subscriber Line), faster speeds will be possible over your regular phone line. Moreover, certain cable companies are offering high-speed access for a monthly price that is equivalent to paying for a separate phone line, something you would add anyway if you really get into using the Net (and you will). All modem manufacturers adopt standards so they can talk to each other. This is coordinated by the International Telecommunication Union (ITU), a United Nations agency that coordinates global communications standards. How do you know you have a modem that has adopted those standards? Look for V. and a number after it. Today, 56K modems should be V.90-compliant. Your iMac modem is, and it also supports the K56flex standard. What does that mean?

In 1997, two competing standards were developed for modems transmitting at 56K. Rockwell and Lucent Technologies developed K56Flex, and U.S. Robotics (3Comm) developed X2. Both had won enough support by Internet Service Providers (ISPs) that it split the market. The consumers, you and I, had a problem. The modem you purchased might not work with your ISP. This also meant that ISPs had to buy a rack of both types of modems to satisfy both standards, not an inexpensive proposition. In early 1998, both sides compromised, and the V.90 standard was established and accepted. All is well for the time being. It means that with a good 56K modem, you can download 22MB per hour of goodies from the Net. You'll read more on that later.

Modems come in two flavors: external or internal. You have an internal 56K modem in your iMac. You can add an external modem if you want to. Most modems today are called smart modems because they have a built-in language command set that will perform functions the computer dictates, such as answer the phone or dial a number. You will find that you can add modem scripts, little text files that your modem will read to perform specific functions. Your iMac comes with modem script for your internal modem that is located in the modem scripts folder in the system folder. When you use a different modem, it will have its own script that you put in this folder. You can also write your own scripts.

If you want to change modems, consider this first: Although modem manufacturers promote many bells and whistles, the most important functions you want are the ability to automatically dial and answer a computer, automatically sense the speed of another modem and drop down to match, provide reliable throughput (few errors and down time), and send and receive faster than 33,000 bps. There are many models to choose from, and your favorite hardware retailer, computer magazine, or Web site will describe the advantages or disadvantages of each one. The modem that comes with your iMac works fine. If it's not broke, don't change it.

Bits And Bytes

When you log on to the Internet, your computer and modem are extremely busy. Both are working hard to make sure all the data is translated correctly. They are "talking" to each other at blinding speed. Your data, whether it's this chapter I typed, a picture you drew, a number in a spreadsheet, or a sound or video file, is composed of tiny electrical pulses called bits, a shortcut for binary digit. Bits represent single digits of data as 1s or 0s. Visualize bits as rapidly turning an electrical wall switch on and off, with 1 being on, and 0 being off.

Bits are transmitted as electrical signals by your iMac to your modem. Your modem transforms these bits into sound and then sends it over the phone line to a receiving modem and computer (such as a bulletin board, another computer on a network, an online service, or your local ISP).

When you type text on your screen, your iMac breaks it down to its binary form—the combinations of 1s and 0s—that represents the words or pictures you see or sound you hear. Each character is based on a worldwide-accepted standard called the ASCII (American Standard Code for Information Interchange) character set, originally designed for the teletype. The ASCII code gives each letter of the alphabet its own ID in a set of eight bits. To the iMac, the uppercase A in binary form is 01000001, and the lowercase a is 01100001. Likewise, the number 1 is 00110001, the number 2 is 00110010, and so on.

Bits And Bytes Is What You Type

8 bits=1 byte

1,024 bytes=1 kilobyte

1,024 kilobytes= 1 megabyte

1,024 megabytes= 1 gigabyte

1,024 gigabytes= 1 terabyte

This group of eight bits is called a byte. Bytes are measured in units of a thousand. One thousand bytes make a kilobyte. (Actually, it's 1,024 bytes, but it's rounded off.) Because a byte represents a single character (a letter or a number), a computer system with one megabyte of memory can store a little more than 1 million bytes, or about 180,000 words in memory. Most computers today have 32 or more megabytes of memory. A single 3.5-inch floppy disk can hold more than 200,000 words. A Zip disk can hold about 80 floppies worth of data, or about 1 1/2 million words. Your hard drive holds 4-6 gigabytes of information. That's almost 10 CD-ROMs full of information. Confused? Simply remember the larger the number of bytes, the more you can do—whether it's in the memory of your iMac or in storage on a hard drive. You have bytes of memory and bytes of storage.

I remember the day when I thought it impossible to fill a 5MB hard drive (which cost $1,500, more than your iMac) attached to my

Mac Plus that had 1MB of memory (which cost $3,000). The cost of bytes has dropped considerably over the last few years.

How To Get Online

The Internet is often referred to as the information superhighway. You need an on-ramp. To drive down any road, you need a car and a license to drive. In this case, your car is a software program called a Web browser, and your license is an email account. You obtain an email account by subscribing to a local or national Internet Service Provider , or you may be able to get access from work or through a local university. Some public libraries and other nonprofit organizations also offer Internet accounts.

Cost

Internet use will have different costs, depending on how you access it. Many of the national commercial online providers charge around $25 or less for unlimited access each month. There is a move by several ISPs to reduce the access time to a set number of hours per month, and some national providers are implementing this. Avoid them if you can or at least fight it.

The average local usage rates can be $10 to $25 a month for unlimited access. Some local providers will give you a "light" version—x amount of dollars for x hours a month. With this monthly fee, you get an email account and access to the Net, and some providers give you space for your own Web page. Some charge extra for Web page space.

Local Or National Provider?

Personally, I like to support local businesses. In my area of New York State, there are more than 100 Internet Service Providers serving my area code. Only a handful are "real" local access providers; individuals or companies that have spent thousands of dollars on Net infrastructure. The rest are scattered around the country and only have access points here (called POPS, explained later) or are local companies that buy bandwidth.

Net infrastructure is built by someone who has several computer servers, racks of modems, peripherals, and a lot of high-speed phone lines entering the premises. That's a commitment that costs thousands of dollars. They are likely to stick around and give good technical support if you have trouble. (They have to pay for all that equipment.) One of the owners of a local ISP here in New York State personally drove to a new user's house because she was having a particularly hard time setting up. Try to get that level of service from America Online!

The other form of ISP is called a virtual ISP. This is a company or person that buys some bandwidth from MCI or other Internet carrier, slaps up a Web page, and offers Internet connectivity and end-user accounts. I'm not saying that this is necessarily a bad thing, or that it doesn't work, but if they don't make the profits they want, or they get bored, it's pretty easy for them to disappear overnight. No money spent on infrastructure, no commitment. This scenario is not cast in stone. There are many good virtual ISPs, but look at their track records and learn something about the owners before you sign up.

Why should you care whether they are real or virtual? The main problem with the situation is that once you have an email account and start giving it to thousands of people, changing it is a real annoyance. I would love to drop my America Online account, but I have been using it for my news business since 1989. All my colleagues know I can be reached there. If I dropped it now, I would have to inform thousands of people of the change. I simply don't have the time (or willpower). Your email account user ID comes from your ISP, unless you spend an extra hundred dollars to get your own domain address that you can bring with you. You can't do that with America Online.

Finally, a word about the national ISPs: I am no longer a big supporter of large national online providers. Some are great, but why would you want to pay an ISP $25 a month when getting on its service is like trying to drive on the L.A. freeway at rush hour? The original idea behind the public Internet was distributed access for all, not the control by one or two companies raking in the profits and deciding what content you should have. Furthermore, just try to get technical support when you need it. You have a better chance of getting struck by lightning than finding someone at the other end of the phone who knows a modem from a shogun. I'm not saying they are bad services; on the contrary, they have great stuff. I just don't like to wait in lines, and I hate crowds.

With that said, Earthlink is not a typical national provider, and that is why Apple bundled it with your iMac. Go ahead and try it. However, all examples of getting online in this book will be based on my two local providers, Global2000.net and Wizvax.net.

Making Sense Of It All

Millions of computers make up the Internet. How do you keep track of them all? It's simple. You have your own name, right? So does every computer on the Net, but a Net computer's name consists of numbers. Most humans don't like numbers, so we give the computer an alias because it's easier to remember mesh.com instead of 204.97.190.254. This number is called the Internet Protocol address (IP address). A computer finds another computer on the Net using the IP address. One of my local ISPs is Global2000.net. To my iMac, Global2000's real name is 209.203.129.2.

There is a good reason to know your IP address. When you are ready to get Net connected and set up your iMac for the first time, you need to know the IP address of your ISP. Because your iMac is really not on the Internet, you will fake it into thinking it is by using PPP, Point-to-Point Protocol, and TCP/IP, the Internet protocols that you set up in a couple of control panels in your system folder. These are the instructions your iMac will use to connect your computer to your ISP, which is sitting on the Internet in realtime.

When you sign up with a local ISP, you receive a dial-up account. It's called that because your iMac's modem must call the ISP to make a connection to the Net. When you dial in to your local ISP, the ISP's computer will automatically assign an IP address to your iMac. This is called a dynamic IP address because it will change every time you call. Remember that both computers must have an IP address to talk to each other. Because you are not on the Net all the time (although it may seem like it), you don't need a static address, one that never changes. However, if you decide to turn your iMac into its own Web or email server, you can usually obtain a static IP address from your ISP for an additional cost.

But Wait: There's More

As I said previously, an IP name in the Net world is the address of a computer expressed as a number. Humans give those numbers real names so we can make sense of it all. We talk in words, not numbers.

To make it even more logical, Internet-linked computers and networks are grouped into similar types called domains. All the computers on the Net that belong to colleges or universities end with the suffix .edu, the education domain. All commercial companies on the Net end with .com for the commercial domain. Nonprofit organizations such as museums end with .org. Government agencies end with .gov, and so on. They belong to a set of domains called top-level domains. After a while, you can look at a domain name and know where it's from. In the U.S., several top-level domains are reserved, but worldwide countries are also part of the top-level domain structure, as shown in the Appendix. Top-level U.S. domains are listed in Table 2.1.

Subdomains are the parts of the address that you create. The Net domain for my Internet magazine, The MESH—Inside Cyberspace, is themesh.com. themesh is my subdomain; .com is the top-level domain. Because it is a commercial venture, a news service, it belongs to the com, or commercial domain. A domain address for a particular site can be quite lengthy. For example, at a university where almost every department has its own computer network, you can get an address that

Table 2.1 Top-Level Domains

U.S. Based	Domains
ARPA	Original ARPANET
COM	Commercial
EDU	Educational
GOV	Government
INT	International
MIL	U.S. Military
NATO	NATO field
NET	Network
ORG	Nonprofit

has three or more subdomains. The bottom line is that the domain address is a specific address that goes to a specific machine.

Getting Ready To Surf

Assuming you set up your iMac correctly when you took it out of the box, you are ready to get on the Net. Be sure you have a telephone line plugged into the phone jack on your iMac. All you need is to set up your iMac software to match the information you get from your local ISP. There are several ways to get that information into your iMac. We will look at them all. There are a few steps involved:

First, sign up with a local ISP (or try the Earthlink Install package that will do all this for you). Your local ISP will give you information to enter into your TCP/IP control panel, Configuration Manager, and PPP configuration. All three are control panels that appear in the control panel folder under the Apple menu at the top-left corner of your monitor. You can also use the Internet Setup program on your iMac, located in the Assistants folder that will walk you through the process. You need to get the phone numbers for dialing into your ISP's computer, not the voice line. You will also need the information described in the following sections.

TCP/IP

Find the Transmission Control Protocol/Internet Protocol (TCP/IP) control panel, located in the control panels folder, which you can access via the Apple menu on the top-left corner of your screen. You need to insert a few items into the TCP/IP control panel. You must obtain and insert the Name Server Address(es) for your ISP. It will be a number, and there can be more than one address. The Search Domain is the ISP's English name (or whatever your language happens to be). My example is Global2000.net. Be sure that the Connect Via: option says PPP and the Configure: option is set to using PPP Server. You will notice in the example in Figure 2.1 that the IP address is already there. Global2000's computer enters this when I dial in. It is a dynamic IP address. The next time I sign on, the number will be different. You do not have to worry about any of the other information because it is only required if you are

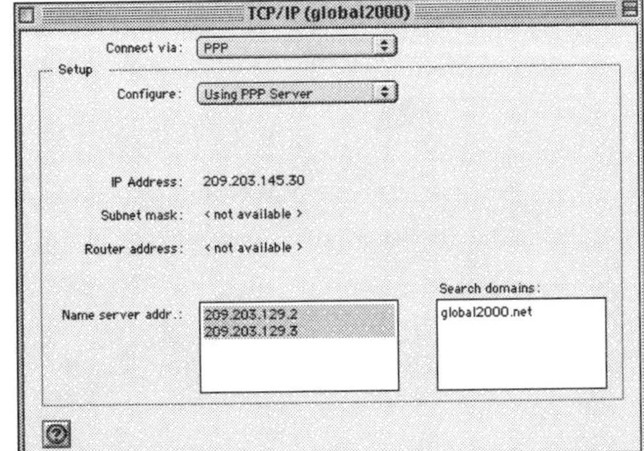

Figure 2.1

The TCP/IP control panel in your system folder lets your iMac talk to your ISP.

connected via a network or live Net connection, such as what your office or school may provide.

The Remote Access Control Panel

You use the Remote Access control panel (or Remote Control Status mini-application under the Apple menu) to dial into your local ISP, as shown in Figure 2.2. You need to insert some information in this control panel to have your iMac dial up. If you have an account with an ISP already, you will have given yourself a user ID or had one assigned to you by the ISP. Mine is themesh in the example. You also need to enter the password and use the checkbox if you want Remote Access to remember it, so you don't have to keep typing it. Do not select this if other people have access to your computer because they will be able to log on to the Net with your user ID. Finally, enter the phone number of your ISP's dial-up computer.

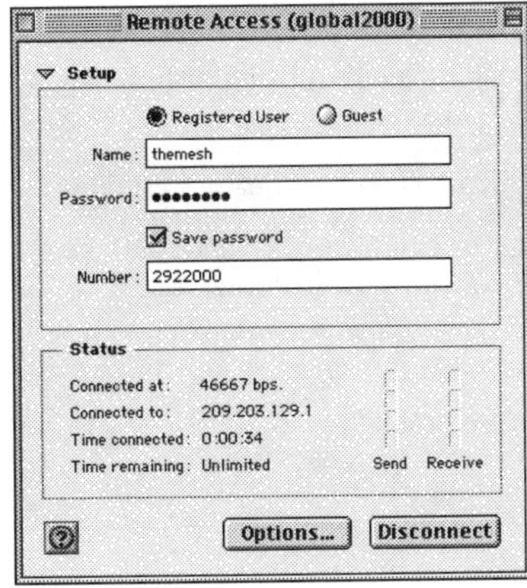

Figure 2.2

The Remote Access control panel logs on to your ISP.

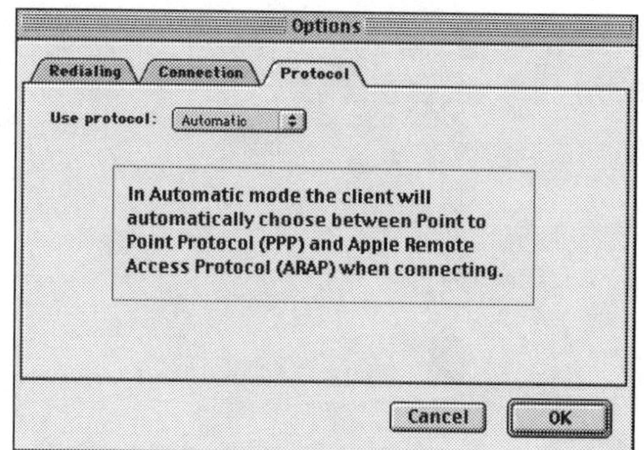

Figure 2.3

Apple Remote Access can automatically select the protocol when logging on.

The Options button gives you some other choices such as redialing, cosmetic type stuff, and an option to choose between PPP or Apple's Remote Access Protocol. Leave it on the automatic selection, as shown in Figure 2.3. It will pick the one that is needed: in our case, PPP.

Other Important Information

You need to set up your personal information and ISP information so you can send and receive mail, surf the Net, subscribe to Usenet newsgroups, and so on. Open the control panels again and select Configuration Manager, a control panel that allows you to set up, among other things, preferences for Microsoft's Internet Explorer.

Internet Shortcuts

Under the Apple menu is a folder called Internet Access. You'll see four choices:

- *Browse the Internet*—This selection will launch your Web browser. You can change the default Web browser in the Configuration Manager.
- *Connect To*—This option will give you a dialog box and will display the Net site address that you enter.
- *The Internet Setup Assistant*—This will assist you in getting your iMac ready to get on the Net.
- *Mail*—This choice opens your emailer. Outlook Express comes with your iMac.

Getting Online At Work Or School

If you use your iMac from an office or other location that is on an office network, called a Local Area Network, or LAN, you still need to know the IP address of your ISP. You will be assigning your iMac its own static IP address when you connect your iMac to the office network.

Your iMac will be connected to the office network probably by Ethernet cabling. Ethernet is a networking connection that is fast and reliable. Your iMac is already Ethernet-ready. The Ethernet connection on your iMac is the large rectangular opening, called an RJ-45 jack, to the right of your USB ports, located inside the panel on the right side of your iMac, not far from your modem port, which is located slightly toward the lower-right corner. You will insert a cable (which looks like a bigger telephone cable) into the RJ-45 port on your iMac. The other end hooks into a device called a hub located somewhere in the workplace.

Your office Network will have a device called a router. The router is connected to a modem-like device called a CSU/DSU and a hub. All the computers on the network will be connected to this hub by the other ends of those Ethernet cables. The hub is like a traffic cop. The router does all the work, making sure packets of data from all the computers on the network get routed to the ISP and out to the Net, and vice versa.

If your office has its own Internet domain, it is assigned a domain address and a bunch of numbers. You can add 253 computers to that domain address. The 254th address is reserved for your router. Each of the computers on the LAN gets its own IP address and is called a static address because it will never change. Once you assign your iMac a static IP address, you are on the network, and if your office allows an outside connection, you are on the Net. Some offices put up a firewall, a server that acts as a security blanket between the LAN and the outside world. After all, you don't want 16-year-old hackers looking at your files.

Configuration Manager

The Configuration Manager control panel is where you prepare your iMac and Web browser to interact with your ISP.

Email Setup

Under the Email option, you enter information similar to the example in Figure 2.4. Enter your real name and your email address that you have arranged with your ISP. The box for Organization is optional. You can use it to identify yourself or your company and it will appear in all the emails you send.

The next option, Sending Mail, is important. Simple Mail Transfer Protocol (SMTP) is the way email gets routed around the Internet. You get that information from your ISP. It can be as simple as mail.isp.net. The next option is retrieving mail. You do want to receive mail, not just

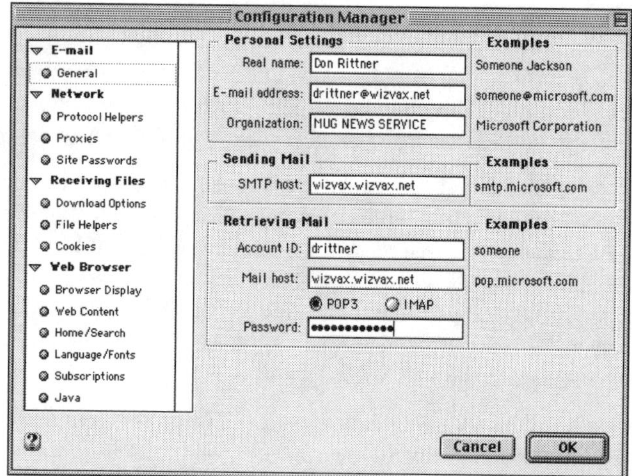

Figure 2.4

Entering your email information in the Configuration Manager.

send it. Your account ID is your user ID without the ISP domain name. The Mail host is the computer at your ISP location where mail is delivered and gets stored before it goes to you. Notice, in my example, it is the same address as the SMTP host.

The next check box is POP3 or IMAP. POP actually has two meanings, depending on how it's used. It's either Point of Presence or Post Office Protocol. In this case, Post Office Protocol refers to the way your email software (Outlook Express, which came with your iMac) gets mail from the mail server. This is a common approach when you use a dial-up account to get your mail. POP was designed to support offline mail processing. Your computer calls a mail server periodically and grabs your mail, so your mail goes from the server to your computer.

Do Not Give Out Your Password

Never give your password to anyone. No one should ask you for it in the first place; however, some people on the Net will try. A common practice on America Online is that a scammer will disguise himself as an employee with AOL and tell you he needs your password to test the system.

Point of Presence, the other meaning of POP, refers to a location where your ISP can be connected to, usually with dial-up phone lines. You will notice that your local ISP may have a POP in various localities around your city or other areas for people to call into. My ISP has a POP in Utica, although it is physically located in Albany, New York.

IMAP, or Internet Message Access Protocol, is a relatively new mail protocol and offers some improvement over POP, the older protocol. Although it works fine for offline processing, its special strength is working in an online and disconnected capacity, and it is used to leave mail on the server so you can access it from other locations. All you need to know is which flavor, POP or IMAP, your ISP requires, and check the box.

Finally, type your password. It will display as dots as you type, so be sure to write it down somewhere. Don't rely on your memory. You should change your password periodically to make sure no one gets it. Make up a password that has nothing to do with what you do or who you are. If you're an electrician and you make your password electron or sparky, I will bet you money that some 16-year-old is going to crack your account. Mix words, numbers, and special characters in your password, such as do#$4M.

Network Settings

You have several options in Network Settings:

- *Protocol Settings*—This allows you to set up or change helper applications that assist you while surfing the Net. You can tell your Web browser to use a particular FTP (File Transfer Protocol) program to download files or add a program here. You do not need to alter this area for now.
- *Proxies*—If you are using a network at the office to get on the Net, you might have to go though a proxy server first. Ignore this if you are dialing from home. If not, you will get the needed information from your office network administrator.
- *Site Passwords*—Here, you can change or delete any user ID or password you have stored on the computer.
- *Receiving Files*—These options let you modify how you are going to deal with sending and receiving files, both online and offline.
- *Download Options*—You can change the location of where files are downloaded and other options.
- *File Helpers*—In this area, you can add or delete helper applications. This list shows you the applications that will be used to open files that use specific extensions or file types. For example, Microsoft Word will open all files that end with .doc. All files that end with .xlt will be opened by Microsoft Excel, and so on.

- *Cookie Helper*—Cookies are text files that store information on your computer when you are surfing the Net. They can store your password or the user ID you created when visiting a site, the last time you visited a Web page, or an item in a shopping cart on an online mall. Some people do not like having cookies on their computers. You have the option to delete the cookie, view the cookie and see what it's for and the date it expires, or simply turn off receiving cookies altogether. Don't worry so much; you can leave them.
- *Web Browser*—In this section, you can modify the look and feel of your Web browser, change the default home page and search page, change the language displayed (such as English), turn Java on or off, and even enable a ratings system based on content. The only thing you are likely to alter in this section is what browser you prefer as the startup browser. The iMac comes set up with Microsoft's Internet Browser (hmmm). You can change it here.

The Internet Control Panel

Apple's Internet control panel lets you set certain functions such as what email application, Usenet news server, or Web browser to use. Some of this information may already be inserted if you used any of the procedures I've already described. Open the Internet control panel.

- *Personal*—Add your real name, email address, and organization (optional). If you have a signature, you can add it here as well.
- *Email*—Add your user account ID. This is your user ID without the name of the ISP.
- *Incoming Mail Server*—The address of your ISP's mail server (also called the POP server).
- *Password*—Add it here; it will display as dots so no one, including you, can see it.
- *Outgoing (SMTP) Mail Server*—This is the name of the mail server of your ISP. Often, it is the same address as the POP or incoming mail server.
- *Email Notification*—You can change the settings to different sounds to alert you about receiving new email.

- *Default Email Application*—It is set for Outlook Express. You can add Eudora or any other email application, and your iMac will launch it when you need to read or send email to the Net.

The Internet control panel is also where you set the following Web options:

- *Default Pages*—Here, you can change your home page and search page if you want.
- *Download files to*—Create and name a new folder like "My downloads." Select an existing folder for your downloads.
- *Colors and Links*—You can change the color of Web links here.
- *Default Web Browser*—Here is where you can change the Web browser to your choice: Netscape or Microsoft.

Make sure you also set your News options:

- *News Server Settings*—Here, you determine how you will grab Usenet newsgroups. It is set up to receive only Microsoft's. Your ISP probably has its own news machine, and you can add the address here.
- *Connect to News Server as*—On some news servers, you need a user ID and password, which you can set here.
- *Default News Application*—Outlook Express is the default. You can use another newsreader such as Internews or Newswatcher. I really like Outlook Express.

You will notice that you can create groups of Net settings. This is useful if you use more than one ISP or you need to switch between calling your ISP and connecting to a remote server using Apple Remote Access. I assume you are using only one for now, as shown in Figure 2.5.

Internet Config

Yes, you have yet another way to configure your Internet settings. Internet Config, shown in Figure 2.6, will set all your preferences just once, and then, all your Internet applications refer to these settings.

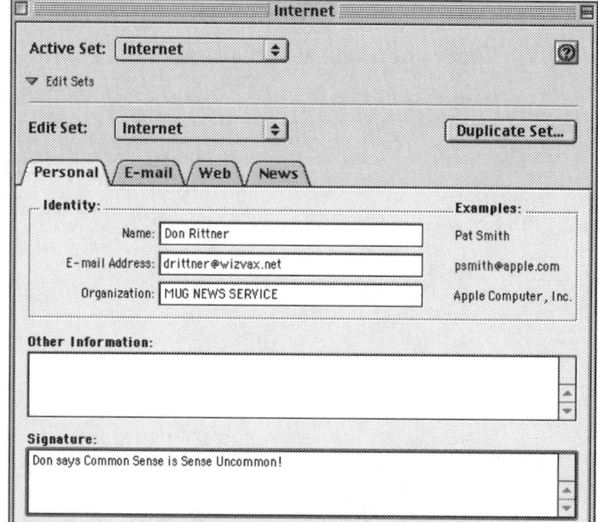

Figure 2.5
Apple's Internet control panel for storing Net information.

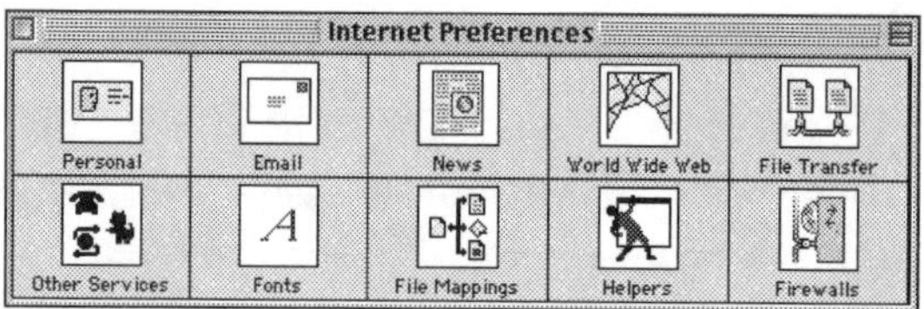

Figure 2.6
Internet Config stores all your Net preferences.

Words You Need Not Fear

- *Bookmark*—You have the ability to save your favorite Web sites by bookmarking them. Later, you can easily return to the site by selecting its bookmark. Bookmarks are features of Web browsers and other Net tools such as FTP clients. Internet Explorer calls them favorites. Basically, they are shortcuts to go somewhere on the Net.
- *Domain Name Address*—This is the name given to anyone registering his or her computer or network on the Internet, the name of the Internet site. The domain will fall into a certain category (.com, .org, and so on). You can have many computers using the top-level part of the domain address, but each computer still must have its own unique address. See Table 2.1.
- *DNS (Domain Name System)*—This is the distributed database that translates computer names, such as **www.themesh.com**, into their numeric addresses (such as 204.190.97.254) and vice versa. Without DNS, you would need a good memory for numbers and a large map.
- *Download*—The process of transferring a file from one computer to your computer.
- *FTP (File Transfer Protocol)*—FTP allows you to access another computer, grab a file, and bring it back to your computer—or to send a file to another computer.

(continued)

Words You Need Not Fear (*continued*).

- *Gopher*—An early search tool that is menu driven to find Net resources on FTP sites.
- *HTML (Hypertext Markup Language)*—This is the formatting in a text file that lets a Web server display its content. Every Web page must be in HTML format.
- *HTTP (Hypertext Transport Protocol)*—This is the language of the World Wide Web. It's how Web servers and Web documents interact.
- *IMAP (Internet Message Access Protocol)*—This is another method of storing your email on a server so you can access it from more than one location.
- *IP address (Internet Protocol address)*—The actual name, in numeric form, of a computer on the Net. Each computer on the Net has its own IP address.
- *ISP (Internet Service Provider)*—This is where you sign up to get connected to the Net. It's like the phone company; you pay a monthly bill.
- *NNTP (Network News Transport Protocol)*—This is the protocol that defines how Usenet newsgroups travel on the Net.
- *POP (Post Office Protocol or Point of Presence)*—Post Office Protocol is the ability to store email on a server and send it to you when you ask for it. Point of Presence is the name for a rack of modems in a location where you can log in to your ISP. It does not have to be in the same area, region, or even state.
- *PPP (Point-to-Point Protocol)*—This allows your computer to connect to your ISP's computer and makes your computer think it's sitting on the Net.
- *Protocol*—Instructions or rules from one computer to another so they may communicate with each other. The way information is supposed to flow and act. All computers on the Net must speak TCP/IP.
- *Server*—Another name for a computer that your ISP uses for connecting you and allowing you to participate on the Net.
- *SMTP (Simple Mail Transfer Protocol)*—The protocol that defines how your email is routed around the Internet.
- *TCP/IP (Transmission Control Protocol/Internet Protocol)*—The two sets of rules or instructions that computers must speak to belong to the Internet.
- *Telnet*—The ability to remotely log on to a computer terminal, anywhere in the world, as though you were sitting in front of it.
- *Upload*—The process of taking a file from your computer and sending it to another computer.
- *URL (Uniform Resource Locator)*—The accepted way to give anyone an address of a destination on the Internet.
- *User ID*—This is your driver's license for the Net. It is the name you will use to identify yourself to the millions of people on the Net. Make it easy to remember.

Get Your Own Domain

A domain is registered with an agency called Internic, although that is changing shortly. You can register your own domain for $100. I have my own domain, themesh.com, for my newspaper and news service. By setting up a mail server at my education center, I can get mail sent directly to me at themesh.com. Although the mail really goes to my ISP, it is routed to my own mail server. This is called a virtual domain because I really am not an ISP. If you plan to create your own company out of the room next to the bedroom, you can get your own domain name and sound like a Fortune 500 company, too.

You grab your email from your local ISP's mail server. Mine is Global2000.net or Wizvax.net. I have two accounts. You can send me mail at themesh@global2000.net or drittner@mesh.com.

The Real Easy Way

Apple went out of its way to make the iMac Internet-ready. Apple installed an application called the Internet Setup Assistant to walk you through the procedures to get your iMac ready to surf in 10 minutes. I purposely left this for last because I think you should have a good understanding of the underlying process that makes your computer connect and interact with the Net. It helps for troubleshooting later. With that said, Apple's assistant is nice, and I demonstrate it here.

You launch the Internet Setup Assistant, shown here in Figure 2.7, by opening the Internet Access folder located under the Apple menu or on the hard drive in the Internet folder. Double-click it. The assistant is designed to ask you some questions and let you enter the necessary information to get your iMac-Net ready. It assumes you already have an account with an ISP; if you don't, it will dial in and help you set up an

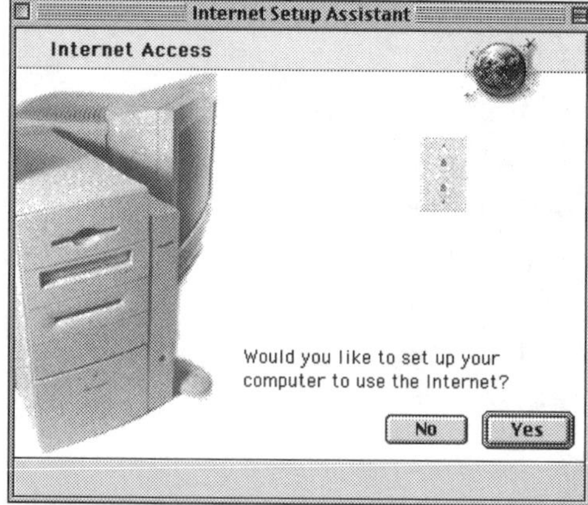

Figure 2.7
Internet Setup Assistant guides you through the process of setting up the iMac for getting on the Net.

account with Earthlink, the national ISP bundled with your iMac. I assume here that you've signed up with a local ISP.

1. Depending on your answer to the question "Do you already have an Internet account?", you will have the option to let Apple sign you up to Earthlink or continue to add info for a local ISP. The answer is yes, of course.
2. I assume you've signed up with a local ISP. The ISP will provide you with the necessary information that is required to connect to its computer. If you select no, the assistant will take you through several more windows and help you sign up with Earthlink.
3. The next window gives you some explanations of what is to follow.
4. For the configuration name and connection type, as shown in Figure 2.8, give yourself a name for the account and continue. If you select Network, you get more windows asking for various kinds of information for a network setup. I assume here that you are dialing in from home.
5. For the modem settings, you turn off call waiting here if you have it, as shown in Figure 2.9. Otherwise, move on to the next step.
6. Type your ISP's phone number, your user ID, and your password as shown in Figure 2.10. Remember that the password will display as dots, so write it down somewhere.

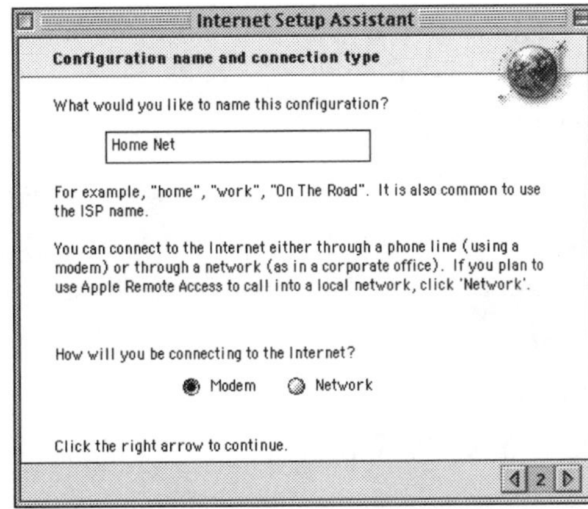

Figure 2.8
Give your Net connection a name; continue by clicking the right arrow.

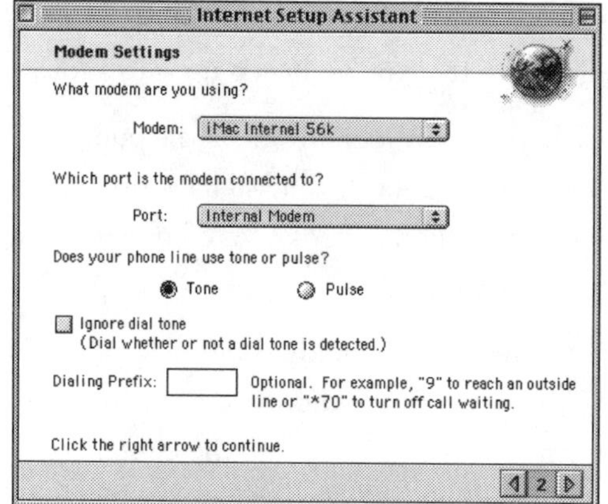

Figure 2.9

This panel sets up your modem.

Internet Setup Assistant

Configuration information

What is the phone number for this configuration? Your computer calls this number to connect to the Internet.

234 5666

What name do you use with this service (also known as your log-in name or user ID)? Leave this field blank for guest access.

drittner

What is your password?

****

You can leave this blank, but you will have to enter your password each time you use the Internet service.

Click the right arrow to continue.

4

Figure 2.10

This panel asks for your ISP's dial up number and your user ID.

7. The answer to the next window, PPP-connect-scripts, is no for 99 percent of ISPs. If your ISP did provide you with a script in a text file, drop it in the PPP Connects Scripts folder in the extensions folder, itself located in the system folder.

8. The next window asks you if you want to assign your own ISP address, unless you specifically asked for a static IP address, the answer is no. Your ISP's computer will assign your iMac a new dynamic IP address every time you log on to its computer.

9. Obtain the Domain Name Servers information from your ISP and place it here, as shown in Figure 2.11. It is the name of the ISP's computer in both numbers and words. These are the on ramps to the information superhighway. I like to think of them as toll booths.

10. Add your email address that you set up with your ISP, and type your password, as shown in Figure 2.12. You're almost ready to log on. The

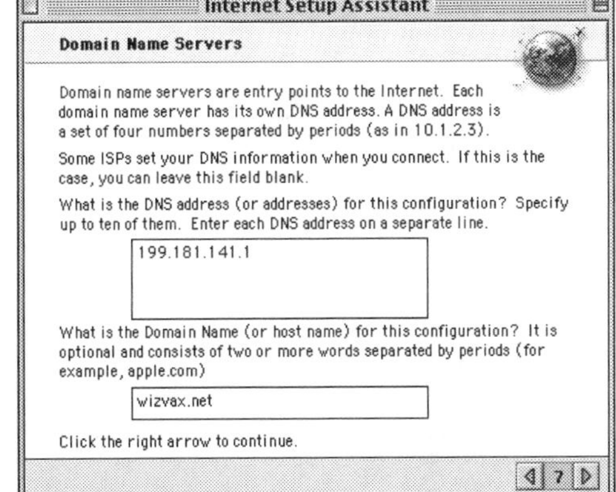

Figure 2.11

This information allows your computer to talk to your ISP.

Internet Setup Assistant

E-mail address and password

What is the e-mail address for this configuration?

This address is where people send you e-mail (for example: chris@isp.com or pat@company.com or kelly@school.edu).

drittner@wizvax.net

What is the e-mail password for this configuration?

You can leave this blank, but you will have to enter your password when you want to receive mail.

****

What is the quoting character you would like to use? This character precedes each line of quoted text of an e-mail message.

>

Click the right arrow to continue.

8

Figure 2.12

Add your user ID and password here.

quoting character should be left alone. It is the most commonly used one on the Net. See Chapter 4 for a description of quoting characters.

11. Add your email account and SMTP host information here, as shown in Figure 2.13. Usually, the addresses for the mail server will be the same, but not always. Some ISPs will use pop.*ispname*.net.

12. If you want to participate in Usenet newsgroups (you will), add the name of the news server here, as shown in Figure 2.14. You will get this information from your ISP.

13. The next window asks if you need proxy servers. You probably don't if you are signing up from home. A proxy server is a server at work or school that acts as a middleman between the Net and your network at work or at school.

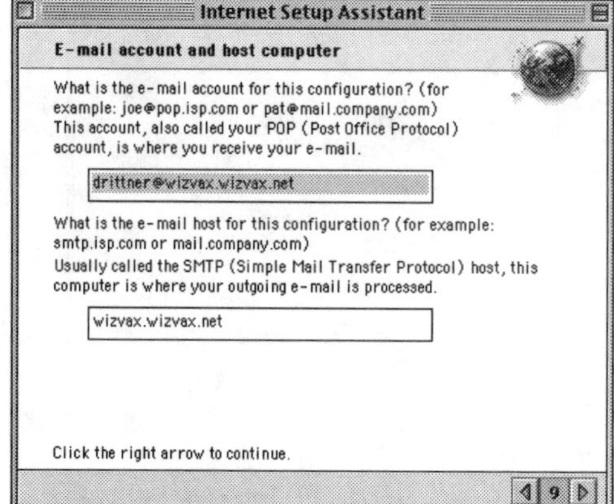

Figure 2.13

Get Email account and host computer information from your ISP.

Internet Setup Assistant

Newsgroup Host Computer

Newsgroups are an Internet service you can use to follow or join ongoing discussions on a wide range of subjects.
What is the news group host for this configuration? (for example: news.isp.com or nntp.company.com)

This computer is sometimes referred to as your NNTP (Network News Transfer Protocol) host. (Optional)

news.wizvax.net

Click the right arrow to continue.

10

Figure 2.14

Insert the name for your ISP's Usenet news server.

14. You are ready to rock-and-roll. Now click Show Details to make sure all the information was entered correctly, as shown in Figure 2.15.
15. If everything has been entered correctly, select Go Ahead. You are now ready to log on.

Logging On For The First Time

If you have entered all the information correctly, it's time to log on to the Net. Make sure your phone line is plugged into your iMac and the wall. Select Remote Access (or Remote Access Status under the Apple menu) and click Connect. You should hear your modem dial into your ISP and the modems "talk" to each other (which will sound like screeching to you). The status box tells you what is happening. If you make a proper connection, you will see two indicators on the right of

Figure 2.15

Check for accuracy and then go ahead. You are ready for the Net.

your Remote Access panel that show send and receive data and the connection speed you logged in at. It should be around 46,000 bps.

Assuming you connected correctly, click the Browse the Web icon on your desktop, or open the Internet folder and double-click the Web browser of your choice. You can also open the Internet Access folder located under the Apple menu and click Connect To... if you know where you want to go, or you can click Browse the Internet, which will launch your Web browser. (It performs the same action as the icon on the desktop.) The Web browser will open the default home page. (Excite is the default page unless you changed it.)

You can avoid all this by simply selecting any of the options stated in the paragraph above. It will automatically kick in Remote Access and dial. If your Web browser starts and opens any home page, you're online. Congratulations!

Hey, It Didn't Work

Even the best laid plans don't always work. Let's see what the common mistakes are.

Won't Connect Properly

If you dialed into your ISP, but you got a message saying the user ID or password is incorrect, retype them. Be careful when typing your password or user ID. If you accidentally put a space before or after them, the connection will not work. Some user IDs and passwords are case-sensitive. Some don't allow the use of extra characters. Make sure your Caps Lock key is not on. Make sure you put all the correct information about your ISP in the proper places. Common mistakes are simple typos, placing com instead of net for your ISP, or simply spelling the name incorrectly. Make sure you entered all the information correctly in the TCP/IP control panel.

If you connect, but your Web browser doesn't display any pages, including the home page, make sure you entered all the information correctly in the TCP/IP control panel. Suppose you connect and type a Web address, but your browser says there is no DNS server. It means that the domain is either down or gone or that you might not really be connected to the Net. Check Remote Access and be sure you are connected to the Net. You can also try that address again later.

Make sure you entered the correct number for your ISP's computer. Some people accidentally put in the tech support number or main office number.

No Dial Tone?

Make sure your phone connection is good. If you are running a long extension, it can become loose and get knocked out of the jack. Make sure you typed the correct phone number—duh! Make sure that phone extension upstairs is not off the hook. Make sure the button on that cordless phone is not off the hook. (My two-year-old likes that one.) Restart your iMac.

Your Web Browser

You explore the Internet using a Web browser. Two Web browsers came with your iMac: Netscape Navigator, the oldest and, in a way, the first (an improvement of Mosaic, the first GUI Web browser), and Microsoft's Internet Explorer. They both do the same thing. They differ in how they implement some features. It's like choosing between a Ford and Honda. They both get you down the road. It's a personal preference. Because the iMac is set to start up Microsoft's Internet Explorer, I start with that. I personally prefer Netscape Navigator, but there is no need to change now unless you really hate Microsoft.

The World Wide Web is the interconnecting mesh of the vast resources of the Internet brought to the user through a rich multimedia interface—your Web browser. Using this one tool, you can view text, graphics, animation, and video, hear music, and use Net protocols such as email, FTP, Telnet, and so on. Your Web browser is like a digital Swiss Army Knife. It can do almost anything.

In 1994, it was decided by those higher on the Net food chain, the Universal Resource Identifiers (URI) working group of the Internet Engineering Task Force (whose editor was Tim Berners-Lee, creator of the Web), that there needed to be a standard way to give Net addresses on the World Wide Web. The result was called a Uniform Resource Locator, or URL. It's pronounced Ural, like the mountain range, or Earl, like the person, depending on what part of the country you come from. A URL is now the accepted way to give an address on the Net. The following are examples of URLs:

- **http://www.themesh.com/netradio/**
- **ftp://ftp.netscape.com**
- **gopher://muse.bio.cornell.edu/**
- **telnet://pldsg3.gsfc.nasa.gov3**

No Period At The End Of A URL

There is never a period at the end of a URL. However, throughout this book, you will often see a URL or email address end with a period if it appears at the end of a sentence. Do not type the period. Because we use proper grammar in this book, URLs at the end of sentences may appear to end with periods. If you do type a period, you will not go anywhere. You will get error messages.

There are three parts to a URL. First is the scheme, which is the protocol, used: hypertext, FTP, or Telnet, for example. The scheme ends with a colon (:). This is followed by a double slash (//) that separates the protocol from the actual action. Everything to the right of the double slash is the destination address. It's hierarchical in form, so the information to the left is the highest order, moving right to the lowest order, with each order separated by a forward slash (/). Another way to look at it is from the broadest to most specific location. In the preceding example, http:// (Hypertext Transport Protocol) means you are going to a Web site, ftp:// means you are going to an FTP site, gopher:// to a Gopher site, and so on. The destination address to the right of the double slash starts from the domain and moves to the actual file, page, or action.

Type the complete URL into the Web browser and press the Enter key. Modern versions of Web browsers allow you to omit the scheme and type only the destination address. Instead of **http://www.themesh.com/netradio**, you can type **www.themesh.com/netradio** and it will work, most of the time.

When you start your Web browser, it opens to a home page. On your iMac, it opens to a modified page from the Search engine Excite. You can further modify it or set your browser to open to your own home page or the home page of any other Web site. Mine opens to a page I created that contains several search engines, online newspapers, and my own Web page. You can change the default settings as explained earlier. Your home page is the starting point or jumping-off point for the Net.

It is possible to type one URL and never touch the keyboard again, jumping from one Web site to another simply by clicking the links with your mouse. The World Wide Web is based on hypertext. A word or picture becomes interactive. You click it, and it takes you somewhere else. It can be a word (usually underlined), picture, sound file, video clip, or animation. Anything is clickable, and it can jump to another page of information on the same server or a server thousands of miles away. In fact, on one Web page full of links, you can actually jump around to hundreds of different countries, simply by clicking your mouse. It's as though an invisible strand connects every bit of information on the Net. You can see why it's called the Web, although I think the word mesh is more appropriate.

Web servers display information to you as specially prepared text files. These files are formatted with hypertext markup language, HTML. You will notice that all Web pages end with the extension .html, or htm, which stands for Hypertext Markup Language.

Learning HTML is not hard. You can have your own Web page up and running in a matter of hours. Many books and online tutorials discuss how to create HTML. Some HTML programs, called HTML editors, will do most of the formatting work for you. You only have to worry about the design of your page. The software will do the coding for you.

If you want to quickly see what an HTML page looks like, start your Web browser Internet Explorer (IE). After IE opens the default Web page, access the View menu and select Source, the last entry. Now, you see what the computer "sees." All those words within angle brackets (<>) are commands, part of the markup language that tells the computer what to do, how to display the words, graphics, and other elements that make up the Web page. Looks Greek, right? It really isn't hard to learn. The following online tutorials will teach you how to do it.

EZY HTML Tutorials

www.algonet.se/~amr-e/ezyhtml/

Nine tutorials cover topics that range from creating links to adding Java scripts. They are written by Amr El-Ghazaly, who has six years of experience building Web pages.

Writing HTML

www.mcli.dist.maricopa.edu/tut/lessons.html

This online tutorial has more than 25 chapters by the Maricopa Center for Learning and Instruction (MCLI) in Arizona.

HTML Tutorial

www3.sympatico.ca/westprep/lessons/

This is a basic tutorial put together by the West Preparatory, a public school in Toronto, Canada, for parents and students. It does not have a lot of bells and whistles, which is perfect for learning the basic concepts of HTML.

If you visit any of these sites, you can create your own Web pages in no time.

What Is The Hype About Java?

You will hear a lot about Java, the programming language from Sun Microsystems that is prevalent on the Net. Java is a programming language, and a program written in it doesn't care whether it's running on Mac OS, Windows, Solaris, and so on. It is independent of the computer platform, and that makes it a great language for the Net.

As a result, Java programs, called applets, are used to expand the capabilities of Web sites. Do you want to learn about how a laser works? Why not pop in some data and watch a laser actually react to that data online? Dissect a frog online. Many online games are now Java-based, allowing you to play them on the Net. You don't have to download them to your hard drive. Your Web browser must be Java-enabled to interact with these kinds of sites on the Net. Both of the browsers that came with your iMac are Java-enabled.

If you would like to see a great implementation of Java, visit the Interactive Physics and Math site (**www.lightlink.com/sergey/java/**). You will be impressed. If you would like a great tutorial on Java, visit the Sun Microsystems Web site, aptly titled The Java Tutorial (**http://java.sun.com/docs/books/tutorial/**).

Getting Around The Net With Internet Explorer

Let's take a quick look at the Internet Explorer interface, shown in Figure 2.16. Start IE if you haven't already.

The Tool Bars

Running across the top of the browser is the tool bar. It contains icons or buttons that allow you to navigate, search the Net, launch your email applications, and so on. Examine each button:

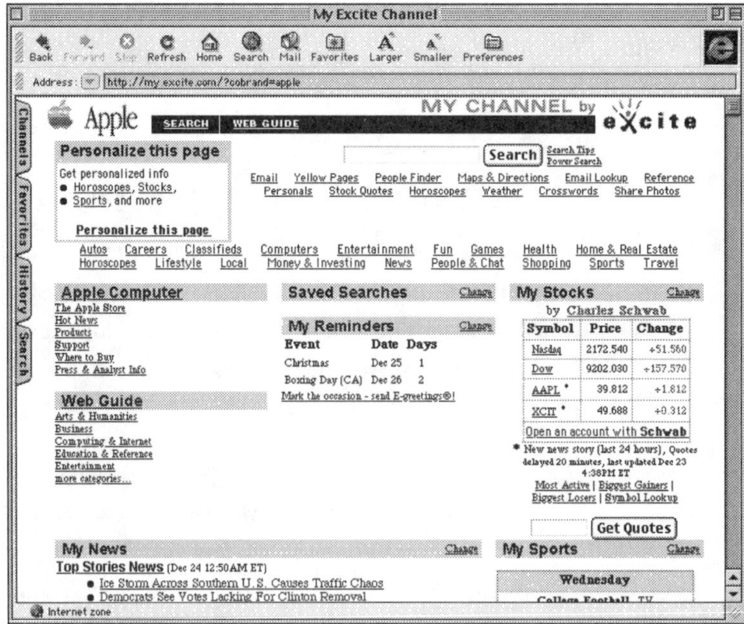

Figure 2.16
The Web browser Internet Explorer by Microsoft.

- *Back*—Takes you back a page.
- *Forward*—Takes you forward a page.
- *Stop*—Stops the browser if it is attempting an action such as going to a Web page, scrolling, loading a picture, and so on.
- *Refresh*—This reloads the current page. This is important if you are viewing a Web camera that needs the page refreshed to display the next snapshot or if a page did not load all the way (for instance, if you stopped it while it was loading).
- *Home*—This button takes you to your home page, the one indicated by your default setup in the Internet or Configuration Manager control panel. You can make any Web page your home page.
- *Search*—This takes your browser to the search engine page of your choice. The default is Excite (directed by Apple), but you can select one of your own choice in the Configuration Manager.
- *Mail*—This launches the email application. The default is Outlook Express. You can change to another email application if you have one.
- *Favorites*—This is a folder that contains all your saved bookmarks. You can do some housecleaning here such as creating and naming folders, moving bookmarks, rearranging folders, and so on.
- *Font A Larger*—This increases the size of the typeface on your page, which is good for strained eyes. Each click magnifies it further.
- *Font A Smaller*—Take a guess.
- *Preferences*—This is the same information you will find in the Configuration Manager. You can modify all your Web settings here.

Second Tool Bar—The URL Bar

Below the tool bar I just described is another tool bar where you can type the URL you want to visit. You can add or delete tool bars in the Configuration Manager.

Under The Menu

There are many features of Internet Explorer available to you under the top menu. I only explain the options that are not obvious. The large display window below the tool bars are where you see the Web page contents.

Figure 2.17
The File menu.

The File Menu

The File menu, shown in Figure 2.17, gives you the following options:

- *Open File*—Use this if you have downloaded an HTML file to your hard drive for later viewing or you are editing your own file and you want to see what it will look like in your browser. When you choose this option, you need to select the file on your hard drive to load into your browser. If you are loading a page that you saved from a Web site you visited, you will not see any graphics unless you downloaded them as well. Instead, you will see a broken link icon.
- *Open Location*—This gives you a dialog box where you can insert the URL of the site you want to visit. You can also have the new site open in a new window, leaving the existing one alone.
- *Download File*—Insert the complete URL of the file you want to download in the box.
- *Download Manager*—Shown in Figure 2.18, the Download Manager shows you what files you have downloaded, the status, the time it took to download, and how big the files are. If you were bumped offline and you did not complete a download, you can

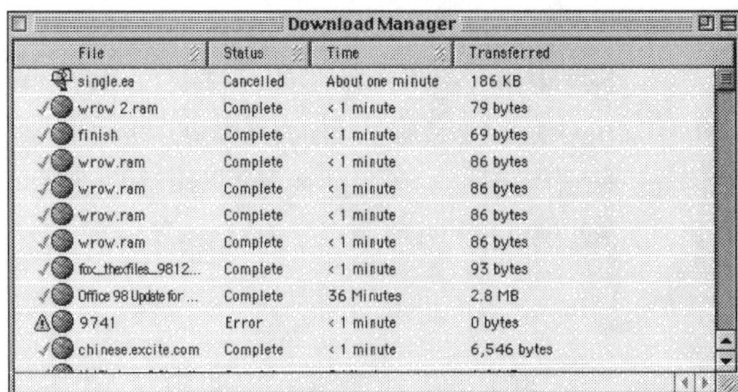

Figure 2.18
The Download Manager.

double-click the name of the file here to relaunch the download. The Download Manager keeps a list of downloads, so it is also a form of backup.

- *Offline Browsing*—If enabled (default), this will connect you to the Web if you are not already online.
- *Quit*—Quits the program altogether.

The Edit Menu

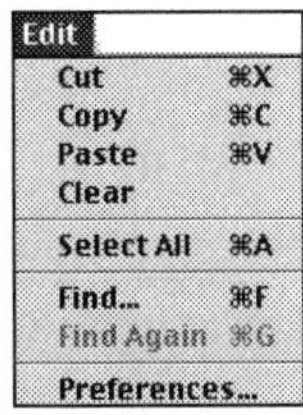

Figure 2.19
The Edit menu.

Shown in Figure 2.19, the Edit menu gives you many tools to work with a Web page's contents.

- *Cut, Copy, and Paste*—These three options allow you to cut, copy, and paste text from your Web browser to a text editor.
- *Select All*—Select All is a shortcut to copying all text on a page.
- *Find*—This search feature will keyword-search a Web page. It's a good tool if you have a Web page with a lot of text, and you are looking for one word or phrase.

The View Menu

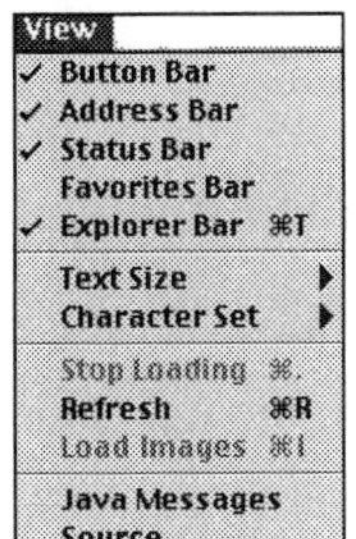

Figure 2.20
The View menu.

The View menu, shown in Figure 2.20, helps you control the way you view a Web page.

- *Button, Address, Status, Favorites, Explorer Bars (toggle bars)*—These options let you toggle on and off various tool bars.
- *Text and Character*—You can modify the size of the fonts and the language set you want to use.
- *Refresh*—Lets you refresh the page you are currently viewing.
- *Java Messages*—Here, you can read any Java messages that have been stored—which is boring unless you are into Java programming or trying to troubleshoot a problem.
- *Source*—Lets you view the HTML source code and save the file.

The Go Menu

Shown in Figure 2.21, the Go menu helps you navigate forward and backward, search the Net, and keep track of each Web page you visit.

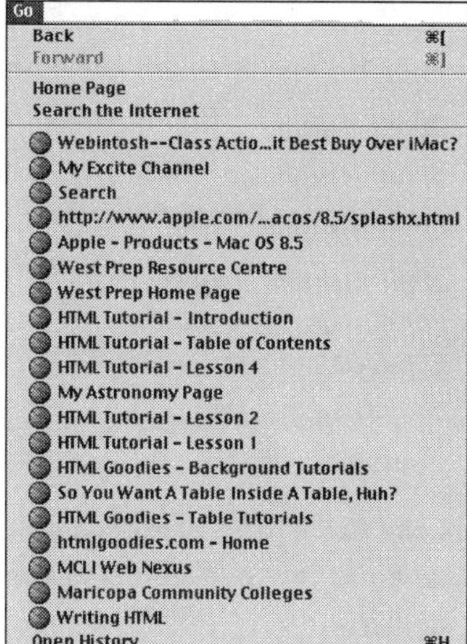

Figure 2.21
The Go menu.

You can quickly go to one by selecting the URL on the Go menu. The last option, Open History, shows you the sites you have visited over a set number of days, and all the links are also live.

The Favorites Menu

The Favorites menu, shown in Figure 2.22, lets you add bookmarks for sites you want to visit again. You can arrange them by folder and type. The Subscribe function keeps track of Web sites for you. It lets you grab a site's Web pages for viewing offline, informs you when a site is updated or changed in any way, at a time you schedule, and much more.

The Window Menu

The Window menu shows you what windows you have open and lets you switch to any of them.

The Help Menu

You can learn about all the features of Internet Explorer from the Help menu, which is shown in Figure 2.23.

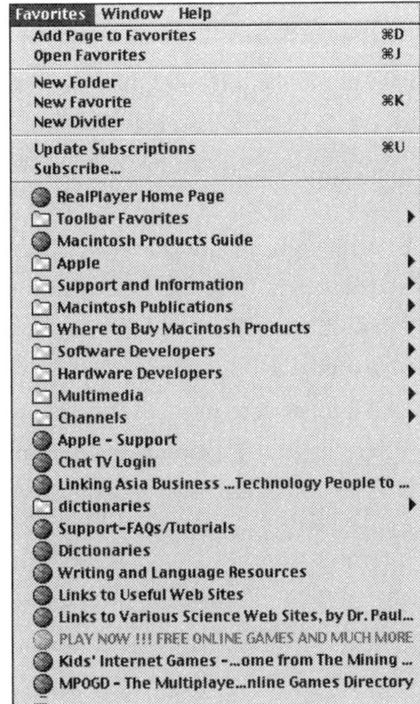

Figure 2.22
The Favorites menu.

The Side Window (Panels)

There are four menu panels on the left side of your browser. Move your cursor over to one, and leave it for a second. It will open to the right. You can also simply click one of the panels, which offer the following options:

- *Channels*—An Internet channel is a Web site that sends you information at a predetermined time, similar to subscribing to a favorite Web site. This is often referred to as push technology. You can receive late-breaking news, delivered right to your browser. If you would like to test the channels feature, visit **www.internetwire.com/feeds/** and receive Internet news from Internet Wire.
- *Favorites*—This is the same as the menu selection. It lists your favorite sites that you bookmarked in the Favorites menu.
- *History*—This shows you the sites you have visited for the last several days. It's the same history you find on the Go menu.
- *Search*—This window opens to an area where you can select one of several search engines for finding things on the Net.

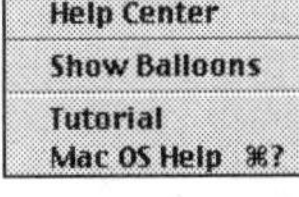

Figure 2.23
The Help menu.

Squeeze That File

The Net, and in particular, FTP sites, has the ability to store any size file and type (text file or binary) on servers. You may find large software applications, graphics files, spreadsheets, book-length text files, or other forms of information that are large in size. Web pages generally are not that big. The larger a file, the longer it takes to download to your computer. Additionally, a large file takes up more space on the host computer. Computer programmers have developed special software programs that will take any size file, or group of files, and squeeze them to a size that is 50 percent or more of their original size, and create one smaller file. This reduces storage on the host computer and the processing time it takes to download to your computer. These programs are called compression or archiving programs.

There are many different compression programs. Because there is no one standard format, you must know whether a file is compressed before you grab it and what program was used for compression, and you need a compatible software program to expand it back to the original file type. In the PC world, you will see names such as LZEXE (PC), PKZIP (PC), WinZip (Windows), Imploder (Amiga), PowerPacker (Amiga), tar.exe (PC), ARC (PC), and others. In the Mac world, there are only a handful of programs, and fortunately, one or two programs will expand most of the others' file types.

You will know whether a program is compressed because it will have certain extensions at the end of a file name. You will see extensions such as .Z, .tar, .uue, .btoa, .zip, .sit, .DD, and .cpt, and combinations. It can be really confusing if you don't know what they mean. Table 2.2 will help you sort them out. Compressed tar and zip files are binary files, whereas uuencoded, shar, btoa, and tar files are text files. DiskDoubled, stuffed, and compacted files can be either text or binary files. A PostScript file may or may not be compressed; it is a specially prepared and formatted file that can be printed on a PostScript printer.

For Mac users, there are only a few programs to know. Disk Doubler expands only files compressed with Disk Doubler and some early versions of StuffIt. Compact Pro expands only Compact Pro. StuffIt Pro expands a host of file formats, including Compact Pro, compress (Z), zip, uuencode, and others. Zip is a popular compressor in the PC world, and there are numerous unzipper applications around. There is a MacZip and ZipIt for zipping Mac files and if you need to send them to PC friends. Many of these companies have free expander versions of their software that appear on most FTP sites or Mac sites described in Chapter 8 or in the compression FAQ mentioned later in this section.

Many of the compression programs allow you to create a self-extracting file called a .sea. Self-extracting files have the extension .sea. You don't need a program to expand it; double-clicking will automatically expand it. Many software installer programs are .sea files.

There are compression programs for all computer platforms. For a detailed list of them, visit The Compression Site (**www.davesite.com/computers/compress.shtml**) maintained by Dave Kristula. You'll find little Mac information here but see good tutorials on the overall subject. The Compression FAQ, which covers the **comp.compression newsgroup**, is available here as well.

You should learn how to use these compression programs because most of the files that you download from an FTP site, with the exception of text files, will be compressed in some way. DropStuff and StuffIt Expander, which came with your iMac, will take care of most of your needs.

Go StuffIt

Back in the early 1980s, I was writing a column for *Macazine* and decided to write about a new compression program called StuffIt. It was getting quite a bit of attention from the Mac community. At the time, there was only one other compression program for the Mac platform, PackIt. I wanted to feature the author so I tracked down his phone number and gave a call. I got his mother.

Much to my surprise, the creator of StuffIt, Raymond Lau, was only 16 years old at the time. I had to wait for him to get home from school before I could interview him. He's grown up since, and so has StuffIt. It is without doubt the leading compression program on the Mac platform. Now sold and distributed by Aladdin Systems, StuffIt has two free versions, DropStuff and StuffIt Expander, which are both already on your iMac.

Internet File Formats

There are several file formats commonly used on the Internet. Although most should be transparent to the user—that is, they work on any platform—once in while, you'll hit a snag. A sound file will not play; an animation or video will not play because you do not have a certain plug-in or application enabled in your Web browser's helper section. Don't fret. The problem can be remedied quite easily. There are standalone applications that you can download from the Net that will perform whatever action is needed. Table 2.2 is a list of some of the more common file formats you will encounter.

Table 2.2 Internet file types.

Extensions	Explanation
Binary or Text Files	
.bin	Macbinary II encoded file. Often, a site will ask whether you want to download as MacBinary or Binary. StuffIt Expander will expand this.
BinHex 4.0	BinHex has been around for ages. It encodes a Macintosh file into 7 bit text. Most Mac files appear in .hqx format and tend to be larger than .bin files.
.cpt	Compact Pro, still out there.
.doc	Microsoft Word documents. Depending on which version of Word it is, you may be able to import it into WordPerfect.
.exe	Ouch, a PC file. If it's a DOS/Windows self-extracting archive, you can only use it if you have Virtual PC or SoftWindows on your iMac.
.gz	You should not be getting many of these files because it is for Unix systems.
.hqx	A binary Mac file that has been binhexed, turned into a text file.
.html or .htm	You already know what that is, right? A Web file.
.image	Apple's disk image format.
.mime	Multipurpose Internet Mail Extensions. The standard for Internet email exchange of ASCII and binary files.
.pit	PackIt file. Yes, there are still PackIt files around on the Net.
.ps	PostScript file. You should be able to print this on any PostScript printer.
.pdf	Adobe Acrobat file. You can read these because the Adobe reader came with your iMac.
.sea	Self-extracting file. Just double-click these. Most software installers are .sea files.
.sit	StuffIt file. Use StuffIt Expander.
.tar	For Unix compression.

(continued)

Table 2.2 Internet file types (continued).

Extensions	Explanation
.txt	Straight text file.
.uu or .uue	Unix uuencoded file used on encoded Unix files.
.Z	Unix compressed file.
.zip	PC files. Pkzip is one of the most common types in the PC world. StuffIt Expander will expand them.
Graphic Formats	
.bmp	Windows bitmapped.
.gif (Graphical Interchange Format)	The most common graphics format on the Internet.
.jpg., .jpeg, or .jfif	A higher resolution (24-bit) format that rivals .gif for popularity on the Net.
.tiff	Tagged Image Format. Great quality, but huge files. Takes a long time to load.
Sound Files	
.au and .aiff	Binary files that can be played with Apple's SoundPlayer.
.ra	RealAudio format, which is becoming a standard among radio stations online.
.snd	Sound file.
.wav	Windows Wave format sound file.
Video Formats	
.avi	Video clips that tend to be large but are fortunately rare.
.mpeg or .mpg	Most common movie type.
.mov, .qt, .movie, or .moov	Apple's proprietary QuickTime format.

What Can You Do On The Net?

You are now ready to explore the Internet. There are five basic activities you can do on the Net:

- *Email*—Correspond with friends, family, and strangers.
- *FTP*—Grab files and bring them to your computer.
- *Internet Relay Chat* (IRC)—Chat in realtime with friends, family, or strangers around the world.
- *Mailing Lists/Usenet Newsgroups*—Participate in discussions about specific topics of interest with people around the world.

- *Telnet*—Search databases, bulletin boards, and library catalogs as though you were there in person.

Mailing lists, Usenet, and IRC are discussed in greater detail in later chapters of this book. I concentrate here on the top three Net activities: email, FTP, and Telnet.

Electronic Mail—No Stamps Needed

The most popular activity on the Net is sending electronic mail—one-to-one or one-to-many correspondence. Email is the simple act of jotting down information and sending it to someone. It fulfills our basic human need to communicate.

Your email address is your personal identifier to the other millions of Internet users. Your email address is important. It's your calling card. The difference between email and the conventional postal service is that email is delivered directly and instantly to your mailbox. There's no extra charge for international delivery, and it doesn't matter what it "weighs."

Email uses SMTP (Simple Mail Transfer Protocol) to get routed around the Internet. Email addresses follow the domain-addressing scheme. One of my Internet addresses, for example, is drittner@wizvax.net. Generically, email addresses are userid@Asite.Adomain. The @ sign separates the person (the user ID) from the computer (the domain address). My personal mailbox or ID is drittner. My domain server is wizvax.net, which is my Internet provider. By combining the user ID with the domain address, each person on the Internet gets a personal mailbox.

You send and receive email using a standalone email application or one that is built into a Web browser. Microsoft's Outlook Express comes bundled with your iMac and is ready to go. I think highly of Outlook Express. It works well as an email client and Usenet newsgroup reader. I share more on its newsreader functions in the next chapter.

Let's take a look at Outlook Express, which is shown in Figure 2.24, and examine its features. First, I provide an explanation of the icons running down the left side of Outlook Express:

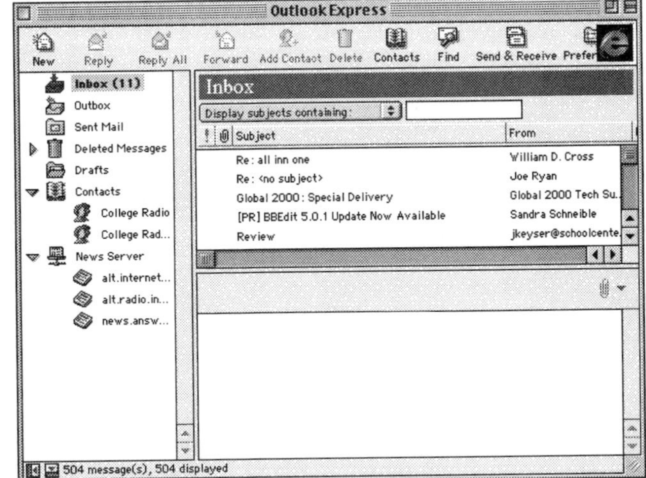

Figure 2.24
Outlook Express, Microsoft's excellent emailer and newsreader.

- *Inbox*—This is where your new mail is stored.
- *Outbox*—This is where mail that is ready to send gets stored.
- *Deleted Messages*—Your email trash can. When you delete mail, it's stored here until you quit Outlook Express.
- *Drafts*—If you are working on composing messages and you are not ready to send them yet, this is where they sit.
- *Contacts*—This is your database of people you correspond with.
- *News Server*—This is where Usenet newsgroups are stored. Outlook Express is also a great newsreader, but this area is covered in Chapter 3.
- *LDAP Server*—This is a directory service to look up names on the Net.

You can launch Outlook Express from Internet Explorer or the Mail icon on your desktop. I'll move across the menu bar and discuss each of the buttons. New creates a blank email form that you fill in, shown in Figure 2.25. The darker area of the email message is where the header information goes. The Account area will have your email account, the one you are using. You can also give the email a priority level.

The To: box is the recipient's address. You can type it, or if the person is in your contacts database, you can select the person by clicking the Contacts button. You have options to send a copy to someone as well as a blind copy (where the original recipient does not know others are

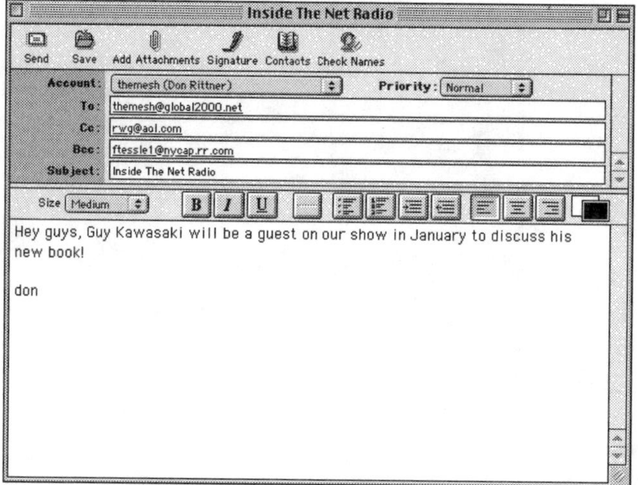

Figure 2.25

A new email message ready for sending.

getting a copy). The Subject box is the title of your email. Because you or the recipient probably get a lot of mail, it's a good idea to be specific in the subject box and use descriptors that both you and the recipient will recognize. If you are like me and get tons of email, believe me, the emails with subject headings such as "Hi," or "What's up," do not get read. If you subscribe to several mailing lists, you will be getting a lot of email. You do want a way to separate the junk mail from the important mail.

After the Subject heading, there is another area with several tools for font size, color, and text arrangement that let you format the email the way you like. The large blank area is where you type the body of the message.

When you are through composing your email, you click the Send button and mail it. You can add an attachment, say a file or graphic, by clicking the Add Attachments button (which looks like a paper-clip). You will be prompted to find the file or files and add them. Outlook Express will compress them automatically.

The next button is a Signature option. If you have typed a signature in the Preferences section, it will appear. If you want random signatures to appear, put the signatures into text files, place them in a folder called Random Signatures, and place that into the Preferences folder in the system folder. Every time you select the button, a different signature will automatically appear. The next button is the Contacts database, which I discuss later. The final button, Check Names, will check for duplicate addresses.

Outlook Express makes composing and sending email easy, as you can see. Let's return to the main window of Outlook Express and discuss replying to a message.

Reply

When you start Outlook Express, the first thing it will do is check whether you have new mail, provided that you selected that option in the Preferences section (in the section called Outlook Express: General). I have the emailer check every 10 minutes because I get a lot of email.

If you have new mail, you will see it in the window titled Inbox. The subject lines of new mail are boldface. If an email has an attachment, you will see the paper-clip icon in front of the subject. Along with the subject heading is the name of the sender and the date.

In my example in Figure 2.26, I sent a test message to myself. You will notice in the bottom-left corner the number of emails in my Inbox: 505. I told you I get a lot of email! Suppose I am not interested in replying to mail, only reading it. I simply select the email that is boldfaced, and the text appears in the bottom. If I decide I do want to reply, double-clicking the subject again will open it and give me reply functions. Also, suppose I want to reply to a message I received a week ago. Instead of scrolling down the list of 500 emails, I can use a built-in search feature right below the title of the Inbox. Here, I simply type the information I want to find

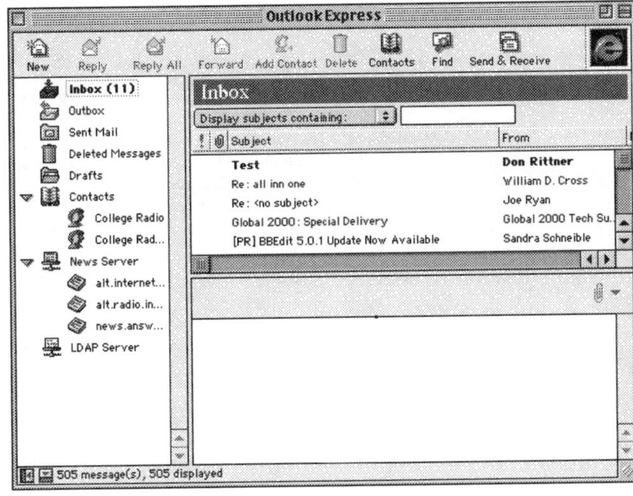

Figure 2.26
A test message sent to myself.

that appeared in the subject, messages from, or messages to line. It's instant searching, so as I type a letter, it displays its guesses.

When you click the Reply button on a message, Outlook Express automatically puts the original message in the proper form for response (adding the >s) and inserts the cursor before the message, also separated by a dotted line. This is where you write your reply. Click the Send button, and off it goes to the recipient. You can save a copy. Add Attachment, Signature, Contacts, and Check Names are also options, as with the original post. Figure 2.27 shows a reply to a message.

That's how easy it is to send and reply to email using Outlook Express. There are more features to this great email application, so let's return to the main window.

Reply All

If the email you received was from a number of people, clicking the Reply All button will place all their email addresses in your reply.

Forward

If you want to forward a piece of email that you received to some other party, clicking the Forward button will give you a copy of the email with a blank To: box. Fill in the new recipient's address and send.

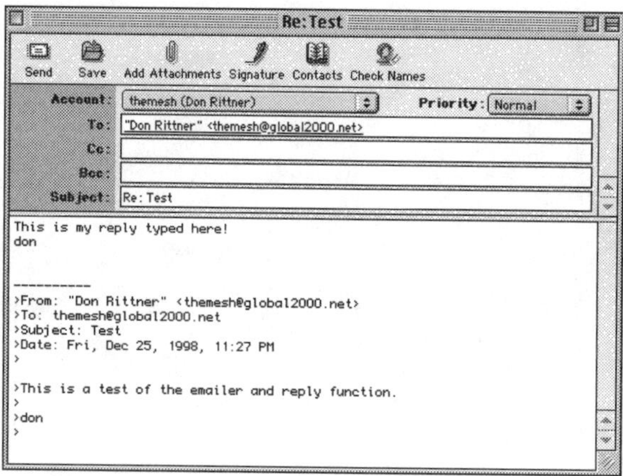

Figure 2.27
A sample reply.

Add Contact

If you received a piece of email and you want to keep the sender's email address for future correspondence, click the Add Contact button to place the user ID into your contacts database.

Delete

Obvious, isn't it? Delete an email. It will move into the trash can called Deleted Email. When you quit, Outlook Express will prompt you before emptying the trash.

Contacts

The Contacts database is your address book. You create a new contact by clicking the New button. Fill out the form that includes personal and business information and notes, and click Save, as shown in Figure 2.28. That's all there is to it.

Mailing Lists

You can create your own mailing lists, as shown in Figure 2.29. This allows you to send one email to many people at once. In the Main Contacts window, you create a mailing list by selecting the button with that name and giving your list a unique name. If the members of your list are already in your main contact database, you simply select their names

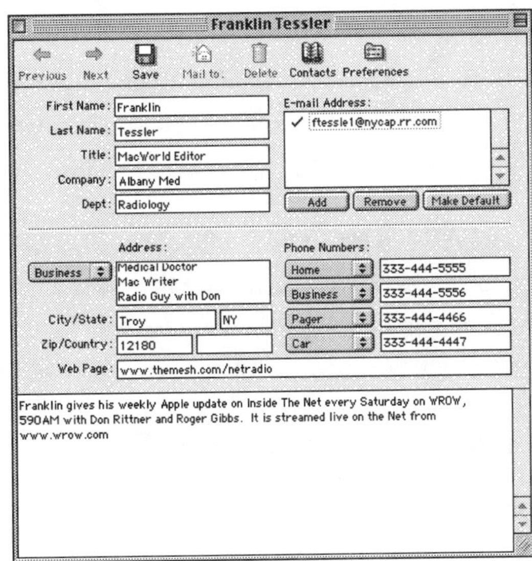

Figure 2.28
Adding a new member to your contacts database is simple.

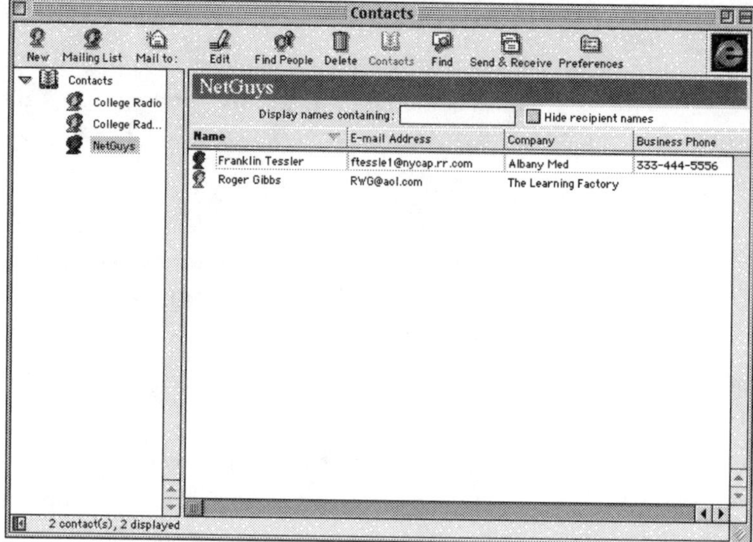

Figure 2.29
Creating a mailing list is simple.

and drag them over to the new mailing list. My example, Net Guys, has two people in it, Franklin Tessler and Roger Gibbs, who present Mac and PC segments on my radio show "Inside The Net."

When you are ready to send an email to the list, select the mailing list by double-clicking it. You will see all the names on the list. In the menu, you will see a Mail to button. Click it to get a blank email form with the names of the list already inserted. Type your message and send it.

Find

Back on the main window on Outlook Express, the Find button lets you conduct a live search for information in almost every part of Outlook Express: email, folders, drafts, deleted messages, and so on.

Send And Receive

You use the Send and Receive button to send email when ready and to check for email waiting on your ISP's server. You can force Outlook Express to check for email at a time interval you set in the Preferences section.

Finding People Using LDAP

You will notice that the last entry on the left of the main window of Outlook Express is LDAP Server. LDAP, short for Lightweight Directory

Access Protocol, is used to provide online directories over the Net. LDAP was designed at the University of Michigan and is used by Netscape, Microsoft Exchange, Lotus Notes, Novell, and others. The default directory service is 411. You can add more. Some other LDAP servers are:

- *Bigfoot*—**ldap.bigfoot.com** (**www.bigfoot.com**)
- *Four11*—**ldap.four11.com** (**www.four11.com**) (The Outlook Express default site)
- *InfoSpace*—**ldap.infospace.com** (**www.infospace.com**)
- *Switchboard*—**ldap.switchboard.com** (**www.switchboard.com**)
- *WhoWhere*—**ldap.whowhere.com** (**www.whowhere.com**)

A worldwide list of LDAP directories appears on the Dante Web site (**www.dante.net/np/pdi.html**), a European network service. For a good explanation of LDAP, visit Altro's Solutions, Inc. Web page (**www.altro.com/LDAP.htm**).

Do not assume that the addresses you find on any of these directory services are current or even correct (see the example in Figure 2.30), but they are a good starting point for looking for people. If you do find someone you are looking for, you can add him or her to the contacts database by clicking the name and selecting Add Contact.

FTP (File Transfer Protocol)—Reach Out And Grab Something

You will see the word FTP used frequently on the Net. It means File Transfer Protocol. I like to think it means "Fetch That Program!" FTP is a method for transferring information, no matter how big, from someone's computer to yours, or vice versa. FTP is one of the best features of the Net. You can use FTP to grab text documents, software programs, spreadsheets, graphics, sound or video files, and just about anything else in digital form.

How does it work? In my office at The Learning Factory, in Albany, New York, I have a three-drawer file cabinet. I like to find and read

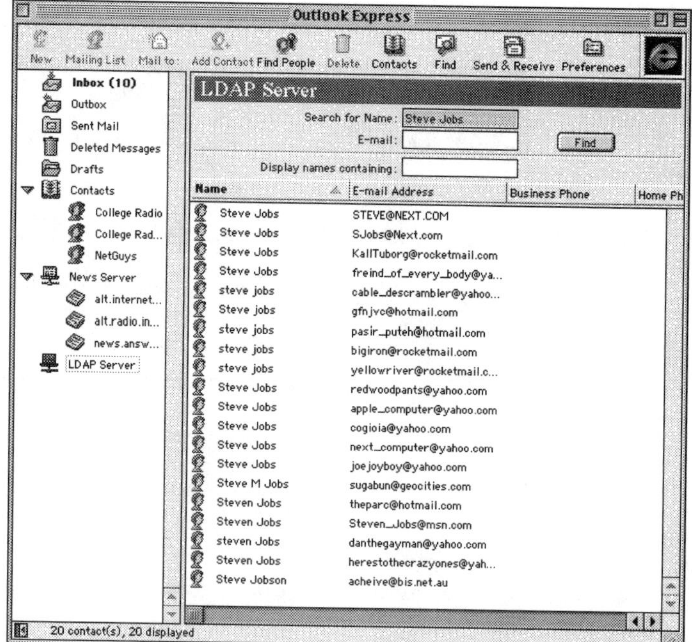

Figure 2.30
Do not rely on the accuracy of email directory services.

interesting environmental articles, having spent most of my life fighting for various environmental causes. When I find an article I think my friends would like, I make several copies and put them in the third drawer of my file cabinet. The first two drawers are locked. I don't allow anyone in there; they're private. But the third drawer is "public." My friends know they can come in when the school is open and look through the public drawer, and if they like anything, they can take a copy. Many times, I don't know whether they've stopped by or not. I might be teaching when they visit, so it happens without my knowledge, anonymously.

FTP operates in a similar fashion with two differences. You don't have to physically visit a site to grab a copy of something, and you don't have to worry about what time it is. An FTP site is open 24 hours a day, 7 days a week.

Grabbing Files

Using FTP today is a no-brainer. When you download a file from a Web site, you are using FTP, although it is often slower than using a standalone FTP program, the second preferred method. There are several good FTP programs for the Mac market:

➢ Fetch (**www.dartmouth.edu/pages/softdev/fetch.html**)

➢ Transit (**www.panic.com**)

➢ NetFinder (**www.ozemail.com.au/~pli/netfinder/**)

➢ Anarchie (**www.stairways.com**)

Because you will be using FTP frequently, I discuss these various programs later.

FTP sites have always been popular. FTP was one of the earliest approaches to organizing information on the Net. However, in the early days, you had to know exactly where those FTP sites were located and the name of the file you were looking for.

Archie was an early search protocol to find FTP sites and their contents. (You still had to know the name of the file.) Archie is still around and doing fine, and it now includes searching Web sites. Check out the Bunyip Archie home page (**www.bunyip.com/products/archie/**). There are still a few Archie sites around the world that are open to the public (**www.bunyip.com/products/archie/world/servers.html**).

Gopher superseded Archie. Gopher provided a menu of FTP sites and a graphical representation of the data and location (icons, folders, files, and directories). Gopher allowed you to retrieve the data. (The Web has been replacing Gopher.) You can access Gopher from your Web browser. A standalone Gopher client, Turbogopher, shown in Figure 2.31, is great for downloading from Gopher sites. Put the URL **gopher://boombox.micro.umn.edu:70/11/gopher/Macintosh-TurboGopher/** in your Web browser and download it.

Many Gopher sites still exist, although they are slowly being replaced by hypertext—the Web. Microsoft's Internet Browser exhibits Gopher sites hierarchically by title, as shown in Figure 2.32, without the graphics, and Netscape Navigator exhibits Gopher sites in the original way, showing folders, files, and directories, as shown in Figure 2.33.

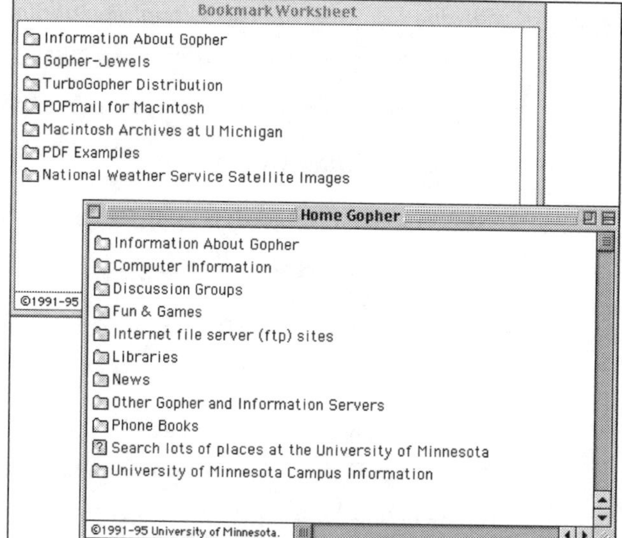

Figure 2.31
Turbogopher lets you quickly grab files from FTP sites around the world.

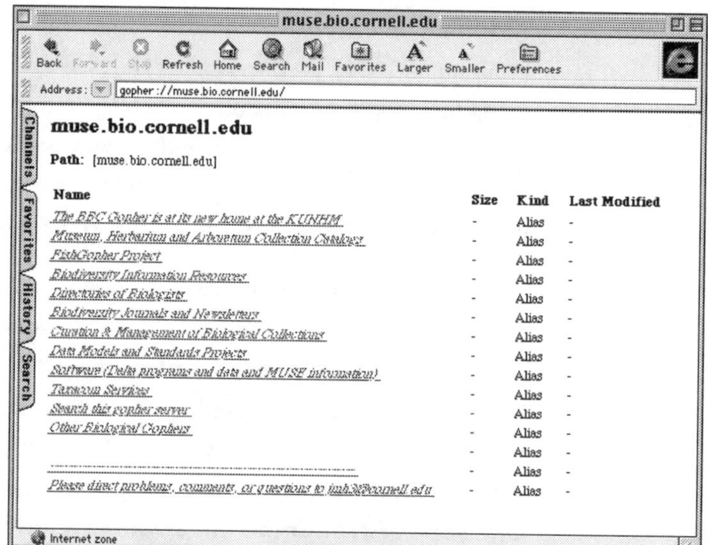

Figure 2.32
Gopher sites look like any other Web link in Internet Explorer.

How Does FTP Work?

Many people and organizations around the world give up a part of their computer hard drives to create an anonymous FTP site. FTP is just a set of files that are reserved so people may anonymously sign on. When you log on to an FTP site, you use the word "anonymous" for the user ID and "guest" or your email address as the password. You are usually allowed

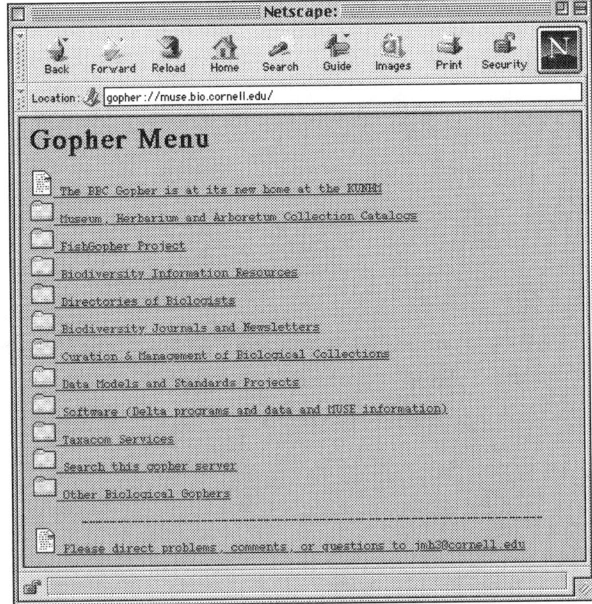

Figure 2.33
Gopher sites look like the traditional folders and file icons familiar to Mac users in Netscape Navigator.

only in the pub (public) directory, where you can poke around and download files to your computer. Some sites require you to use your email address instead of the word anonymous.

To find out more about the workings of FTP in a non-GUI environment, read the excellent FTP FAQ that is maintained by Perry Rovers. You can get it by dropping the following URL into your Web browser: **ftp://garbo.uwasa.fi:pc/pc/doc-net/ftp-list.zip**. This FAQ will give you all you need to know about the subject. Drop it on StuffIt Expander because it is a PC zip file.

Using FTP

Let's look at how easy it is to grab a file using FTP. Most of the Mac FTP programs have a group or set of bookmarks of popular Mac-oriented FTP sites already built in. You just select one and go to it. Let's look at some of the more popular Mac FTP clients:

Fetch 3.03

Fetch, as shown in Figure 2.34, is one of the oldest and most reliable FTP clients for the Mac. Fetch has many advanced features as well as the

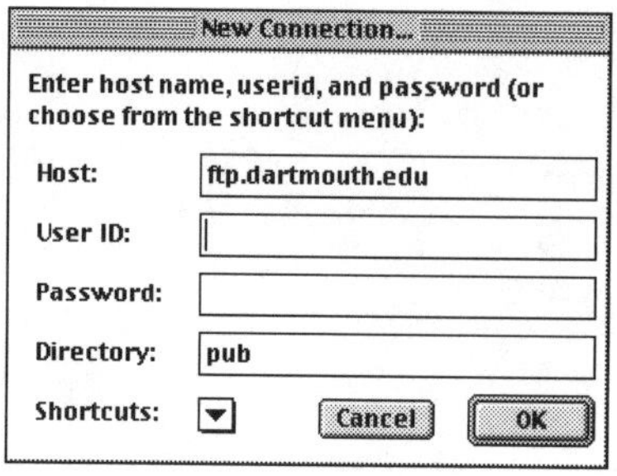

Figure 2.34

Fetch is one of the most popular FTP clients on the Mac platform.

basic upload and download options. You can download Fetch via your Web browser by typing in the following URL: **ftp://ftp.dartmouth.edu/pub/mac/Fetch_3.0.3.hqx**. You launch Fetch like any Mac program: double-click it. You'll see a New Connection... window with the Dartmouth FTP site as the default setting.

You will notice that the User ID and Password windows are blank. This is because anonymous and guest are the default ID and password. Some sites require you to use your online address or other information. The next box has pub for public as the default. The pub directory is the directory normally set aside for anonymous FTP. If you know the exact path of the file you want to download, you can type or paste that instead. Below that are shortcuts, shown in Figure 2.35. If you click the window, you will notice several FTP sites already listed. By selecting one, you can go to the site. You can create your own shortcuts in the Customize window.

Suppose you select the default site, Dartmouth. Fetch will go to the Dartmouth pub directory automatically and show you a list of folders and files in that directory. A welcome screen, shown in Figure 2.36, will give you some basic information or directions. The FTP window opens

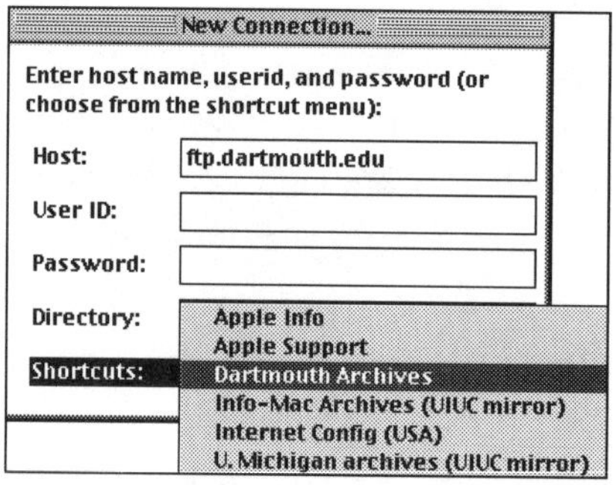

Figure 2.35

Fetch has built-in shortcuts to your favorite FTP sites.

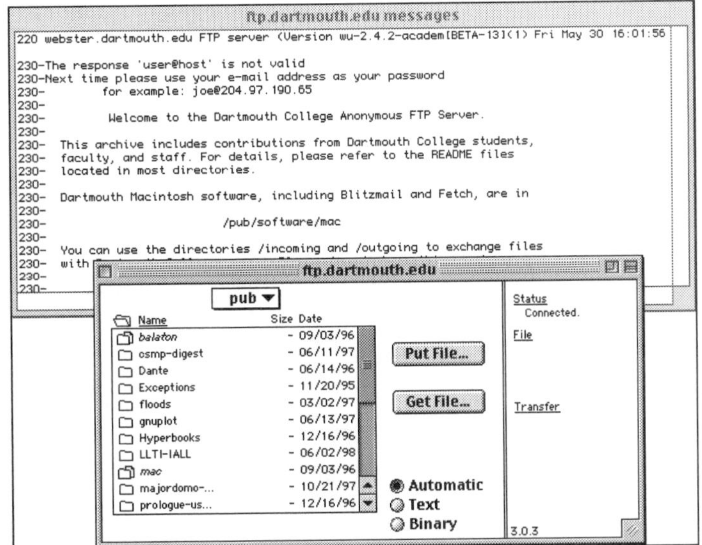

Figure 2.36

FTP sites present a welcome screen and list of directories.

the pub directory and lists files and folders along with dates of the last entry. Look for the Mac folder and double-click it. This takes you to the Mac subdirectory, which lists more files and folders.

You will notice at the center of the bottom of the screen that you have the ability to choose how you want to upload (put) or download (get) a file. If you choose Automatic, Fetch will look at the data you want to send or receive and make a guess. If you are only dealing with text files, select the text option, or if you are dealing with binary files, you can select that option. It's best to leave it automatic if you are not sure.

After you open the Mac subdirectory, look for the latest version of Fetch (you may have to scroll down the window), select it, and click the Get File (download) button. A dialog box is displayed so you can download the file where you choose and rename the file if you like, as shown in Figure 2.37. You want the latest version of Fetch. Click the Save button.

After you click Save, the file will download to your hard drive. As shown in Figure 2.38, a time indicator on the right will display the download progress. When it's finished downloading, you can select another file or check out other folders or files for downloading. There is always an index or readme file in a pub directory that lists the files in the directory, so download that first and read it. If you have permission to upload

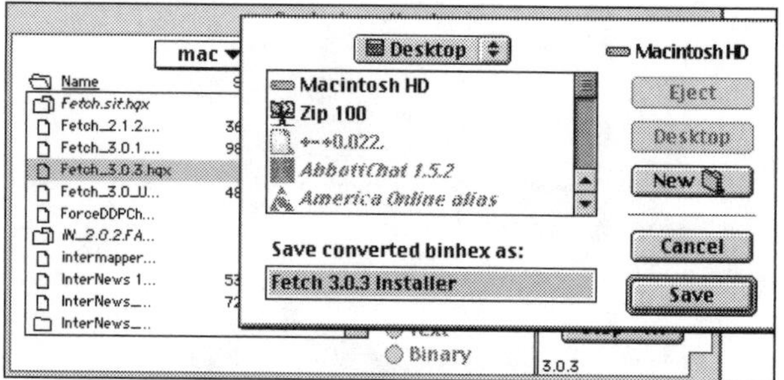

Figure 2.37
You can choose to rename a file and direct where to download it.

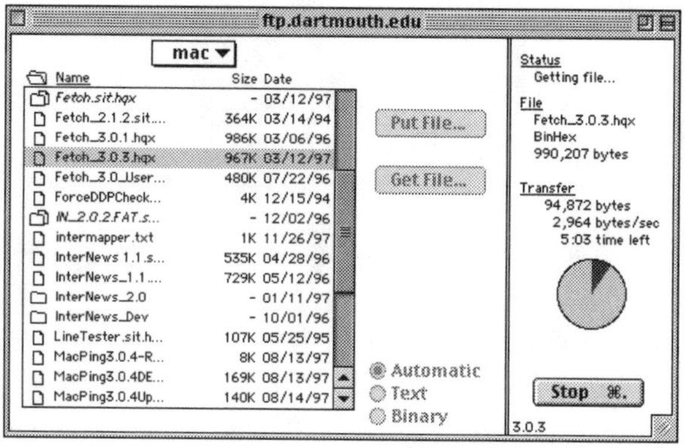

Figure 2.38
You can see how long it will take to download with the progress circle.

files to an FTP site, the Put File button allows you to perform the upload. Clicking it will open a dialog box and let you select the file and its format as raw data, text, BinHex, and so on, before you upload it.

NetFinder

NetFinder is a shareware FTP client by Peter Li and Vincent Tan that is similar to the Finder in operation, as shown in Figure 2.39. You can transfer files via FTP and HTTP and browse locally on your hard drive. You can save a list of favorite sites as bookmarks. Download NetFinder from the NetFinder Web site (**www.ozemail.com.au/~pli/netfinder/**).

Transit

Transit, shown in Figure 2.40, is a shareware FTP client by Panic Software that couldn't be any easier to use. When you connect to an FTP site, simply grab the file you want and drag it over to the window of your hard drive. Visit **www.panic.com** to download the latest version.

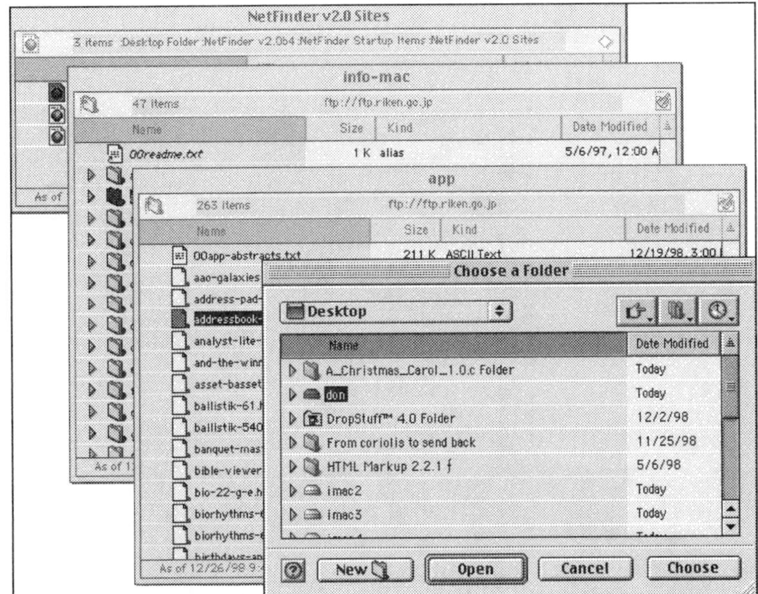

Figure 2.39

NetFinder has a Finder-like appearance and lets you point and click your way to downloading.

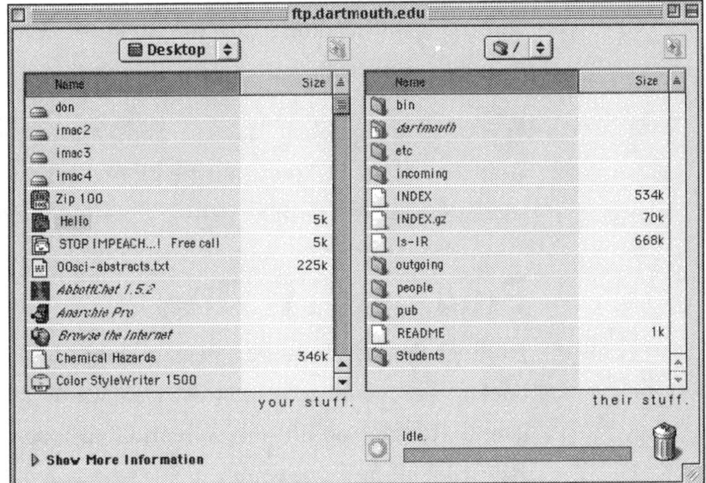

Figure 2.40

Using Transit is as simple as grabbing a file from one window and dragging it to another.

Anarchie

The Swiss Army knife of FTP was created by Peter N. Norton. The shareware program Anarchie does FTP big time. You can download entire Web sites or view them in link form, make Netscape or Internet Explorer use Anarchie for FTP downloads, and use the built-in Sherlock for Web searching. Anarchie even lets you do Archie inquiries to the few remaining public Archie sites. It has many FTP sites already bookmarked.

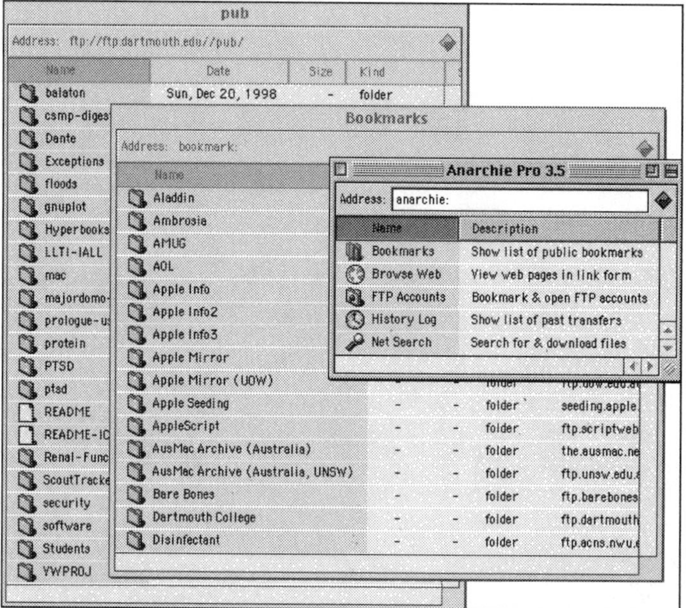

Figure 2.41

Anarchie is the Swiss Army knife of FTP.

Visit the Stairways home page (**www.stairways.com**) and download Anarchie, shown in Figure 2.41.

As you can see, grabbing files from another computer is quite easy on your iMac. Any of the FTP programs mentioned in these sections will give you an easy-to-use interface for getting the latest goodies for your iMac.

Finding FTP Sites

Although the FTP client programs mentioned here all have FTP sites bookmarked, you should also visit a great site for finding Mac-related FTP sites. Go to the Mac-FTP-list (**www.quillserv.com/www/macres/ftplist.html**) by Bruce Grubb. It hasn't been updated in over a year, but it still lists many FTP sites. Another good site for FTP and Mac programs can be found at Datatek (**www.datatek.net/Mac_Files/Macintosh_FTP_Sites**). EzAccess (**www.ez-access.com/macftp.html**) has a good list of Mac FTP sites. Visit Tile-Net (**http://tile.net/ftp/**) and type "Macintosh" to get a list of about a dozen of so Mac FTP sites.

Filez

www.filez.com

Filez every week scans over 7,000 ftp sites around the world and creates a catalog of all the files, currently over 75 million. You can then search its database which gives you a list of where the files are located and you can download immediately.

Telnet—Just Like Being There

Telnet is the main Internet protocol for logging in to a remote machine, and it is especially suited for searching through databases, library card catalogs, large datasets, and even computer bulletin boards. There are about 10,000 Telnet sites around the world. Telnet is often a non-graphical interface, unlike the Web, even though you can launch it within your Web browser it opens as a separate window, as shown in Figure 2.42. Even Gopher uses Telnet to connect to remote host computers. When you use Telnet, you are actually using the other computer—unlike FTP, where you grab a file and bring it to your machine.

When you log in to a Telnet site, you need to type a user ID and password. Some government or public sites will identify themselves in the welcome window. If you are logging on to a bulletin board, you can usually sign up on the spot as a new member. Usually, a welcome page will give you login information as well.

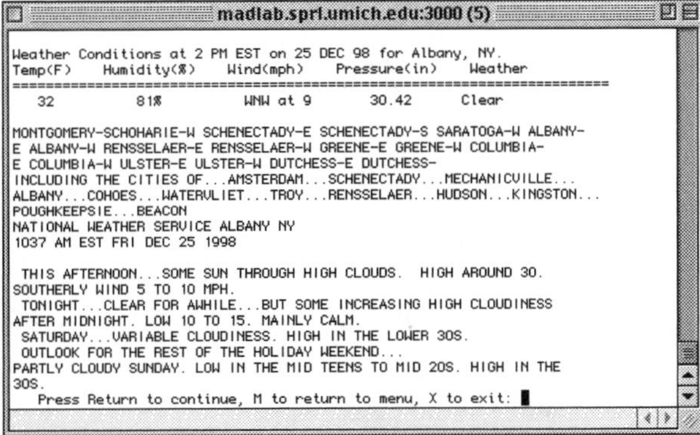

Figure 2.42
Telnet to the Weather Underground and check local weather.

The most common Telnet application for Mac users is NCSA Telnet, developed by the National Center for Supercomputing Applications (NCSA) at the University of Illinois at Urbana-Champaign. Rolf Brawn from Sassy Software modified and improved it with his BetterTelnet, which I recommend. Download BetterTelnet (**www.cstone.net/~rbraun/mac/telnet/**) and use your application helper in Internet Explorer preferences area to make it the default Telnet application.

You usually launch Telnet by selecting it as a link on a Web page, although you can open the application by itself and type the URL. The NCSA group prepared an excellent full tutorial on using NCSA Telnet (**http://helpdesk.uvic.ca/how-to/support/mac/telnet/docs/MacTelnet.Home.html**).

Some Telnet Sites To Explore

Use Telnet to virtually visit hundreds of sites on the Net.

Big Dummy's Guide To The Internet

http://trex.nanzan-u.ac.jp/bdgtti/bdg_toc.html#SEC93

A bit dated, this guide was written in 1994, but many of the Telnet sites still work.

Hytelnet

www.einet.net/hytelnet/HYTELNET.html

This is a huge searchable database of Telnet sites.

Safety, Environmental, Health, And Other Industry-Related Information

http://www.if.uidaho.edu/ehs/telnetsh.html

This Web page features a handful of environmental Telnet sites.

Telnet Sites On The Web

http://anzio.com/telnetsites.html

This sites lists hundreds of Telnet sites arranged in broad categories from education to entertainment.

Mailing Lists And Newsgroups

Mailing lists and Usenet newsgroups are explained in more detail in Chapters 3 and 5, but I also want to mention them here. Humans have been communicating for thousands of years, using every possible method from cuneiform on tablets to ASCII on computers. Pick up your newspaper, and you can find daily meetings of groups of people who share some common interest. It might be a book club, garden club, a PTA group, a user group, or a seminar at your local library.

The Internet has extended your ability to communicate with like-minded people from the far corners of the world. The Internet mailing list (also called the discussion list, listserv, or list) and Usenet newsgroups are nothing more than roundtable discussions about different subjects. Membership is free. Business is conducted every day, regardless of time, and no one cares where you live.

To participate in an Internet discussion, all you need is your email account. Once you know the name and address of the mailing list you want to join, you simply subscribe to it by sending an email to a special address. In the subject heading or body of your email message, you type "subscribe *name of the list*". Sometimes, you insert your email address, or name, instead of the list name.

A mailing list is operated automatically by special software commonly called a list server. A popular list may have heavy traffic and generate 100 or more emails a day. If you subscribe to more than one list, you may get a clogged mailbox overnight. Fortunately, the list might offer a "digest" version. The software automatically collects all the email generated that day and sends it to you as one big email. You can then download it and read it at your leisure.

Actually, Listserv is the name of a specific software program but has also become the generic name for mailing-list software, much to the displeasure of L-Soft International, Inc, (**www.lsoft.com**), the company that developed it. There are several other mailing-list software programs available, and you can usually identify them by their type of subscription address. For example, the following are common list type addresses:

- listserv@somewhere.domain (common among university lists)
- majordomo@somewhere.domain (common among commercial lists)
- requests@somewhere.domain (Macintosh list software)

  For a more complete of list software programs visit **www.catalog.com/vivian/mailing-list-providers.html**.

The important thing to remember is that you subscribe or unsubscribe to one address, and you send your requests, or discussions, to a different address. The list server software automatically sends a copy to everyone who has subscribed to the list, so you don't have to worry about copying everyone. There does seem to be one recurring problem with this arrangement. List subscribers, especially new ones, often get the two addresses mixed up, and you will often see "unsubscribe" or "subscribe" in a post during the normal course of receiving your list emails. Although it is tempting to scold the person and start a flame war, it's good etiquette to send the person a private email telling him how to get off or on the list. Some listserv software programs are now placing subscribe and unsubscribe instructions directly in the headers of a post.

You can subscribe to the list that announces new lists, naturally called new-list. Send email to listserv@vm1.nodak.ed, and in the body of the message, put "SUB NEW-LIST *Your Name*". Because there are many new lists being developed, you can expect a bit of traffic in your mailbox on this one. Mailing lists are discussed further in Chapter 5.

Usenet Newsgroups

Usenet is a distributed news network that was created before the Internet by a couple of college graduate students. Worried they were going to miss news about their favorite Unix programming language,

File Not Found

Sometimes a Web page will get moved or renamed so you will get the error message, File Not found, when trying to connect. Try deleting the part of the address on the rightmost end of a Web address and work your way back to the left, a / at a time. Then, you may find the moved page.

they wrote software that allowed a person to post public news from one Unix computer to another Unix computer anywhere in the world. They called their public postings "articles" and their topics "newsgroups," following a newsletter metaphor. They were in fact trying to mimic a Unix newsletter and thought that was the only subject that would be discussed.

Usenet has grown from two computers to millions. Usenet news rides along the entire Internet as well as personal computer bulletin board systems. Because of its broadcast beginnings, you do not participate in Usenet using your email account. You need special newsreaders to subscribe, read, post, and otherwise use the network. Before the development of special graphical user interfaces, called GUIs, you had to have a good working knowledge of Unix or use special text-based newsreaders. Outlook Express, bundled with your iMac, is a fine newsreader.

Newsgroups are arranged in seven main hierarchies:

- comp—Discussion of computers and related subjects.
- misc—Topics that fall outside the other six (law, kids, and so on).
- news—Deals mostly with Usenet the Network
- rec—Recreation and sports, arts, hobbies, literature, and such.
- sci—Scientific research discussions.
- soc—Social issues, religion, politics, culture, and so on.
- talk—Gab, gab, gab. News and discussion around Usenet and related issues.

There are both public and private newsgroups, but the majority are open to all. There are more than 80,000 newsgroups, and the number is growing daily. Usenet has become the largest single discussion network in the world. A special online etiquette (called netiquette) has been created because of Usenet and now is used on the Net as well. Not

Who Makes Up The Net?

In my 20-plus years of being online, I have been exposed to enough people to see a pattern of personality types emerge. I have grouped people into seven kinds of Net personalities (blame it on my anthropology background) that are visible on the Net and Usenet in particular:

- *CyberOp*—These are the movers and shakers of the Net. They are mostly volunteers who write and distribute FAQs, respond to help requests in public chat rooms or mailing lists, put up useful Web pages to help people, and help in the voting process for creating new newsgroups on Usenet. You will see their names pop up frequently. You should be very nice to these folks.
- *CyberSquirrels*—They love to collect things—every FAQ, list, guide, software, graphic, flame, or any other piece of information they can find on the Net. No one knows what they do with it all, but they probably have a stamp collection and the entire set of *Star Wars* collectors cards in their attic.
- *Netgrumps*—These are the old-timers who were on the Net when it was a "real" Net; back in the days when you only talked about bits, protocols, and defense grants. They dislike all newbies. They will eventually go the way of the Apple II and PCjr.
- *Netters*—These are the folks who do everything right. They contribute, help others, follow the rules, rarely flame, and are all-around nice people. Most of the 100 million folks on the Net belong to this group.
- *NetWeights*—These make up the large majority of Usenet and Internet users. You know they are there, but they rarely ever post or reply to anything. However, they do read just about everything, and their presence is known. Some people refer to them as lurkers. On the Net and Usenet, they subscribe to tons of mailing lists but rarely write anything.
- *Newbie*—If you bought this book, chances are you're a newbie, a brand new computer user. You will stick out on the Net like a sore thumb unless you study Chapter 4. A newbie can be a brand new computer user or Internet user.
- *RAMheads*—This group is always complaining about something or will disagree with you no matter what you post. If you post "The sun is up," they'll make you prove it. They post in many different newsgroups and mailing lists and take exception to almost everything posted. They frequent public chat rooms, too. They live to see their own postings and names. They love to start flame wars. This is a group you wish would experience a power outage for a long time. They insist their postings are important and the Net can't survive without their input. They are the kind of people you accidentally invite to dinner once and then can't wait until they leave. Also known as *Buttheads*.

You should work on becoming a Netter and strive to become a CyberOp.

Linking To Computer Bulletin Boards

If you plan to use your iMac to connect only to the Internet, then you do not have to read this sidebar. However, if you do plan to use your iMac to find and connect to local bulletin boards, or university computing centers, read on. You need special communications software to allow your computer to communicate with your modem. Once you select and set up your communications package, most of the communication functions are performed automatically by your computer and modem.

There are several software choices available for your iMac. Some of these are commercial products that cost a couple of hundred dollars, and some are freeware or shareware (available from a user group or the Net). Some of the free programs have as many, if not more, features as commercial products.

What should you look for in a software program? Make sure you can easily change the parameters such as bit rate (the modem speed in bits per second), parity, and stop bits. Additionally, it should have two or more error-checking protocols such as Xmodem or Ymodem. (They all have ASCII download capability.) Make sure you can select different terminal emulation (the ability to emulate different kinds of computers, mostly minicomputers or mainframes). Options such as storing phone numbers will allow you to call all your favorite boards without typing the phone number each time. Several of the packages allow you to write macros or scripts (shortcuts you can write to automate signing on and signing off and other things such as downloading or uploading files). Remember to purchase communications software written for the Mac operating system.

Stop Bits

Because your iMac and modem are not sending all your data in one burst, it's necessary to add an extra bit at the beginning and end of each byte while it is being transmitted. These extra bits are called start bits and stop bits. The way it works is simple. Your iMac and modem tell the receiving computer that the next bit being sent is the start of the data flow (the start bit) and then sends a stop bit to tell the computer it received the complete byte.

Most bulletin boards and university networks require you to set up your communications software as one stop bit in order to communicate successfully. Others will ask for two stop bits. Regardless, you will need to know how many. Most bulletin boards will require one stop bit, so if in doubt, that is how you should set up your communications software.

Parity

Parity refers to the number of 1s in a binary number. If the quantity is even, the number has even parity; if odd, then it has odd parity. Parity checks for mistakes in transmission. If parity is used, it is placed right before the stop bit. It can be either a 1 or 0, depending on whether you select even or odd parity. If you select even parity but the byte contents have odd parity, the parity bit will be a 1, so the parity of the entire byte will be even. On the opposite end, if you select even parity, and the data byte already has even parity, the parity bit will be set to 0, so even parity will be maintained. Why do you need to know this? The sending and receiving computers must have the same parity. Most bulletin boards require no parity.

Duplex

Duplex and half duplex are terms that refer to the direction of the data transmission. Half duplex means that data is sent between two computers in one direction at a time. Duplex, or full duplex, is data transmitted in both directions simultaneously. Some error-checking protocols such as Xmodem are half duplex. The sending computer must wait for the receiving computer to tell it that it received each block of data before it sends another. This often slows transmission because line noise on the phone can disrupt transmission and the block of data must be retransmitted. Most bulletin boards require a duplex setting.

File Transfer

On the Internet, transferring files is done with FTP, file transfer protocol. Computer bulletin boards have several file transfer protocols. The information you grab from bulletin boards can be in the form of text (ASCII) files or binary files (files that may be programs, applications, graphics, spreadsheets, or specially formatted ASCII files). Downloading is the process of taking information from a bulletin board or network. Uploading is the process of sending information stored on your iMac to a bulletin board or network computer for others to use.

Your communications software will allow you to download information using several protocols to make sure the resulting download is error-free. You can capture text documents or straight ASCII right from the screen. Most software programs let you capture the text as it scrolls down the screen and save it into a text file. You also can download the file using the ASCII download command. ASCII contains no error checking, so if you have a bad phone line, the resulting text download may be jumbled beyond recognition.

Most communication programs carry two or more error-checking protocols. Xmodem sends data in small blocks of 128 bytes and then checks for accuracy of the transmission, telling the other computer to resend the block if there are errors. Xmodem-CRC is a version of Xmodem that uses a more accurate error checking called Cyclic Redundancy Check. Ymodem uses larger blocks than Xmodem, 1,024 bytes, and allows batch transfer, or downloading more than one file at a time. Kermit is the name of both a protocol and a communication program (and a frog). Kermit is popular for downloading from mainframes and minicomputers on college campuses. It's slow, but you can use it for batch downloading (getting more than one file at a time). Zmodem also downloads multiple files and can recover its transfers intact if you temporarily lose the connection.

The only thing you need to remember is that both computers must use the same protocol when downloading (to your computer) or uploading (to the other computer). That's why when you select your communications package, you should select one that supports a number of file transfer protocols. Nine out of ten times, you will use ASCII, Xmodem, or Ymodem for grabbing files.

knowing netiquette can prove embarrassing to a new user. Before you participate in Usenet or the Net, study Chapter 4 and save yourself the embarrassment of looking foolish in front of millions of readers. The next chapter explains Usenet in more detail.

Ready To Rock-And-Roll?

You are now ready to use your iMac and go onto the Net. You know how to use email, FTP, and Telnet, the three tenors of the Internet. The following chapters will complete your understanding of all that is waiting for you on the Net.

3 Usenet: The News Network

Rittner's Computer Law: There are 5,000 great people for every jerk on Usenet. But that still is a lot of jerks. Proceed with caution and eyes wide open.

Usenet (or Users Network) is a worldwide electronic soapbox for online users. Each day, millions of people discuss, debate, and share their ideas, opinions, and information via Usenet. Like the Internet, Usenet has no geographic boundaries or time constraints, and it operates 24 hours a day, 7 days a week. And like the Internet, Usenet isn't owned by anyone. It belongs to the people.

Let's be clear about Usenet right from the top. Usenet is not the Internet. The Internet is not Usenet. They are two different computer networks. However, Usenet does ride over the Internet bandwidth, and someday, it probably will become just another part of the Net, like email, Telnet, or FTP.

Usenet is not really a computer network like the Internet. It's a distributed news service; a collection of public conferences, or discussion groups, called newsgroups, where you can discuss thousands of different topics. The messages are collectively called netnews, or the news, and more than 80,000 newsgroups span the Usenet digital frontier, covering every topic from Agriculture to Zambia. More newsgroups are formed every day by millions of users in more than 100 countries. Usenet is a very busy place.

Although anarchy is the rule rather than the exception on Usenet, this policy does promote freedom of expression, and Usenet is slowly transforming the way we meet and communicate with one another. It's a form of high-tech socializing. However, your social group is not limited to your local neighborhood. Like the Internet, Usenet is global, and you can discuss any topic with men and women in New York, London, or just about any location on earth that has a digital connection.

Millions of people find Usenet an important place to get valuable information, to share research, reports, or data, to find jobs, to learn how to fix their computers, to get reviews of software or hardware, to retrieve software, to argue, to debate, to tell jokes, to get therapy, and even to find dates and potential spouses. Usenet then is an electronic extension of a vital trait that makes us human—one-on-one communication.

Like the Internet, Usenet represents a cross section of humanity. You will find that most users are civil, some are ill mannered, and some will try to rip you off with some business scam. In short, Usenet is a reflection of human society as we know it. Enter at your own risk and with eyes wide open.

Not Only For Talk

Usenet is primarily for public discourse, and although it's really not a repository for software programs, several newsgroups do provide access to binary files (software applications, graphic files, spreadsheets, and other non-text items). A few newsgroups carry the actual binary file in the newsgroup post by converting the file into ASCII text. This conversion allows the file to be sent over Usenet without any special formatting. To change the text file back into its binary or usable condition, you use special programs that are available free (explained previously in Chapter 2). Although Usenet is primarily for discussion, you can obtain some software there as well.

Usenet Is Older Than The Internet

Where did Usenet come from and why? Blame it on college kids. Tom Truscott and Jim Ellis, two graduate students from Duke University in North Carolina, created Usenet in 1979. Both students wanted to hook up some computers so they could share news and information about the Unix community. Usenet ran only on Unix-based computers in those days, but today, any computer from a mainframe to a small home PC (and a modem) can get Usenet access.

The commercial online services such as America Online, CompuServe, and Prodigy carry Usenet. Versions of Netscape Navigator and Microsoft Internet Explorer have the ability to participate in Usenet using your local Internet provider. Many email clients such as Outlook Express can act as a news reader as well. Even home computer bulletin boards, perhaps in your own city, carry Usenet, so there are plenty of ways to join in this global dialog. Quite frankly, Usenet is everywhere.

I use Outlook Express to demonstrate how to participate on Usenet because the program comes bundled with your iMac.

What Is A Newsgroup?

Newsgroups are the heart and soul of Usenet. A Usenet newsgroup is simply an electronic collection of posts created by a group of computer users, centered around a specific topic, and unaffected by geography or time. Newsgroups are open to everyone. However, some newsgroups restrict what can be posted.

Think of a newsgroup as a monthly book club at your local library, a computer user group, or even a Boy Scout troop monthly meeting. It's the coming together of strangers to discuss a subject of common interest. The major difference between your hometown meeting and a Usenet discussion is that each newsgroup may comprise people from many different cultures who are separated by thousands of miles.

There are thousands of newsgroups—80,000 and growing, as of this writing—and sorting through them could take weeks. To make newsgroups a little easier to navigate, they are arranged into seven main hierarchies. These seven hierarchies are distributed around the world to thousands of Usenet servers (a computer with a big hard drive). A system administrator has complete control over what flows through the Usenet news server.

Every newsgroup name consists of two or more words separated by periods; the first is the name of the hierarchy to which the newsgroup belongs, and the other names are categories or subcategories. For example, **rec.arts.startrek.current** is in the recreation (rec) hierarchy within the subgroups arts, startrek, and current. From this description, you can usually figure out what kind of discussion takes place in the newsgroup. In this case, **rec.arts.startrek.current** deals with current *Star Trek* shows, movies, and books.

The seven main hierarchies are called the mainstream categories; those that are left are called alternative categories. All Usenet news servers carry mainstream newsgroups. The alternative groups are optional. The news or system administrator does not necessarily carry all the newsgroups in any of these hierarchies. The system operator is god and can do what he or she pleases.

Additionally, not all Usenet discussions originate or are discussed on Usenet only. Some Usenet groups are ported from the Internet through special software or hardware gateways. Some Internet mailing lists are ported to Usenet as newsgroups. Even conferences, called echoes, from the amateur computer network Fidonet are ported over to their Usenet equivalents. Regardless, as long as the groups pass through Usenet, you can participate in all of them if your Usenet site carries them.

It's important to remember that the administrator of a site determines which set of newsgroups his or her particular site carries.

The Mainstream Hierarchies

Throughout your Usenet experience, you will find yourself mostly dealing with the seven main Usenet hierarchies and the alt group, the largest of the alternative groups. Following are the main seven categories and a brief description of each:

The Green Eggs Report

The Green Eggs report (**www.ar.com/ger/**) is a collection of URLs spotted by the Rumor database system. Rumor collects all the URLs from the Usenet spool (currently about 1,500 new and unique URLs every day). Rumor gets only FTP, Gopher, and HTTP Web sources.

The newsgroups are listed alphabetically. Once you select a newsgroup, the Web sites are listed by their title, followed by FTP sites, Gopher, and so on. Selecting any of the listed titles takes you to the Web, FTP, or Gopher site.

The Green Eggs Report is a handy tool because not all Web sites on the Net get listed by major search engines such as Yahoo!, Alta Vista, and so on. Because most URLs are categorized in a particular newsgroup subject area, it is a good way to find new and useful sites on your topic.

- *comp*—This category deals with the discussion of computers and related subjects.
- *misc*—This potpourri category concerns topics that don't fall into the other six categories. You will find groups on law, kids, alternative news sources, education, and other topics.
- *news*—This category contains newsgroups that mostly deal with Usenet, news software, newsreaders, questions and answers for new users, FAQs, and announcements. Several newsgroups in this category are carried on all Usenet servers.
- *rec*—The recreation category is the place to look for hobbies, games, humor, music, sports, arts, literature, and the like. This is one of the most popular categories on Usenet.
- *sci*—These newsgroups are the heavy scientific research groups in which science, engineering, technology, some social sciences, and other traditional research-oriented topics can be found.
- *soc*—Look at these groups for discussions on social issues, religion, politics, and culture.
- *talk*—These groups tend to offer forums where you can argue or debate.

Although these newsgroups are the main newsgroup hierarchies, they are by no means the only categories. There are 565 top-level newsgroup hierarchies. Many of them are categorized as regional, and some are specific to states, cities, companies, projects, and even countries. You might not have access to all or any of them.

The Alternative Groups

In addition to the mainstream seven categories, you will probably come into contact with the following "alternative" categories:

- *alt*—Many of these newsgroups mirror subjects and discussions in the main seven. However, they provide alternative ways of looking at the topics. You will find some interesting and unusual newsgroups in this category. The alt category is by far the most popular and carries the most traffic.

- *bit*—These are popular Bitnet mailing lists (Listserv lists) that have been ported to newsgroups. Bitnet was an academic Internet that coexisted in the early days of the Net (and for all practical purposes is defunct).
- *biz*—Here you can post commercial advertisements and discuss business issues.
- *clarinet*—This is a commercial news service containing up-to-the-minute news from the Associated Press, stock reports, business news, Newsbytes computer news, and other traditional news sources. Your system administrator must pay for this feed, but the groups are free for you to read.
- *k-12*—These newsgroups originated on Fidonet and have been ported to Usenet. This is a great series of groups in which students from around the world can talk to each other and work on school projects together.
- *inet*—These Internet mailing lists are ported to newsgroups.

Remember that the main Usenet groups are broken down into subgroups, and each subgroup is separated by a period. This provides a coordinated way to arrange various topics under one category.

NOTE: *In Net conversation, you'll hear periods referred to as "dots." "Dot" is Net language for "period" because "dot" is easier to say than "period." If you want to refer a friend to the newsgroup **sci.environment**, you say "go to the newsgroup **sci-dot-environment**."*

There are naming variations. Some groups have a .d at the end to stand for discussion. The group with the same name without the .d is for posting the information, and the group with the .d is for discussing the information that was posted in the non-discussion group. For example, in the group **rec.humor** (rec-dot-humor), you post jokes, but the group **rec.humor.d** (rec-dot-humor-dot-d) is for discussing the jokes that were posted in **rec.humor**. Confusing? Don't worry; not too many groups have these double arrangements.

Ignore The Last Period!

A note to folks new to the online world: World Wide Web sites and email addresses do NOT end with a period. Throughout this book you will see a period at the end of World Wide Web sites and email addresses. This is only a publishing convention; therefore, you should ignore that last period when typing in the addresses.

Types Of Newsgroups

Newsgroups come in two flavors: moderated and unmoderated. More than 90 percent of newsgroups are unmoderated. They are free-flowing and unregulated, and pretty much any kind of post is allowed. There is no control over what is posted. As you might imagine, the unmoderated groups can be hectic, with an abundance of useless posts. As new users join the group, the same questions are often asked over and over. To preserve sanity, many newsgroup coordinators, or even regular participants, will create a special document for their newsgroup called a FAQ (frequently asked questions). The purpose of a FAQ is to answer the most common questions or to describe the philosophies and activities of the group. There can be some control over what is posted to a newsgroup if there is a FAQ and people pay attention to it—but don't hold your breath.

When the members of an unmoderated group can't take it anymore, or want to insist that posts stay on the subject, they have the option to either propose a new moderated group on the same topic or turn the existing unmoderated group into a moderated one. A moderated group means one or more people actually control the content flow of the newsgroup. You cannot post directly into the newsgroup; you must send your post to the moderator's address, and it will get posted if the moderator finds it relevant to the newsgroup. Although some folks complain that this is censorship, others insist it's a great way to filter out stupid posts. Both opinions are accurate.

Many of the moderated newsgroups have a low volume in posts, but a high degree of important information distributed within them. On the other hand, some unmoderated newsgroups that have high traffic contain a lot of nonsense. You must be the judge on whether a particular newsgroup is worth subscribing to.

Newsgroup Popularity?

Popularity is by no means a measure of a newsgroup's importance. If you are a scientist working on fusion, a newsgroup specializing in physics will likely provide important information. You can also assume that it won't

Usenet Archives

You can browse through previous Usenet newsgroups by visiting archives posted by Cameron Laird of Network Engineered Solutions. Use a Web browser to visit **www.pitt.edu/~grouprev/Usenet/Archive-List/newsgroup_archives.html**. The Usenet News Stand by Critical Mass Communications lets you do a quick search of archives belonging to the .comp hierarchy. Use your Web browser to visit **www.criticalmass.com/concord/**.

have an abundance of users. On the other hand, graphic newsgroups that cater to more mature topics are very popular. In fact, week after week, the **alt.binaries.*** newsgroups (* means there is more than one newsgroup in that general topic) rate number one in total traffic. There is no way to mandate good taste on Usenet or the Net, and as many people in the online community argue, there shouldn't be anyway. After all, it's a network that supports freedom of expression, right?

A Warning For Parents

If you are a parent, be aware that some newsgroups are explicit both in the discussion of sex and availability of images. The growth of Usenet and the Internet in general have raised serious issues about the easy access of pornographic or obscene material to youngsters via Usenet and the Net. The commercial online services have taken measures to give parents control over what their children can access, and some commercial software programs filter out certain unwanted phrases or words. In 1996, the U.S. Congress, in its reform of the Telecommunications Act, passed wording that prohibited the use of pornographic, obscene, or indecent discussions on the Net (including Usenet). The law was challenged, and those portions dealing with speech were struck down as unconstitutional, but the battle is not over yet. A new child protection act was introduced in 1998. As I mentioned earlier, online communication is open to all, and there is a good cross section of the world online, so what constitutes good taste is as varied as your choice of toppings at Pizza Hut. Proceed at your own risk with caution. If you are offended by certain language, or if you allow your child to explore the online world unsupervised, obtain a software filtering program, or simply never go online.

Even though Usenet was originally created to share information about Unix, alternative and recreational newsgroups make up the bulk of Usenet's total traffic. Even though you're using a computer network to participate in Usenet, most of the actual discussions taking place concern non-computer, more traditional (and not so traditional) issues.

Although newsgroup participation takes place through the computer, we sometimes forget that it's human beings who make Usenet productive. The hardware and software are only the pipeline over which Usenet travels. Without the dedicated work, much of it voluntary from system administrators, and the willingness of the Usenet community to share, Usenet simply would not exist.

Keeping Out Unwanted Information

There is a growing fear that children can gain access to unwanted information such as pornography, foul language, or other information a parent wants to block from children. A number of software programs now available allow the parent to block out this unwanted material effectively. Some work with your online software; some work alone. The following programs all allow you to filter out newsgroup information:

Bess

http://bess.net/about_bess/

This Internet provider on the Web pre-selects material and blocks unwanted material on its server before it gets to a user. The service is subscription-based. Email at bess@bess.net.

Usenet-Addresses

This Web service (**http://usenet-addresses.mit.edu/**), previously accessible only via mail-server@rtfm.mit.edu, allows searches of more than four million email addresses by name and by organization collected from Usenet posts between July 1991 and February 1996. It also has links to more than 2,000 local email directories, phone books, and home page indexes. Never assume the addresses are current and reachable. None of the addresses listed for me are valid anymore.

Cyber Patrol

www.cyberpatrol.com

This is subscription-based software. Each month, you get a list of blocked sites. Mac and Windows versions are $49.95 (includes six-month subscription). Home versions are free. It works with all newsreaders.

InfoScan

www.machinasapiens.com/english/products/infoscan/infoscanang.html

This program will scan email or newsgroups for user-selectable keywords already downloaded to your hard drive. Mac and Windows versions are $35. Demo versions are available.

SurfWatch

www.surfwatch.com

(800) 458-6600; Versions for Windows 3.1, Windows 95, and Mac; $49.95. SurfWatch is probably the leading software blocker on the market. It works on chat, FTP, Gopher, Web sites, and newsgroups. An optional service lets you update the program to block out new sites.

Give Me The FAQs

Because newsgroups are open to all, thousands of new users enter the Usenet community each day for the first time. It's common for a new user to subscribe to many different newsgroups when he or she first discovers Usenet. Filled with excitement, the new user often jumps into a group and "announces" his or her presence with a dumb question or makes a request that has been answered a hundred times before.

Unfortunately for those regular members of the newsgroup, it becomes very tiring because this happens too frequently. The newsgroup creator or one or more regular users of the newsgroup will attempt to alleviate this clutter by collecting all the frequently asked questions, answers, comments, main points, or even a summary of the main elements of discussion in the newsgroup. They create a document called a FAQ (short for Frequently Asked Questions, pronounced "fack"). Sometimes, a FAQ is not really a set of answers to any questions, but more of a tutorial on the newsgroup.

The FAQ is usually posted in the newsgroup once a month, even if there are no changes in it. The intention is that new folks should read it. The FAQ for each newsgroup is almost always posted in the **news.answers** newsgroups, which is the official repository of FAQs.

Incidentally, FAQs have evolved into providing way more than originally intended. Many FAQs have become professional-quality publications. Some are as large as books; some are concise summaries of specialized fields; some are workbooks; and some are great how-to guides. Information is so diverse that if you scan the **news.answers** newsgroup, you will likely find FAQs that:

- Describe science fiction TV shows and movies with complete plot and cast histories
- Discuss childhood vaccinations
- Even show you how to spam-proof your email
- Guide you to personal investments
- Inform you about everything you want to know about Sandra Bullock
- List a variety of support groups
- Provide a complete guide on body art
- Provide a complete movie database
- Show you where all law-related resources reside on the Internet
- Tell you everything you want to know about Bulgarian culture or Hungarian electronic resources

There are hundreds more FAQs, some more serious and some lighter in tone. There are FAQs on computer topics and even FAQs that have no real newsgroup home (suicide prevention, for example).

What has evolved on Usenet is a large self-publishing house in which you can publish for free and have millions of readers. No agent or contract is required. There is a great deal of personal satisfaction in knowing that your FAQ has helped many people on the Net. Most FAQ maintainers, as they are called, are bestowed a sacred and holy trust as the keepers of the "facts" (FAQs). If you want to be admired or even worshipped, and your favorite newsgroup does not have a FAQ, consider writing one. For more help and details, read "FAQs about FAQs" by Russ Hersch.

One of the most rewarding aspects of FAQdom is the quality of information you can find in a FAQ. FAQ contributors pride themselves on producing accurate information. If they don't, any knowledgeable member of the group will quickly point out the errors and demand that they be corrected.

Before you subscribe or participate in a newsgroup that interests you, look for a FAQ on that newsgroup. Read it and then read it again. Make sure you know the purpose of the newsgroup and how you can make a contribution to it. Finally, if you want a free education on diverse topics, take the time to read a handful of FAQs per month. You can always benefit from the combined experience of the Net community.

A few highly recommended FAQs for beginners are:

- "A Primer on How to Work with the Usenet Community" by Chuq Von Rospach
- "Emily Postsnews Answers Your Questions on Netiquette" by Brad Templeton
- "FAQs about FAQs" by Russ Hersch
- "Hints on Writing Style for Usenet" by A. Jeff Offutt, VI
- "How to Find the Right Place to Post (FAQ)" by Aliza R. Panitz
- "List of Moderators for Usenet" by David Lawrence
- "Rules for Posting to Usenet" by Mark Horton
- "Usenet FAQ" by Jerry Schwarz
- "Usenet Software: History and Sources" by Gene Spafford
- "Welcome to **news.newusers.questions**!" (weekly posting) by Leanne Phillips
- "What is Usenet?" by Chip Salzenberg
- "What is Usenet?" a second opinion by Edward Vielmetti

You will find these FAQs posted periodically in the **news.answers** newsgroup. You can read some of these guides online at **www.glink.net.hk/GuideToUsenet.html**.

If you can't find a FAQ in a specific newsgroup or the **news.answers** newsgroup, all of the FAQs are archived and can be obtained via File Transfer Protocol (FTP) or email. To receive the file via FTP, anonymous FTP to **rtfm.mit.edu** and go into the Usenet directory within the pub directory (/pub/usenet). Every newsgroup and major subject has its own subdirectory. If it has a FAQ, you will find it there.

As an example, if you are looking for the "X-*Files* FAQ", located in the **alt.tv.x-files.creative** newsgroup, you FTP to **rtfm.mit.edu** and then go through the directories /pub/usenet/alt.tv.x-files.creative. In this directory, you will find the FAQ that you can download to your computer: "ATXFA_FAQ;_Frequently_Asked_Questions".

If you do not have access to anonymous FTP, and you do have access to email, send email to mail-server@rtfm.mit.edu, and use the index command to get FAQs. The index command gives you a list of the contents of a directory you specify. If you are looking for the "X-*Files* FAQ", send an email with the following text in the body of the email: "index usenet-by-group/alt.tv.x-files.creative". You then receive as return mail the example in Figure 3.1.

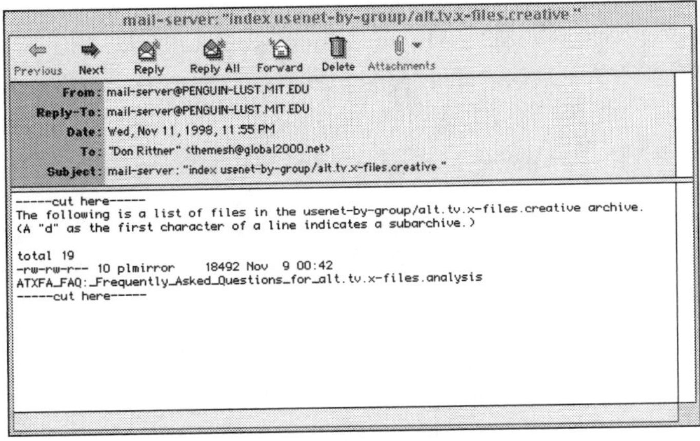

Figure 3.1
FAQ email.

You then use the send file command to retrieve any of the FAQs you want. To grab the file from the list, for instance, send the following text in an email message to mail-server@rtfm.mit.edu:

```
setdir usenet/alt.tv.x-files.creative
send ATXFA_FAQ;_Frequently_Asked_Questions_for_alt.tv.
z-files.analysis
```

The file will be sent to you via email (in chunks if it's large).

Usenet FAQs

If you have access to the World Wide Web, you can use a great Usenet service from Thomas A. Fine at The Ohio State University (**www.cis.ohio-state.edu/hypertext/faq/usenet/**). It is an alphabetical list of all Usenet FAQs. Simply click on the FAQ you want to read or do a limited search for only the newsgroup names, archive names, subjects, and keywords.

Newsgroups—The Ins And Outs

You know what a newsgroup is now, so let's get to the basics. All newsgroups reside on a news server, a computer that has a big hard drive. (It is better because there are gigabytes of news generated daily.)

A news server is owned or maintained by a news or system administrator, who decides which newsgroups he or she wants to carry. The server may carry all 80,000+ newsgroups or just a handful. News administrators are the bosses. Regardless of the number of newsgroups your administrator decides to carry, you are free to subscribe to as few or as many of the available newsgroups as you want.

You, the user, need two things: a client or reader application, called a "newsreader," and the ability to subscribe to newsgroups.

Subscribing to a newsgroup is easy. It takes seconds. However, to subscribe to newsgroups, you must have a newsreader. Newsreaders have been an integral part of Usenet software since the beginning of Usenet. However, in the beginning, you needed to be a Unix techie to read newsgroups or to memorize arcane commands to use Usenet.

Early newsreaders had interesting names. For example, readnews and vnews were two early newsreaders. In addition, rn was recommended with the C news version of Usenet software. Another one, nn, is one of the earliest readers but lacked a lot of functions, especially the ability to ignore certain posts. A newsreader called trn is an evolution from rn that allowed the use of threads. Finally, tin, the most recent and easiest to use, is a menu-based newsreader. However, you don't really need to know about that nor should you care. You have the easiest newsreader in the world on the iMac. Newsreaders like the one in Outlook Express are as easy to use as sending regular email.

Whenever you access Usenet, there is a newsreader (or two), such as those previously mentioned, available for your use if you are in a non-Mac environment. You cannot really participate in Usenet unless you use a newsreader (or are really adept in Unix commands). This book is for non-technical users so you will not have to learn a single Unix command.

What does a newsreader do? A newsreader is like a personal secretary. It does all the menial work for you and lets you do the important task of reading and replying to your favorite newsgroups. A newsreader is used to subscribe and unsubscribe to newsgroups and to read, to post, to reply, to ignore, and to keep track of what articles you have read. Newsreaders can keep track of hundreds of messages in hundreds of different newsgroups at the same time, and they make the news easy to read—and you don't have to give it flowers on Secretary's Day!

The commercial online services such as America Online and CompuServe provide their own nice, graphical-based, easy-to-use newsreaders for their Usenet feeds. Microsoft's Outlook Express, which came bundled with your iMac, is an excellent newsreader, and it is the one I use in the examples.

You are not restricted to using Outlook Express. You may use any one of several stand alone newsreaders such as Nuntius, Internews, or NewsWatcher for Mac users, or if you prefer to use PC emulation on your iMac, there is Trumpet or Free Agent for PC users. You can obtain these by downloading them from a software site on the Web explained in Chapter 8, or go to **www.newsreaders.com**.

Anatomy Of A Newsgroup

A typical newsgroup article has three parts: the header, the body (the actual text of the article), and the signature (optional). Header information can help you determine whether you want to read an article, to which address you should reply, the origin of the article, and other information. There are 20 possible header lines, although most articles only contain about 15 of them. Most of the header information you can ignore.

The following example is a call for papers from the **news.announce. conferences** newsgroup. Depending on the source of your news feed, the header information may appear at the beginning, the end, or both ends of a post. This example came from America Online. Take a look at the header info and the explanations that follow.

```
Subject: CFP: Simulation of Information Systems (S&G)
From: majrw@cis0.levels.unisa.edu.au (Jim Warren)
Date: 26 Sep 1994 16:41:48 -0500
Message-ID: <367f6s$9qk@sparky.sterling.com>

Title: CALL FOR PAPERS - Simulation of Information Systems
(S&G)
From: James R. Warren, University of South Australia
 (james.warren@unisa.edu.au)

Call for Papers

Simulation & Gaming: An International Journal of Theory,
Design, and Research (S&G) Special Issue on Simulation of
Information Systems

Guest Editors: James R. Warren and Jerzy A. Filar

Increasingly, information systems serve active roles as in on-
line systems, decision support applications, real-time control
and EDI.

Success depends upon complex interactions of hardware, soft-
ware, people and procedures. Unacceptably long delays in
system response can have substantial monetary or human costs.

We are looking for papers that represent state-of-the-art
method and practice in Simulation of Information Systems,
including:

-- Interorganizational and logistics system dynamics
-- Validation of dynamic models
-- Simulation as a BPR tool
-- Evolving and adaptive IS
-- Integration of CASE and simulation
```

```
-- Data, process, and behavior modeling in an integrated
framework
-- Object orientation in the analysis of IS dynamics

S&G is an interdisciplinary journal. Authors should consider
the human and organizational context as well as the computer-
based system.

Papers may be technical in nature, but only as necessary to
draw out the principles and concepts. Authors should identify:
(a) the referent of their models (i.e., what is modeled); (b)
the information provided (e.g., reachable states, performance
rates, animation); and (c) the role in the decision process
(e.g., determine throughput, assess system safety).

Submission deadline: October 21, 1994. Submit 3 copies to:
Dr. James R. Warren
School of Computer and Information Science
University of South Australia
The Levels, SA 5095, Australia
Voice: +61 8 302 3446
Fax: +61 8 302 3381.

S&G is published by Sage Publications.

----------- Headers -----------
Path:
newsbf01.news.aol.com!newstf01.cr1.aol.com!uunet!sparky!not-
for-mail
From: majrw@cis0.levels.unisa.edu.au (Jim Warren)
Newsgroups: news.announce.conferences
Subject: CFP: Simulation of Information Systems (S&G)
Followup-To: poster
Date: 26 Sep 1994 16:41:48 -0500
Organization: Sterling Software
Lines: 47
Sender: rick@sparky.sterling.com
Approved: rick@sparky.sterling.com
Distribution: world
Expires: 22 Oct 1994 8:00:00 GMT
Message-ID: <367f6s$9qk@sparky.sterling.com>
Reply-To: majrw@cis0.levels.unisa.edu.au (Jim Warren)
NNTP-Posting-Host: sparky.sterling.com
```

What Is The Address?

Although there are no Yellow Pages for the Net yet, there is a way to find someone's email address on Usenet. A Usenet database server at MIT keeps track of each post. You can try to find someone's address by sending email to mail-server@rtfm.mit.edu. In the body of the message, you type

```
set dirusenet-addresses/
send name
```

where *name* is the name of the person you are looking for. You can also try this in the body:

```
send usenet-addresses/name
```

You can use more than one word separated by spaces or any other identifying feature that might be in the person's address. As an example, to check for my name, I send:

```
setdir usenet-addresses/
send rittner
```

Figure 3.2 shows what the reply looks like.

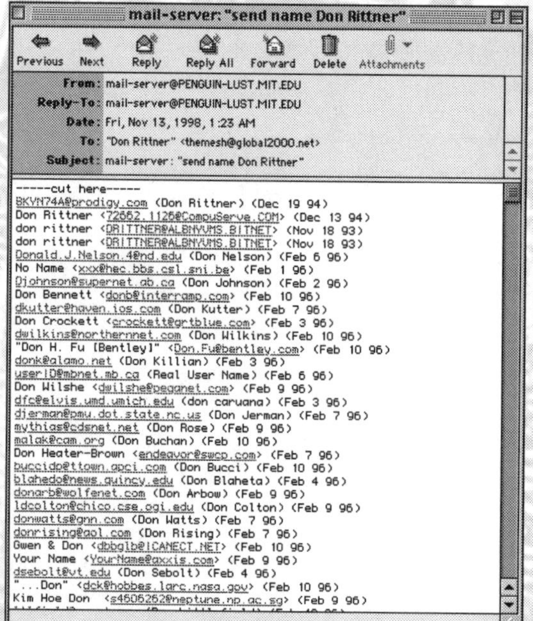

Figure 3.2
Search results for the name Don Rittner.

This is also a cool way to see if you have any relatives online!

Searches are limited to 40 matches, so don't search for "Smith". For more information about this server, send the command "send usenet-addresses/help".

Header Terms

Depending on what newsreader you use, one or more of the following headers will appear in a Usenet article post. Much of it you can ignore because it is information your newsreader and computer uses for maintenance purposes. Information I feel you should be aware of or notice I marked "important."

- *Approved*—Because this post is from a moderated newsgroup, it has been approved by the moderator and shows the moderator's Net address. Sometimes, other types of control messages are in this header. Ignore this line.
- *Control*—You may never see this header because it is used by the news administrator to control the working of Usenet. Ignore this.
- *Date*—The date and time of posting. Time is usually given in GMT (Greenwich Mean Time), also known as Universal Time (important).
- *Distribution*—On many newsreaders, you can determine the distribution of your post. Some will allow you to restrict distribution to a few areas or, as in the previous example, to distribute worldwide. (You will see options such as local, ny, usa, world, na, and so on.) On the commercial online services I am mentioning in this book, you have no control over distribution; they are sent worldwide. Ignore this. For the most part, posts are now sent worldwide.
- *Expires*—This is the date posts will be deleted. The system administrator determines when to delete posts, so this is a recommended kill date (important).
- *Follow-up To*—This tells you where or to whom to send a follow-up post. You might want to send it to the original poster, but it could be that the poster wants a follow-up to go somewhere else. You may have sent the original post to several newsgroups, but want only a follow-up discussion to take place in one particular newsgroup (important).
- *From*—This is the name and Net address of the person who posted the article (important).
- *Keywords*—This line will contain one or more keywords that categorize the content of the article. Ignore it.

- *Lines*—The total number of lines in the body of the article, including the signature but not the header. Ignore this.
- *Message ID*—This is generated automatically by the program that sent the article. The last part of the address shows you the computer from which it was sent. Ignore this information.
- *Newsgroups*—This shows you the newsgroups upon which the article was posted (important).
- *NNTP-Posting-Host (Network News Transfer Protocol)*—The transport protocol to send Usenet news. This header shows the name of the Internet computer that the poster used. Ignore this line.
- *Organization*—The name of the organization to which the poster belongs or the company that owns the computer from which the post was sent. You can ignore this information.
- *Path*—This is the route your computer follows (via various computers) to get to America Online, CompuServe, or whatever site from which you are reading. The computer systems are separated by an "!" (exclamation point, called a bang). This line could be very long depending on how many systems through which the article passes. You can ignore this information.
- *References*—This appears only in follow-up articles. It contains the identification info from the Message-ID header of the original article. This allows you to read a series of connected articles called threads. Your newsreader uses this information, but you can ignore it.
- *Reply To*—This has the same information as the From line. If you use the automatic reply on your newsreader software, this is where the reply will go. If you want a reply to go to someone else, you enter a different address here (important).
- *Sender*—This is the Net ID of the computer or person from whom the article was sent. It is not always the poster of the article. In the previous example, the sender is the moderator of the newsgroup, not the original writer of the article. The computer that posted the article automatically generates this line. Ignore this information.
- *Subject*—The subject of the post is the information you supply when you create a post (important).

- *Summary*—This is a brief one-line summary of the article, useful in follow-up articles, but not used very often. Ignore this line.
- *Xref*—This stands for cross-reference and allows you to see which other newsgroups contain this article. Ignore this; your newsreader uses this header.

Signatures!

Often at the end of a user's post, you will find three or four more lines of information called a signature. It generally contains a name and may include such information as the user's Net addresses, fax number, telephone number, company affiliation, and a motto, quote, or even ASCII-based artwork. People typically do not change their signature on a regular basis. However, some folks like to rotate various quotes or artwork in theirs.

You create your signature and store it, and when you are using certain newsreaders, you can call it up with a single command. In the Mac environment, you can create a signature, store it in your Scrapbook, and then copy and paste it into your articles. In Outlook Express, you can store your signature by going to the Preferences selection, selecting Message Composition, and adding your signature in the bottom box. Be sure to select the checkbox that allows your signature to automatically get posted.

Remember to keep the signature small and to the point. Three or four lines are recommended. Big signatures can really annoy people, especially system administrators, because they take up more system space. The famous netsurfer Kibo (James "Kibo" Parry) probably holds the record for the biggest and, to some, the most irritating signature, with more than 1,000 lines. A common, more acceptable signature may look like this:

```
**********************************************************
Don Rittner             | MUG News Service (MNS)
drittner@mesh.com       | Serving Apple MUGs Worldwide
(518) 374-6444 BBS      | "Common sense is sense uncommon"
**********************************************************
```

Mandatory Subscriptions

When you first become part of the Usenet community, it's a good idea not to post to a newsgroup for several weeks. It's for your own good. This is to prevent people from making a lot of common mistakes and looking like fools in front of millions of people worldwide. The first thing you should do is to subscribe to the following newsgroups and to read them all for about a month:

- **alt.internet.services** (unmoderated)—This is a good newsgroup to ask questions about the Internet.
- **news.announce.conferences** (moderated)—Here you will find dates and times for seminars, workshops, symposia, conferences, calls for papers (CFP), expeditions, and unique opportunities for work or travel. This newsgroup usually has a high degree of traffic.
- **news.announce.important** (moderated)—This newsgroup features just what it says: news about the Net that is really important for all to read, but there is no discussion. Very little traffic is here, but you want to read it so you don't miss what does get posted.
- **news.announce.newgroups** (moderated)—This is where you go to see proposals and public discussion of new groups, how to's, the results of voting on proposed groups, and the success or failure of those proposed. You can also find lists of mailing lists and newsgroups that are formed.
- **news.announce.newuser** (moderated)—Here you will read introductory messages for the new user. It's a moderated newsgroup and usually does not accept posts from everyone.
- **news.answers** (moderated)—Like it says, this is the place to get answers. You will find a lot of FAQs, lists, guides, and more. This is the place to look first for information about newsgroups. It's the official repository for FAQs.
- **news.groups** (unmoderated)—Here you can ask questions or make comments.

- **news.groups.reviews** (moderated)—This features reviews of other newsgroups and mailing lists. It's a good place to get an idea of whether you want to subscribe to a particular newsgroup.
- **news.lists** (moderated)—This is where you can find lists of all newsgroups, statistics such as the top-25 newsgroups in a month, how-to articles, changes to lists, mailings lists from Bitnet or the Internet, and lists of moderators and moderated newsgroups. Basically, you can find any kind of Usenet stats here.
- **news.misc** (unmoderated)—This group features general discussion about Usenet; pretty much anything goes.
- **news.newusers.questions** (unmoderated)—Got a question about the Net? Looking for an address? Not sure how to do something on the Net? This is the place to ask those questions. Play here for a while before you start getting your feet wet in the real newsgroups.
- **news.software.readers** (unmoderated)—If you need answers about various newsreaders, this is the place.

How To Create A Newsgroup

The creation of a newsgroup is democratic in nature but can be considered a political process as well. Although it is not advisable for you to start your own newsgroup until after you've participated in Usenet for a long time, the Web site **www.cis.ohio-state.edu/hypertext/faq/usenet/usenet/creating-newsgroups/part1/faq.html** describes how you can do it.

Anyone who sees a need for a newsgroup can take on the role of the proponent. The proponent must write a preliminary charter for the proposed newsgroup and indicate whether it is to be moderated. Then, the proposer discusses a name with the moderator of **news.announce.newgroups** and his affiliated group advice mailing list committee and sends the proposed Request For Discussion (RFD) to the moderator of **news.announce.newsgroups**, who then (at his leisure) posts it to the relevant newsgroups.

What follows is a 21- to 30-day discussion in **news.groups** (and private mail as well) for any revisions to the group name and charter. At the end of the discussion, the proponent (or anyone else for that matter) will arrange for the Usenet Volunteer Votetakers to take the poll. The UVV forwards the revised name and charter to the moderator of **news.announce.newsgroups**. If no one has complained about the discussion process and the name of the group is acceptable to the moderator, a Call For Vote (CFV) is posted. The volunteer votetaker takes the poll (which usually runs from 21 to 31 days) and forwards the results to the moderator of **news.announce.newsgroups**. Finally, if no one has a valid complaint about the poll (there usually is a five-day waiting period), the moderator of **news.announce.newsgroups** issues the control message to create the group throughout Usenet, and it becomes available to carry by any Net administrator.

A successful vote includes two thirds of the voters' approval, and there are at least 100 more yes votes than no votes. All of the voting takes place in public, and the actual results of the poll are published with the names of those folks who voted for it. An unsuccessful poll means the newsgroup cannot be proposed again for at least six months. Creating a newsgroup this way can become nasty (with flames), time consuming, frustrating, and rewarding, depending on the reaction of the Usenet community. There is a better way.

Create an alt newsgroup (which one Netter says stands for anarchists, lunatics, and terrorists). You should suggest the creation of your group to any existing group that may have an interest in it and to the group **alt.config**, which discusses proposals for new alt groups (but do not ask for votes there). If you get a good deal of interest and not too much flack (or flames), you can then ask your local Net administrator to send the control message to create it. However, anyone who knows how to send the control message can do it. Again, the Net administrator on each computer decides whether or not to carry it. There is no voting for an alt group. Any voting you do is purely for your own gratification (or as ammunition against the naysayers). Do not be intimidated by negative posts against your idea. Some people on the Net will tear apart anyone's proposal to create a newsgroup.

Don't Spam

Remember that sending the same Usenet article to 20 or more newsgroups that are not related is considered spamming. What will happen if you spam? Sometimes, nothing. Sometimes, the entire Usenet community will come after you. One past event resulted in a spammer being threatened with bodily harm. Keep your post to your area of interest. Do not use Usenet to try to get rich or to promote some business scheme.

Let's Join Usenet!

Now that you understand what Usenet is and isn't, let's join a few newsgroups and learn how to be a good Net citizen.

Double-click your Outlook Express program (or launch it by double-clicking the Mail alias on your desktop). I assume you already set up Outlook Express as explained in Chapter 2.

You will notice on the left side, in your main window of Outlook Express, the words "News Server" as a last entry. This is the default Usenet server that is linked to Microsoft's news server, and if you select it, you are asked whether you want to download the list of newsgroups from this list. Choose no for now.

Instead, double-click the Preferences icon on the top of your Outlook Express main window. You will see , E-Mail, News, and Directory Services under Accounts. Select News. You will see the window shown in Figure 3.3.

You see two buttons on top. Clicking the button on the left, News Server, would show a list of news servers if you had more than one. The button on the right allows you to create a new news server. You can have more than one.

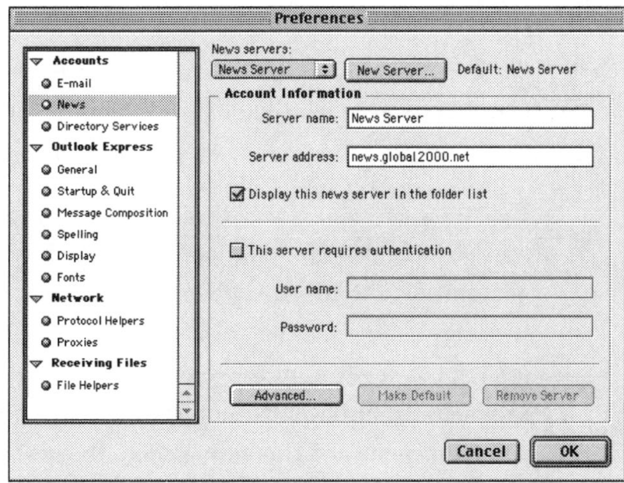

Figure 3.3
Creating a news server.

Mark As Unread

Remember that when you first subscribe to a newsgroup, you should wait awhile before you jump into the discussion. There may be a large number of posts and discussions. If there are a large number of posts, you can mark them all as read so the next time you enter the newsgroup, only the new articles are highlighted. That way, it is a bit easier to start following a discussion.

Under Account Information, give your new news server whatever name you want. Mine is simply called News Server, the default name. The second selection is the address for your news server, obtained from your local Internet provider. In my case, Global2000 is my Internet Service Provider, and its news server name is news, so the complete address is **news.global2000net**. That's how simple it is. All you need to do is to type the name of the news server from your local Internet Service Provider and press the OK button. Forget the rest of the information. You don't need it.

After you have successfully completed the setup, log on to your Internet Service Provider, open Outlook Express, and double-click your new News Server button. You are asked whether you want to download a complete list of newsgroups. Answer yes.

Before you download the complete list, make sure you have given Outlook Express ample memory allocation because chances are your Internet Service Provider carries more than 30,000 newsgroups and you will get an out-of-memory error. To ensure you have enough memory, select the icon for Outlook Express (not an alias), go up to the Show button, select Memory, and allocate more memory. I allocated 4,000K and have 33,000 newsgroups listed. Use that as a guide. It will take a few minutes for Outlook Express to download the complete list from your Internet Service Provider.

Once you have the complete list downloaded, select a category that interests you and double-click the title. A window will pop up to list all the current articles posted. Select an article to read, as shown in Figure 3.4.

That's how easy it is. Notice that you can reply to the article either to the author or newsgroup (or both) as well. However, because you have not subscribed to the newsgroup, the next time you log on, you must select the category, again. It will not appear as one of your subscribed newsgroups. If you want to subscribe to the newsgroup, return to the complete list, highlight the newsgroup by clicking it once, and then access the menu and choose Subscribe. The next time you log on, the newsgroup will be listed under the News Server icon.

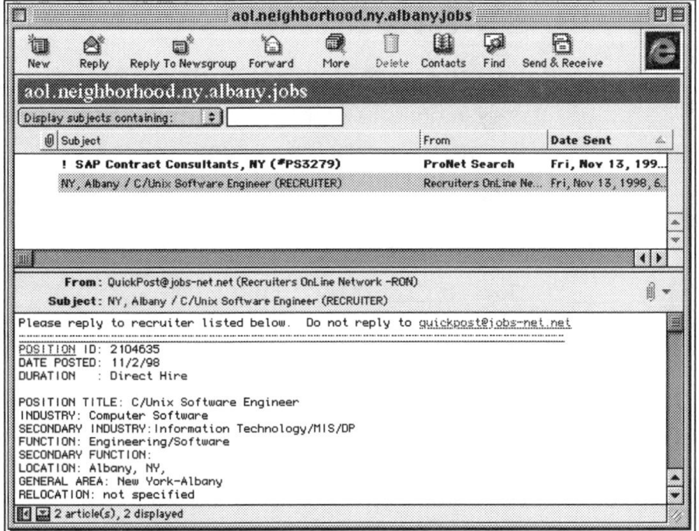

Figure 3.4
Newsgroup article.

Once you start reading articles in a newsgroup, you will notice that many different conversations are going on at the same time. You might decide that you want to read only articles posted about a particular line of questioning or discussion. You will notice that when you double-click an article to read, you have several options. You may click the Next button to take you to the next article to read, no matter what the subject is about, or you can continue to follow a discussion by pressing the Thread button, as shown in Figure 3.5. A discussion thread is a series of posts following a particular topic line, usually the topic listed in the Subject header. You can read articles about a particular discussion by clicking the Thread button.

You now know the basics of Usenet. Have a happy and rewarding newsgroup discussion.

Figure 3.5
Thread button.

Mac-Related Usenet Newsgroups

You can subscribe to any or all of these Mac-related newsgroups using your copy of Outlook Express. The following list is an example of unmoderated and moderated discussions (noted) and whether a FAQ is available. The annotations are from the official list that gets published and distributed.

alt.bbs.first-class
The First Class Mac GUI BBS.

alt.bbs.public-address
Public address BBS software for the Macintosh.

alt.binaries.clip-art
Distribution of DOS, Mac, and Unix clip art.

alt.binaries.mac.games
Macintosh games.

alt.binaries.sounds.macintosh
Lots of sound files for your Mac.

alt.games.marathon
Discussion of the Macintosh sci-fi game marathon (FAQ).

alt.hackintosh
Clever programming on Apple's Macintosh.

alt.irc.channel.macintosh
See **www.poundmac.org/** for details.

alt.mac.bin.req.only
Macintosh requests for demos and sample programs.

alt.mac.copy-protect.kdt-terminator
Kdt and copy-protection for Macintosh (moderated).

alt.mac.updates
Macintosh software and hardware updates.

alt.sources.mac
Source code for Apple Macintosh computers.

alt.sys.mac.newuser-help
A forum for Macintosh users new to the Internet.

alt.online-service.america-online

Or should that be "America Offline?"

asu.sys.mac

Talk about Macintoshes.

bit.mailserv.word-mac

Word processing on the Macintosh.

biz.marketplace.computers.mac

Macintosh hardware/software.

clari.nb.apple

Newsbytes's Apple and Macintosh news (moderated).

comp.binaries.mac

Encoded Macintosh programs in binary (moderated).

comp.binaries.newton

Apple Newton binaries, sources, books, and so on (moderated).

comp.infosystems.www.browsers.mac

Web browsers for the Macintosh platform.

comp.infosystems.www.servers.mac

Web servers for the Macintosh platform.

comp.lang.lisp.mcl

Discussing Apple's Macintosh common lisp (FAQ).

comp.lang.pascal.mac

Macintosh-based Pascal.

comp.lang.prograph

Prograph, a visual object-oriented dataflow language.

comp.mail.eudora.mac

Eudora email software for Macintosh.

comp.protocols.appletalk

Applebus hardware and software.

comp.sources.mac

Software for the Apple Macintosh (moderated).

comp.sys.mac.advocacy

The Macintosh computer family compared to others.

comp.sys.mac.announce

Important notices for Macintosh users (moderated).

comp.sys.mac.apps

Discussions of Macintosh applications (FAQ).

comp.sys.mac.comm

Discussions of Macintosh communications (FAQ).

comp.sys.mac.databases

Database systems for the Apple Macintosh (FAQ).

comp.sys.mac.digest

Apple Macintosh: information and uses, but no programs (moderated).

comp.sys.mac.games

Discussions of games on the Macintosh.

comp.sys.mac.games.action

Action games for the Macintosh (FAQ).

comp.sys.mac.games.adventure

Adventure games for the Macintosh (FAQ).

comp.sys.mac.games.marketplace

Macintosh games for sale and trade.

comp.sys.mac.games.misc

Macintosh games not covered in other groups (FAQ).

comp.sys.mac.games.strategic

Strategy and planning games on the Macintosh (FAQ).

comp.sys.mac.graphics

Macintosh graphics: painting, drawing, 3D, CAD, animation.

comp.sys.mac.hardware

Macintosh hardware issues and discussions.

comp.sys.mac.hypercard

Macintosh hypercard: information and uses.

comp.sys.mac.misc
General discussions about the Mac (FAQ).

comp.sys.mac.oop.macapp3
Version 3 of the MacApp object-oriented system.

comp.sys.mac.oop.misc
Object-oriented programming issues on the Mac.

comp.sys.mac.oop.tcl
Symantec's THINK class library for object programming.

comp.sys.mac.portables
Discussion about laptop Macs.

comp.sys.mac.programmer.codewarrior
Macintosh programming using Codewarrior.

comp.sys.mac.programmer.games
Macintosh game programming.

comp.sys.mac.programmer.help
Help with Macintosh programming.

comp.sys.mac.programmer.misc
Other issues of Macintosh programming.

comp.sys.mac.programmer.tools
Macintosh programming tools.

comp.sys.mac.scitech
Using the Macintosh in scientific and technological work (FAQ).

comp.sys.mac.system
Discussions of Macintosh system software (FAQ).

comp.sys.mac.wanted
Posts of "I want XYZ for my Mac."

comp.sys.newton.misc
Miscellaneous discussion about Newton systems.

comp.sys.newton.programmer
Discussion of Newton software development.

comp.sys.powerpc
General PowerPC discussion.

comp.unix.aux
The version of Unix for Apple Macintosh II computers (FAQ).

eug.comp.sys.macintosh
Macintosh computers and software in Eugene, Oregon.

misc.forsale.computers.mac
Apple Macintosh computer items.

misc.forsale.computers.mac-specific.cards.misc
Macintosh expansion cards.

misc.forsale.computers.mac-specific.cards.video
Macintosh video cards.

misc.forsale.computers.mac-specific.misc
Other Macintosh equipment.

misc.forsale.computers.mac-specific.portables
Portable Macintosh systems.

misc.forsale.computers.mac-specific.software
Macintosh software.

misc.forsale.computers.mac-specific.systems
Complete Macintosh systems.

net.computers.os.unix.rhapsody
Apple's next-generation OS for the Macintosh.

Usenet Glossary

Review these terms before you participate in Usenet discussions:

- *Article* (or *post*)—The message you send to a newsgroup on Usenet.
- *Browser*—An application that lets you explore the World Wide Web. Netscape Navigator and Microsoft's Internet Explorer are two examples.

- *Cross-post*—Sending your article to more than one newsgroup at a time.
- *FAQ (Frequently Asked Questions)*—Documents written by various folks on the Net to help people avoid posting the same questions over and over again in a newsgroup. Before you participate in any newsgroup, you should see whether it has a FAQ and read it first.
- *Feed site*—The computer from which the news server is receiving its newsgroups.
- *Flame*—A written, usually vicious, attack on someone's posts in a newsgroup. When more than two folks get involved, it becomes a *flame war*.
- *Follow-up*—Reply to an article you read.
- *Foo*—Also *foobar*. When you want to refer to something that really has no name.
- *GUI (Graphical User Interface)*—The Mac operating system is a GUI.
- *Kill list*—Allows you to ignore certain posts from authors you don't like or on certain topics. You can also ignore newsgroups containing controversy, flame wars, frequent off-topic posts, or other unwanted material.
- *Netnews*—Collectively, all the traffic on Usenet. Also called the *news*.
- *News administrator*—The person who controls what newsgroups live or die on a news server.
- *News feed*—The total number of newsgroups a news server is receiving from its feed source.
- *Newsgroup* (also called *group*)—A public discussion group on Usenet.
- *Newsreader*—A software program you need in order to subscribe, to read, and to post newsgroup articles.
- *News server*—A computer from which you get your newsgroups.
- *Offline reader*—An application that will automatically sign on to your Usenet account, download your news articles, sign off, and let you read and reply to them offline, thereby saving money.
- *Post*—Submit an article to a newsgroup.

- *Rot-13*—A code to scramble a message in a newsgroup that may contain material offensive to some readers.
- *Signature*—Three or four lines of personal information at the end of your post. Can be your address, a quote, your Net ID, or even ASCII art.
- *Smiley*—A shortcut using symbols to express emotions in your posts. :) is a smile, for example.
- *Subscribe*—Join a newsgroup.
- *Unsubscribe*—Quit a newsgroup.
- *Usenet*—A news distribution system that uses computers and networks to exchange public discussions on thousands of topics.
- *Thread*—A series of related articles (usually based on the subject line).

Web-Based Usenet Helpers

A number of great Web sites are designed for Usenet folks. Here I list a few good ones.

A List Of Archives Of Newsgroup Traffic

http://starbase.neosoft.com/%7Eclaird/news.lists/newsgroup_archives.html

Some people archive particular newsgroups because trying to keep all the articles posted on any particular group would require gigabytes of space. This site directs you to various locations of archives of specific newsgroups. Not all newsgroups are archived, but if they are, you will probably find its location here.

Advertising On Usenet

www.shopsite.com/resource/usenet.html

An article by Joel Furr on advertising issues relating to Usenet.

BorderWare Usenet Storage Space Calculator

www.netpart.com/janus/usenet.html

If you are thinking about creating your own news server, use this calculator to determine how much storage you will need. You may change your mind.

DejaNews

www.dejanews.com

DejaNews is a complete Usenet search engine that lets you do keyword searches throughout its Usenet database. You can fine-tune your search by number of hits or format, sort by date, author, and so on, and use the Boolean search limits OR and AND. You can also search using an age bias for old or new posts. It is a great service.

The software searches your keywords and gives you a list with dates, header info, the newsgroup it is in, and the name of the poster. Simply click the title and read the post. You can even reply or post to the subject if you want to.

DejaNews allows you to gather a profile of any user, so be careful where you post and what you post. Don't post anything you don't want your mother or the FBI to know about.

Doug Moses's Top-10 List Of Usenet Newsgroup Search Engines

www.geocities.com/Heartland/2841/search3.html

Doug Moses has linked on one page 10 search engines that will find newsgroups: Altavista, DejaNews, Excite, Infoseek, Anchorman, InReference, Liszt, tile.net/news, Usenet Info Center, and Usenet News Finder. A convenient way to start your search.

Excite Search Engine

www.excite.com/reference/usenet_newsgroups

Excite NetSearch by Architext Software Inc. provides a Usenet search engine that will go through all netnews using your keywords or words that describe a concept.

Figlet Service

www.inf.utfsm.cl/cgi-bin/figlet

If you want to create some ASCII line art of your name or a saying, this Web site will automatically convert your text in one of more than 100 different fonts (styles).

GAIS (Global Area Information Servers) Usenet News Search

http://gais.cs.ccu.edu.tw/GaisNEWS.html

This search engine looks into posts and finds your keyword. You have a lot of choices for matching, such as prefix, case sensitivity, and even allowance for misspellings. You can search the whole file or just the subject field, line, or paragraph, and other info.

Inter-Links

www.nova.edu/Inter-Links/cgi-bin/news-lists.pl

This site is run by Inter-Links and maintained by Rob Kabacoff at Nova Southeastern University in Ft. Lauderdale, Florida. It has a search tool for mailing lists and Usenet groups. Enter keywords to search, or click the Usenet title, and go to a listing of Usenet hierarchies that you can also select. When you click the hierarchies, it gives an alphabetical list of every newsgroup in that hierarchy. Clicking the title of any newsgroup then gives you a list of posts you can read, arranged by subject. You can read the posts and respond if your Web browser allows it. You can also use a list of people who have contributed to news to find people's email addresses.

Liszt Newsgroups

www.liszt.com/cgi-bin/news.cgi

Another very good Usenet search engine. Type a keyword, and the engine scans the complete 15,000+ newsgroup database and returns a list. You need a news server to be able to access it.

Master List Of Newsgroup Hierarchies

www.magmacom.com/%7Eleisen/master_list.html

If you are only interested in finding a hierarchy within Usenet, check out this site. It is an alphabetical list of all newsgroup hierarchies.

Reference.com

www.reference.com

Reference.com is a search engine that lets you keyword search Usenet and mailing list archives, or just newsgroups, to find a newsgroup and posts on your topic. Once you find one, you can browse the archives, post, or search for a FAQ if it has one. It shows the hierarchy of the newsgroup you select so you can actually display each of them. You can also do advanced searching such as looking only for a certain author, address, organization, group, or block of specific dates. You can set your output so that the list is short or verbose and sorted in a certain order. If you subscribe to the service—it's free—you can search by category, subject, author's name and address, organization, or group. Moreover, the engine will automatically search for that information for a pre-defined period (run every day or every two days and so on for x days) and provide a list of hits, even in HTML format. You can read the articles online and reply to them. There isn't much this site doesn't do.

SupportHelp.com

www.supporthelp.com

Looking for technical help from a software or hardware vendor? This Web site has hot links to the majority of newsgroups that provide tech support at the click of the mouse.

The Usenet Cookbook

www.astro.cf.ac.uk/misc/recipe/index.usa.html

Want more proof on how community minded Usenet folks are? The Usenet Cookbook is just that, hundreds of recipes from Usenet members who frequent the food newsgroups: vegetarian dishes to Chernobyl Chili (high-energy microwave chili) to baked apples, all laid out for you. Just follow the recipes and enjoy.

Tile.net/News

http://tile.net/news/

Tile.net/News is another news listing service that contains an alphabetical index of newsgroups, as well as a list by description or hierarchy. Like Anchorman, it is not a server. You need to access an Internet Service Provider to actually read the articles. Tile.net/News is keyword searchable as well using Excite's search engine.

Usenet FAQs

www.cis.ohio-state.edu/hypertext/faq/usenet/top.html

This site does not provide a full-text search, but the newsgroup names, archive names, subjects, and keywords are searchable, or you can use the alphabetical listing.

Usenet Job Hunter's Companion

http://206.117.85.190/jobs/

Looking for a job on the Net? There are hundreds posted. This site contains a list of all job-related newsgroups for easy reading.

Usenet News (Information And Public Access)

http://pegasus.uthct.edu/OtherUsefulSites/UseNet.html

This site is a compilation of Usenet sources. The Bible of Usenet, Usenet Information Center, and FAQ sites are here. Lists and search engines for finding Usenet newsgroups and posts are located here as well as a number of sites where you can read and post to newsgroups.

Usenet Newsgroup Resources

http://scwww.ucs.indiana.edu/NetRsc/usenet.html

This is a nice collection from Indiana University of Usenet information. You can find articles on how to create newsgroups, FAQs, various help guides for some newsreaders, and more.

Usenet Support Page

http://206.117.85.190/usenet/

This is another helpful Web site that supports Usenet. It contains help files, all newsgroups, FAQs, and a link to the DejaNews search engine, the best Usenet search engine around.

Usenet Volunteer Votetakers Information Center

www.uvv.org/

This is the official Web page for those folks who handle the voting procedures for creating new newsgroups. The site also contains the text of most of the various how-to articles about Usenet.

Usenet Info Center

Kevin Atkinson created and maintained an ambitious project called the Usenet Bible in 1994 with hopes that it would become a comprehensive guide to newsgroups. To access the Usenet Bible, you simply use email to request in-depth descriptions of any newsgroup (he had 337 newsgroups described when this book went to press), or log onto his Web site at **http://sunsite.unc.edu/usenet-i/intro.html**.

The Web site has a list of many of the Usenet FAQs, allows you to search for a newsgroup from a database, and contains other useful information.

In February 1995, Kevin changed the name to the Usenet Info Center. Using the service is easy. To ask the Bible what information is available for a group, send a message to usenet-b@clark.net with a subject line of "See: Newsgroup". For example, to see what's in **alt.music.progressive**, you send a message with the subject line "See: **alt.music.progressive**". Upon receiving the request, the server will mail you the raw database file of that group with the following information in it:

1. A short description of the group
2. A long description of the group
3. Any FAQs that go with the group
4. The moderator's name and email address (if moderated)
5. Where, how, and if the group is archived
6. Its average volume
7. Its average number of readers
8. Any mailing lists to which the group is gatewayed

In our sample group, **alt.music.progressive**, we get the following reply:

```
Subj: alt.music.progressive newsgroup data...
Date: Wed, Jan 18, 1995 3:18 AM EST
From: usenet-b@clark.net
X-From: usenet-b@clark.net (USENET Bible Request)
To: AFLDonR@aol.com

SD: Yes, Marillion, Asia, King Crimson, etc.
ST: 33000 454 55% 2784 4.7 4% 0.11 0.9%
LD:
Discussion of progressive rock; that is, the art rock movement of the
1970's, headed by Yes, Genesis, ELP, Kansas, Gentle Giant, and others.
This music is characterized by strong classical and jazz influences,
lengthy pieces, and attention to compositional details (perhaps
noticeable mainly to trained musicians) rather than catchiness or
marketability. New artists that write compositionally complex music
are also discussed.
```

(continued)

Usenet Info Center (*continued*).

```
There are other definitions for "progressive" music. For one group of
people, it is a synonym for today's "alternative" music.
alt.music.progressive does NOT address this music; see
alt.music.alternative instead. For a second group of people, it means
any music that progresses beyond popular music in some significant
way. alt.music.progressive sometimes addresses this type of music.

The most common argument concerning "progressive rock" occurs when two
people use different definitions of "progressive." One or both of
them start screaming, "the music you like is NOT progressive." These
arguments get nowhere and should be avoided.

Note that alt.music.genesis and alt.music.yes exist for discussions
particular to Genesis and Yes, respectively.
FAQ:
Subject: MUSIC: Marillion and Fish FAQ [*/*]
From: kbibb@jafar.qualcomm.com (Ken Bibb)
Frequency: monthly
Archive-name: music/marillion-faq/part1
Summary: A list of frequently asked questions and their answers about
       Marillion and Fish, their music and the mailinglist Freaks.
       Read this document before subscribing to Freaks.
Date: 3 Dec 1994 14:14:03 GMT
STP: 71% 76% 58% 95% 95% 35% 93% 76%


----------- Headers ----------------
From usenet-b@clark.net Wed Jan 18 03:13:36 1995
Received: from clark.net by mailgate.prod.aol.net with ESMTP
     (1.37.109.11/16.2) id AA237896816; Wed, 18 Jan 1995 03:13:36 -0500
Return-Path: <usenet-b@clark.net>
Received: (usenet-b@localhost) by clark.net (8.6.9/8.6.5) id DAA10355; Wed, 18
Jan 1995 03:16:08 -0500
Date: Wed, 18 Jan 1995 03:16:08 -0500
Message-Id: <199501180816.DAA10355@clark.net>
To: AFLDonR@aol.com
From: USENET Bible Request <usenet-b@clark.net>
Subject: alt.music.progressive newsgroup data...
```

(continued)

Usenet Info Center (*continued*).

For a description of the information in the raw database files, send a message as previously written (with "See:" in the subject line), but type "database-info" as the newsgroup. To get the list of newsgroups that lack descriptions, send mail as previously written, but type "desc-still-needed" as the newsgroup. Kevin requests that you help out the project by writing a long description of any undescribed newsgroup and sending it in. To see all the newsgroups that have a description, type "desc-have" as the newsgroup. If you want to see a detailed breakdown of how many descriptions he needs (or has), type "desc-status" as the newsgroup.

These files are also available via FTP at **ftp.clark.net:/pub/usenet-bible/info**.

4 Netiquette: How To Communicate On The Internet

Rittner's Computer Law: No matter how well you know the rules of netiquette, you will eventually offend someone who doesn't.

The "i" in iMac stands for Internet. As you learned in Chapter 2, getting on the Net is easy. However, before you start surfing the Net, you need to read this chapter carefully. It will help you avoid looking foolish to a world audience, and where can you hide after that? This is probably the most important chapter in this book. I recommend that you read it more than once.

Online etiquette, or *netiquette* as it's called, is about behaving properly in the online world—practicing good online manners. In the 15 years of the Internet, Usenet, and online services, the Net community has developed a code of behavior. Like all cultures, it has acceptable and unacceptable etiquette and taboos to avoid. You will save yourself a great deal of embarrassment and avoid some major headaches if you learn proper online etiquette.

These common sense helpful hints are designed for participating in Internet discussion lists, Usenet newsgroups, public chat rooms, and generally about anything you do on the Net that affects more than one person. Remember that the Internet spans the globe in more than 100 countries. You will come in contact with many different cultures and customs. This chapter will show you how to avoid offending millions of people at the click of a mouse.

Don's Guide To Good Manners

The following set of online guidelines will ensure that you have a great online experience. Remember at least one important law is to write to others as you would want others to write to you. Common courtesy is a universal language.

Smileys And Shortcuts

Most people on the Internet write in English, and the English language can be a bit confusing when you read it (yes, even to Americans). For example, I can send you an email that reads "I think you're nuts!" Because it's impossible to translate inflections or emphasis of speech when communicating online, I might be paying you a compliment or telling you off.

Written language on the Internet has developed a special shortcut for displaying emotions: smileys, or *emoticons* (emotional icons). Smileys help you communicate what you mean. They can add an element of fun and levity, emphasize a point, display an emotion, and even prevent misunderstandings. Smileys have become an integral part of computer writing. There are hundreds of them. You could call smileys a form of "computerese."

How do smileys work? You tilt your head. You create smileys by designing icons with letters and symbols and adding the result to the end of the sentence or phrase. You can recognize the characters by tilting your head to the left. For example, this is a smile:

:-) Two eyes, a nose, and a mouth; the nose is optional.

Using my previous example, if I send you email with

I think you're nuts! **:-)**

You can tell that I am kidding by the smiley.

During your journey as a Net citizen, you will encounter hundreds of smileys. Table 4.1 is a sample of the more common ones. Memorizing these will get you through your digital day in good shape. However, as in normal conversation, don't overuse these gestures.

Table 4.1 Smileys and emoticons.

Emoticons	Meaning
:-o	Wow!
:-|	Grim
:-v	Speaking
:-,	Smirking
:-||	Anger

(continued)

Table 4.1 Smileys and emoticons (continued).

Emoticons	Meaning
:-)	Smiling
:-p	Sticking out your tongue
:-(	Frowning or sad
:-*	Kissing
:-[	Pouting
:-#	My lips are sealed
:-O	Yelling
;-(	Crying
[ ]	Hugs (Usually, you put the initials of the receiver between the brackets.)
}:-(	Bull-headed
:-&	Tongue-tied
;-)	Winking

More Shortcuts

Along with emoticons, you should recognize shortcuts—acronyms—for commonly used phrases. Some common acronyms you will see online appear in Table 4.2. As with smileys, don't overuse them.

Be Considerate

Because you are dealing with millions of people on the Net, it's easy to offend someone. You might accidentally reveal the ending of a movie, express a strong opinion, or insult someone from another country (because you're not familiar with his custom or culture), so accept the fact that someone out there is bound to be offended by your comments. Don't sweat it. He'll get over it.

In case you frequent public forums or chat rooms, newsgroups, or mailing lists where you might share information that people may or may not choose to read, there is a solution. To minimize offending posts, the Net community developed Rot-13, a simple method for encrypting posts. Rot-13 is popular on Usenet (where it originated) and is commonly used in certain newsgroups that feature questionable humor, profanity, or spoilers such as the end of a movie or plot line.

Table 4.2 Acronyms for the online world.

Acronym	Meaning
LOL	Laughing out loud.
GMTA	Great minds think alike.
IMHO	In my humble opinion.
BTW	By the way.
BRB	Be right back.
GA	Go ahead.
/	Done (after making a remark).
ROTFL	Rolling on the floor laughing.
...	More to come.
?	Wants to ask a question.
!	Wants to make a comment.
BBIM	Be back in a minute.
FYI	For your information.
CU	See you later; signing off.

Rot-13 works by taking a letter of the alphabet and rotating (rot) it to the 13th letter; for example, a becomes n, b becomes o, and so on. Rot-13 is built into certain email programs and Usenet newsreaders.

The pre-installed versions of Netscape Communicator and Microsoft Internet Explorer that come with your iMac do not have Rot-13 capability.

MacROT For iMac Users

Mac software guru, Andrew Welch of Ambrosia Software, wrote a special Rot-13 program exclusively for this book, and you can download it by visiting **www.themesh.com**. Andrew has written several popular shareware programs (games and utilities) for the Mac community.

Using MacROT is simple. Place the MacROT application or an alias for it in your Apple menu folder (pressing the Command+M or the Apple key+M), which is in your system folder, so it's always available.

When you want to encrypt or decrypt a post or email, select the application under the Apple menu. Copy and paste your article or email into the box. You can also use the built-in editor to write your piece. Select the piece you want encrypted by placing the cursor in the beginning of the text, click and drag it to include the selected text, or if you want to encrypt the whole article, use the Command+A combination. Click the encrypt/decrypt button (the one with arrows, or Command+T shortcut), and presto, your article is either encrypted or decrypted.

MacROT is freeware exclusively for owners of this book. Figure 4.1 shows you how MacROT looks when encrypting a message.

Online Do's And Don'ts

There are a few simple ways to get people mad at you online. It's not advisable to develop a bad reputation on the Net. Afterall, where can you hide after that? If you follow the suggestions in this section, you will avoid becoming a casualty.

Spam Is More Than Lunch Meat

Once you get online, you will be introduced to spam about as fast as you get your email account. Spamming is sending (flooding is a better term) the same email message or post of little or no value (except to the sender) to many people, discussion groups, or Usenet newsgroups all at the same time. You can recognize spam almost immediately with headers such as "Make Money Fast," "Lose Weight Fast," or "Stop Creditor Phone Calls." Figure 4.2 is an example of SPAM. It's obnoxious. If you like SPAM, join America Online. I get most of it there. Spamming grew to almost epidemic proportions until many Internet providers and commercial online services started suing the spammers. Spamming is still pretty common, but there are ways to filter out spam.

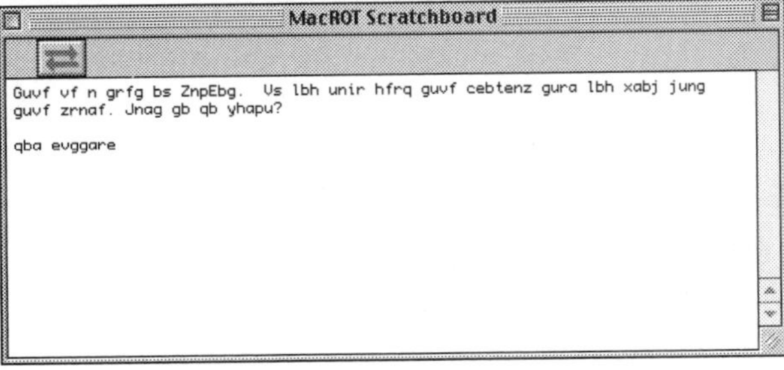

Figure 4.1 *The MacROT application showing an encrypted message.*

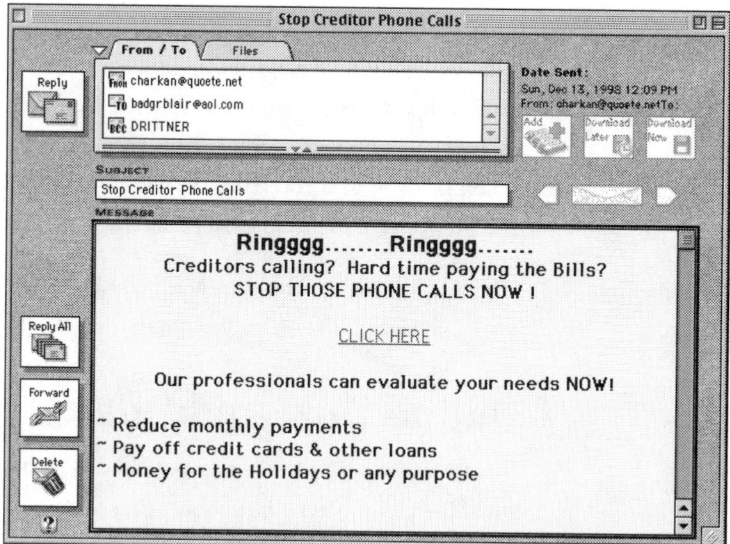

Figure 4.2
Spam.

Spamming is not a good practice unless you have a desire to be hated or threatened by people around the world. However, some people have thick heads and never learn, so there are constant offenders. An official World Wide Web site blacklists the repeaters. To see a list of the perpetrators, you can visit the Blacklist of Internet Advertisers Web site, as shown in Figure 4.3, at **www-math.uni-paderborn.de/%7Eaxel/BL/**. Other good Web sites for learning about spam are Fight Spam on the Internet! at **http://spam.abuse.net/spam/** and the Coalition Against Unsolicited Commercial Email (CAUCE) at **www.cauce.org**.

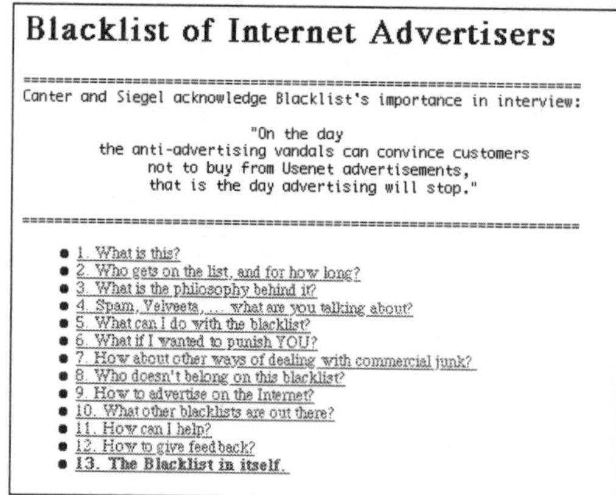

Figure 4.3
Blacklist of Internet Advertisers site.

Don't Test The Waters

If you subscribe to a discussion list or newsgroup, do not post a test message to check whether it's working. Post a real question instead. If you get an answer, it's working. Usenet has newsgroups set up for test purposes, such as **misc.test** or **alt.test**. Use them instead. I recommend visiting **news.answers**, as shown in Figure 4.4, to see if there is a FAQ for your newsgroup before you start contributing.

Fanning The Flames

Flaming is another problem you want to avoid at all costs. A flame war is a post war that wastes time and bandwidth and usually creates many hard feelings.

A flame war starts when someone sends a message that is critical of another person's post (often a personal attack), someone else sends a post criticizing the critic, and so on. Before long, hundreds of people are flooding the list or newsgroup with attacks back and forth. Flame wars die eventually but can waste a lot of time, and they can even destroy a mailing list or newsgroup. It is best not to get involved. If you feel you must jump into the fray, get up from your iMac, go get a drink or take a break, and come back later when you have calmed down.

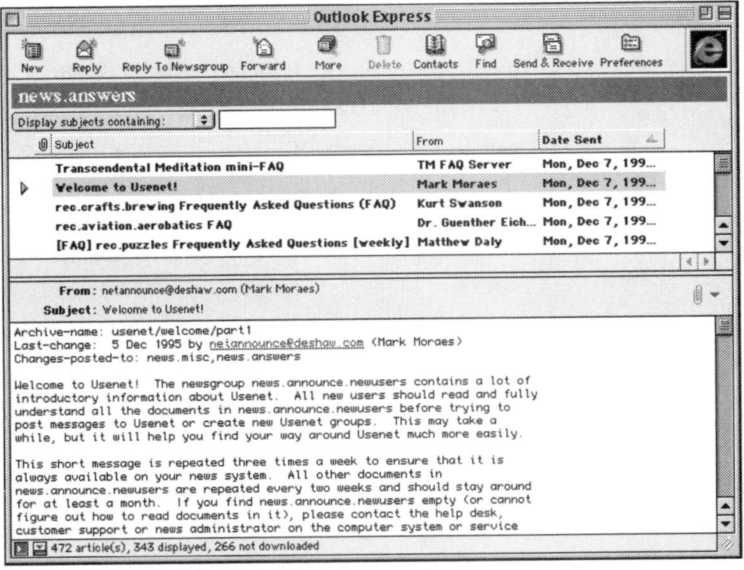

Figure 4.4
News.answers *newsgroup.*

Be wary of the "spelling flame." Someone pounces on a poster who uses bad grammar or makes a typo, and this brings out all the English teachers who then flame each other's posts.

If you're the kind of person who likes to rant and rave, you can subscribe to the Usenet newsgroup **alt.flame** and get it all out of your system (and spare the rest of us).

Beware Of Cascading Posts

A cascade occurs when users in a discussion list or newsgroup continue adding (mostly useless) responses to a post so that there may be 20 or more replies contained in a single message. If you want to see the creative side of cascading, subscribe to the **alt.cascade** newsgroup.

I Have A Special Deal Just For You

The Net was not created as an advertising medium, although commercial interests have made giant inroads, and electronic commerce is now a growing part of the Net.

The Net would be in total chaos if every company on the Net used it to advertise in public forums, discussion lists, newsgroups, and so on. Blatant advertising is taboo in discussion lists and newsgroups unless they are created specifically for that purpose. If you must rave about a product, there are newsgroups to serve you. The biz hierarchy allows advertising, and the newsgroups **comp.newprod** and **comp.forsale** are examples of newsgroups designed explicitly for advertising.

When you see posts such as "Make Money Fast" or "Lose Weight Fast," don't even bother reading them (unless you are interested in being scammed). If or when you decide to plug something yourself, be sure to mention that in the subject line to let people know ahead of time. It's common to see $$$ in the header of a post to indicate it's of a commercial nature. Some posters also write "blatant ad" in the header. You can then choose not to read it.

An acceptable way to advertise, in a low-level way, is to include a one-sentence plug in your signature at the end of a post. The other acceptable way to advertise on the Net by a retailer is through a free Net email service, mailing list service, or Net search engine. For the service to be free, the user must allow banner advertising to appear in the body of the email. It really isn't that intrusive, and you might find yourself clicking a banner to find a good deal. To be honest, someone has to pay the bills. It isn't a bad trade-off. I call it the Robin Hood approach. Businesses pay the server or provider, and you, the user, get the information for free.

Psst, Can You Keep A Secret?

Let's face it: Not everyone is comfortable talking to strangers even if people cannot see them. Sometimes, you might want to express an opinion without claiming ownership because you don't want a fellow co-worker or friend who may be online to see it. No worry. Anonymous servers let you post in privacy. These servers strip your name and header information and replace it with the word "anonymous."

However, you should be warned. Do not use anonymous servers to conduct anything illegal because there is no guarantee that you cannot be traced or that something won't happen to reveal you as the poster. A famous lawsuit between the Church of Scientology and a former member forced a remailer to give up the address of a person or else lose his entire confidential database.

You can use a number of anonymous remailers. To get a current list, use your Web browser to visit **www.cs.berkeley.edu/~raph/remailer-list.html**. You can also subscribe to the newsgroup **alt.privacy.anon-server**.

25 Common Sense Tips

If you follow some basic, sensible rules and observe proper protocol, you will have little trouble communicating in the Net community. The following useful tips will help you communicate on the Net:

1. Look before you leap. Before you post anything, as a rule you should read at least two months' worth of posts in a newsgroup and at least two weeks of posts on a discussion list to see what is being discussed. If the Usenet newsgroup you joined has a FAQ (Frequently Asked Questions) document, read it.

2. If you are responding to someone's post, be sure to quote the passages on which you are commenting in your reply. It's important to make references to the original post because the person might not remember his or her entire post. Figure 4.5 shows the proper way to respond to someone's email or post.

   The accepted way to respond is to write your response and then follow it with the original posts, each line of the original prefixed with a **>** (Outlook Express and other mailers do this automatically).

3. Don't bore everyone. If you are responding to a message that appeared in a discussion list or newsgroup, and your reply is of little interest to the rest of the readers, respond to a post privately if possible. If someone posts a simple request, one in which the

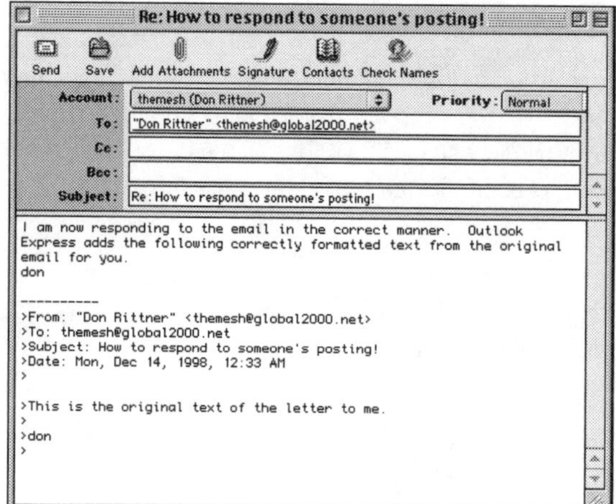

Figure 4.5
Proper email or post netiquette.

general readership is not likely to be interested, it's better to send the person a reply to his email address rather than have 100 people post the same answer to the newsgroup. No one wants to read 100 replies with the same answers. Moreover, when someone asks for information, he will (or at least should) collect all the individual replies, condense them, and then post the collected replies as one public article for all to read as a courtesy.

4. Be on top of things. When you join a discussion group or newsgroup for the first time, take a week and read before you jump in. This rule is important when joining a newsgroup for the first time because all articles are marked as unread. Go ahead and read a few, but you should tell your newsreader software to mark them all as read so you can start new the next day. You can do this with Outlook Express by selecting the newsgroup article and choosing Unread Only under the View menu. You can also use the key combo Command (or Apple)+Y. There is a real good reason why you should do this. When America Online (AOL) provided a link to Usenet for the first time to its huge membership, it made the mistake of not explaining netiquette. Because members did not mark their posts as read, AOL users answered inquiries that were as much as a year-old. It became so unbearable to the Usenet community at large that a large flame war erupted, and to this day, there are a couple of "I hate AOL" newsgroups in which people vent their hostility toward AOL. AOL users are not popular on

Usenet (or for that matter, anywhere else). Take heed; make sure your replies and posts are current.

5. Don't be redundant. Before you write a response from a general inquiry, read further to make sure someone else hasn't already responded.
6. Keep your posts short and to the point, and be succinct when replying. The average Net citizen may belong to several discussion lists and newsgroups.
7. Do not abandon good grammar, proofing, and writing styles. Don't assume everyone knows what your acronyms mean. (Avoid them when possible.) Write in the active voice. Use smileys when needed to emphasize meaning. Remember, you have an international audience. Do not use slang that is strictly American.
8. Do not try to impress folks with your knowledge of the English language—unless you are in a language group.
9. DO NOT TYPE IN ALL CAPS unless you're shouting at someone. Reading posts in all caps strains the eyes, and using them will probably get you flamed. As Figure 4.6 shows, if you do type in ALL CAPS, you are guaranteed to get flamed!
10. Be clear in the subject line of your post. A subject line that reads "I Love Lucy" could mean you're a TV buff or an anthropologist with a strange sense of humor.

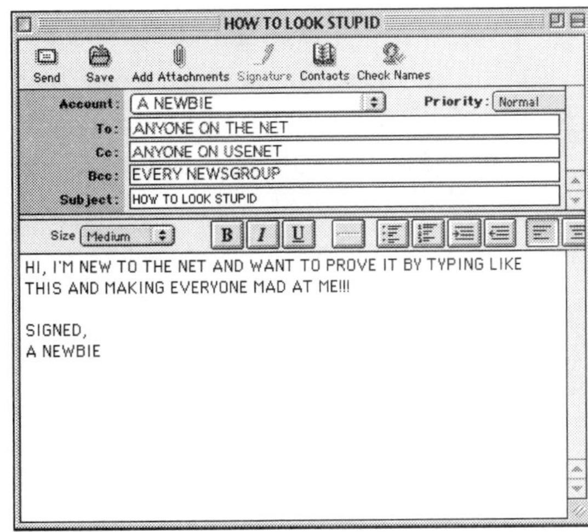

Figure 4.6
Ticket to being flamed.

11. Proof it. Reread your article before you send it. Then, reread it again.
12. Don't try to be cute. Most of those who read your post don't know you.
13. Be tolerant. Do not start a flame war because someone misspells a word. Spelling flames are immature. Perfect people don't belong on the Net anyway. :)
14. Think first. Do not send anything on the Net that you will regret later. Once it's posted in cyberspace, you can't get it back. Chances are, if you insult someone online, that person, a friend, or even a relative of that person will read it. Everything on the Net is archived. Never post anything in a public forum that you don't want your mother or the FBI to know about.
15. Know where you are (in cyberspace). In a discussion list or newsgroup devoted to rare butterflies, asking whether anyone has a used snow blower for sale is likely to get you flamed.
16. Know where you are (on the planet). When participating in Usenet newsgroups, be sure to check the headers of a post, and make sure you send your reply to the correct newsgroup or email address. Someone may send a post to several newsgroups (cross-post it) but intend only one for actual discussion. Refer to the message ID of the article, not the article number. Message IDs are preserved on all the news servers because article numbers vary from server to server.
17. Be honest. No smoke screens, misrepresentations, or scams, please. If you are posting about how fabulous a piece of software or hardware is, and you work for the company (or have some financial stake in it), make that association evident in your post. Don't hide it. All the responsibility for a post lies with the individual posting it. Don't assume that Mr. Doe is speaking for Apple because he's a salesman for the company. You will often see in a poster's signature a statement saying that the opinions expressed are hers, not her employers. You should assume that anyway.
18. Don't be a jerk. Learn the difference between free speech and civility. If you visit your friend's home and insult his wife, chances are you will be shown out the door. So much for free speech. It's okay

to argue and criticize someone's post or opinion, but do not make personal attacks on anyone.

19. Be careful what you say. Understand what slander means. Net folks have been sued. Many electronic free speech and privacy issues have not been tested in court yet, and you don't want to become a test case do you?
20. Keep it to yourself. Do not reveal someone's private email to the Net, even if you are responding to a flame. Email is considered copyrighted by the writer, and you could get into serious legal trouble if you post it publicly without permission.
21. Speaking of copyright: Watch out for copyright infringement. If you are using material from a published source or otherwise copyrighted source, be sure to cite it. Do not publish copyrighted information without permission.
22. Don't be a moron. "Can you help me find my lost girlfriend from Buffalo?" "I am a physics student and need an idea for my term paper or I will fail. Can you suggest one?" Do not use the Net for personal requests that obviously show a lack of initiative on your part. Although it's true that Net folks are helpful and giving when it comes to real requests, no one wants to be bothered with helping you fumble your way through life.
23. Post once on Usenet. When you want to post an article to more than one Usenet newsgroup, post to all of the groups at the same time. Don't post the same article to each newsgroup separately. This practice lets your software send only one copy of the article—not three or four. You create less traffic, you won't be accused of spamming, and folks with smart newsreaders will only read it once anyway.
24. If you find you must cross-post to several discussion lists, you should put in the header of all copies "cross-posted" with the title of the post, which should be the same title as the original. Readers can then choose to ignore it if they belong to more than one mailing list and receive your multiple posts.

25. The Net is not America. Not all Net users are American, although there are certainly more Americans than non-Americans on the Net. Keep in mind when posting that the Net involves many countries and cultures. American slang or inside jokes don't go over well in other countries.

The bottom line when you are online is to treat others on the Net as you want them to treat you. Although you might not see whom you are communicating with, nonetheless, it is a human on the other side of the digital stream. Practicing civility in cyberspace is a cardinal rule.

Netiquette Sites On The Web

In case you want to learn more about how to handle yourself on the Net, the following Web sites are all excellent for explaining online etiquette:

- Dear EmilyPost News—**www.clari.net/brad/emily.html**
- MAP07—from the Roadmap for the Information Superhighway—**www.hart.bbk.ac.uk/~trish/maponline/MAP07.html**
- The Net User Guidelines and Netiquette—**www.revealed.net/IRWeb/INM/netiquette.html**
- RFC1855: Netiquette guidelines (The "Official" Netiquette Guide)—**www.cis.ohio-state.edu/htbin/rfc/rfc1855.html**
- Help! I've been Spammed! What do I do?—**www.tezcat.com/~gbyshenk/ive.been.spammed.html**

5 iMac Resources: Internet Mailing Lists

Rittner's Computer Law: The Net is the ultimate empowerment tool. You have the right to express your opinion to a global audience, but everyone has the right not to pay any attention to it.

There are more than 25 million Macintosh users in the world according to Apple. That's equal to the combined population of New York City and Paris. The Macintosh community is a large, intelligent, and creative group of people. Many people volunteer their time to create Internet mailing lists and Usenet newsgroups, to produce newsletters, to maintain Web support sites, to manage news sites, to maintain archives of shareware software, to provide technical support areas, to publish electronic magazines, and even to broadcast radio shows. They all love the Macintosh. In the Apple world, these people are affectionately known as "Mac evangelists." In the next few chapters, you will meet many of these evangelists and benefit from their contributions to the Mac community.

In a nutshell, this chapter will show you how to subscribe to Mac-related Internet mailing or discussion lists and electronic newsletters.

Corresponding With Mac Users Worldwide

Learn how to use your email account to discuss issues with people around the world.

Internet Mailing (Discussion) Lists And Electronic Newsletters

In Chapter 2, you learned that an Internet mailing or discussion list allows you to participate in dialog with fellow iMac users using your email account.

There are several kinds of mailing lists. Some mailing lists are designed as a one-way street; you receive them but don't have the ability to reply. This kind of list is often referred to as an automailer or announcement list. It's primarily used to update you on a software upgrade or news about a product introduction.

Some mailing lists are electronic newsletters, containing articles, tutorials, reviews, and news. Often, they are plain-text emails, but some are produced with special software programs that allow the publisher to include color covers and graphics throughout the publication, just like a printed newsletter or magazine.

Most mailing lists are multi-way electronic discussions in email form and are rewarding sources for information because they are current and active on a daily basis.

Many Internet mailing lists and electronic newsletters deal with Apple Computer, the iMac, and all other models of Macintosh, as well as software, peripheral hardware, development, the industry, and other issues relating to the Mac. Many of the lists are for general, non-technical consumption. There are lists for the new user, the more technically inclined user, and software- or hardware-specific topics. As a new iMac owner, I have taken the liberty to emphasize which lists I consider important enough for you to join.

Regardless of the type of mailing list you join, it's easy to get on a list. You subscribe to a list using your email account, and subscribing is simple. You send an email to a specific address, called the administrative address, and in the subject line of your email, type a command, usually subscribe *name of the list* and your name or email address. Often, you don't need to include your name, only the name of the list. The whole process is just that easy.

Many mailing lists offer two flavors, normal and digest. If a digest is available, subscribe to it instead of the normal list. Otherwise, you might find your mailbox full of emails if the list you join is very active; some lists generate hundreds of emails a day. A digest sends you one file with all the day's or week's posts rather than hundreds of separate emails. Simply download the file and read at your leisure.

Once you subscribe to a list, you'll receive an email with instructions on how to unsubscribe, how to search any archives for previous postings, and how to perform other administrative functions. Keep that email in a safe place because it is frustrating when you want to discontinue your subscription and can't remember how to sign off. Believe me, you will get sick of reading all the emails that ask "How do I sign off from this list?"

It's important to remember that when you want to post to a list, you do not use the administrative address, the one you used for subscribing. There is always a second address for posting. Learning these details is why it is important to read the confirming email you receive after you subscribe to a list.

Some list maintainers send you an email that you must reply to in order to activate the subscription. This ensures that you really want to join the list and proves to the list maintainer that you are real and the address is reachable.

Finally, some list maintainers, especially in moderated lists, must approve your subscription request. It is not automatic.

All of the mailing lists described in this chapter are available to you for free. I provide a summary of their purposes, taken from the original sources, and instructions for subscribing.

iMac Specific

The following resources will keep you informed about the latest news and developments specifically about the iMac.

iMac Update

Apple Computer publishes iMac Update. You can subscribe to the newsletter by visiting the iMac Web site at **www.info.apple.com/support/index.taf?product=imac**.

The iMac List Digest

This email-mailing list developed for iMac users is sponsored by **NoBeige.com**. You can subscribe by visiting **www.nobeige.com**.

The iMac List

This list features general discussion about the iMac. To subscribe, send email to lists@reformed.net, and in the message, include "subscribe iMac *Your Name*".

Apple And Related Mailing Lists

The following mailing lists cover all aspects of Apple and its products.

Apple Desktop Bus Input/Output Discussion List (ADB I/O)

This discussion list incorporates all aspects of data acquisition and controlling electronic devices. According to Apple, it's frequented by students, interactive artists, researchers, and developers as well as the engineers who designed (ADB I/O). Because ADB was abandoned for the Universal Serial Bus (USB) on the iMac, you might not be interested in this list unless you have an older Mac as well.

To subscribe, send email to ADB_IO_Discussion@lists.bzzzzzz.com. Include "subscribe" in the subject heading.

To subscribe to the digest, in the subject heading, include "subscribe digest".

Aimed-talk

Aimed-talk is a list for anyone interested in the Association of Independent Macintosh Engineers and Developers and developing for the Macintosh. To subscribe, send email to aimed-talk-request@aimed.org, and in the message, include "subscribe".

Apple eNews

Apple eNews is a newsletter published by Apple Computer that highlights developments, products, and news from Apple. It's published twice a month. You can subscribe to the newsletter by visiting **www.apple.com/hotnews/subscribe.html**. You can find more information about the list at **www.lists.apple.com/applewire.html**.

Apple Developer News (ADN)

Apple calls this "an electronic news bulletin that delivers critical, developer-related technical and business news." It's published as needed. To subscribe, visit **http://support.info.apple.com/support/supportoptions/lists.html**.

Apple Forever Support Project

This is an interesting mailing list for those interested in investing in Apple. For more information, visit **www.appleforever.org**.

Apple Information Access Toolkit (AIAT)

According to Apple, "the Apple Information Access Toolkit (formerly known as V-Twin) is an object-oriented library for creating a new breed of content-aware applications. This list is for developers using AIAT to discuss problems and solutions, to ask questions, to share tips and advice, or to make feature requests."

To subscribe, send email to majordomo@public.lists.apple.com, and in the message, include "subscribe AIAT-Dev". If you want to subscribe to the digest version of the list, include "subscribe AIAT-Dev-digest".

Apple Media Toolkit Developers

This list is for developers using the Apple Media Tool. To subscribe, send email to amkdev-request@earthchannel.com. In the message, include "subscribe AMKDEV *Your Name*".

Analog Web Log Software For The Macintosh

Hosted by Innovative Technologies, this list discusses Analog, a free Web log software program. For more information, write to amkdev-request@earthchannel.com.

Anarchie Pro Discussion List

Hosted by Stairways Software, this list features discussion of Anarchie Pro and related software. To subscribe, visit **www.stairways.com/mailinglists/**.

Apple Guide

This list, hosted by Stairways Software, offers discussion of issues related to writing or designing Apple Guides. You can subscribe to the list by visiting **www.stairways.com/mailinglists/**.

Apple Network Administrators Toolkit

According to Apple, this list is for "users of the Apple Network Administrator Toolkit (ANAT). The Apple Network Administrator Toolkit includes At Ease for Workgroups, Apple Network Assistant, and Apple User and Group Manage."

To subscribe, send email to majordomo@public.lists.apple.com, and in the message, include "subscribe ANAT-Users". If you want to subscribe to the digest version of the list, you should use "subscribe ANAT-Users-digest".

Apple Press Releases

This list will send you Apple's press releases as they are issued. Subscribe by visiting **http://support.info.apple.com/support/supportoptions/lists.html**, or send email to pressrel@thing2.info.apple.com and in the subject heading, include "subscribe pressrel".

Apple Software Update Locations

This list will send you Apple's software locations once. Subscribe as needed by visiting **http://support.info.apple.com/support/supportoptions/lists.html**.

Apple-Net-Announce

This moderated list posts announcements and press releases involving products related to Apple computers and intranets or the Internet. To subscribe, send email to majordomo@public.lists.apple.com, and in the message, include "subscribe Apple-Net-Announce".

Apple-Net-Authoring

This list discusses issues pertaining to authoring or creating Web sites, including content and graphics, design, site architecture, and other items of interest, according to Apple. To subscribe, send email to majordomo@public.lists.apple.com, and in the message, include "subscribe Apple-Net-Authoring".

To subscribe to the digest version of the list, include "subscribe Apple-Net-Authoring-digest".

Apple-Net-Clients

According to Apple, this list discusses client-side tools such as Web browsers or FTP clients. To subscribe, send email to majordomo@public.lists.apple.com, and in the message, include "subscribe Apple-Net-Clients".

To subscribe to the digest version of the list, include "subscribe Apple-Net-Clients-digest".

Apple-Net-Connectivity

According to Apple, this list discusses "the low-level aspects of Apple networking, including LocalTalk, EtherTalk, Open Transport and LAN issues, as well as modems, PPP, and low-level network connection issues." To subscribe, send email to majordomo@public.lists.apple.com, and in the message, include "subscribe Apple-Net-Connectivity". If you want to subscribe to the digest version of the list, include "subscribe Apple-Net-Connectivity-digest".

Apple-Net-Servers

According to Apple, this list discusses "server-side tools such as WebStar and other Web servers, as well as issues involving the use of Apple products in an Internet Service Provider environment. Tools that publish or present data on networks should be discussed here, also Web CGI usage and authoring issues. To subscribe, send email to majordomo@public.lists.apple.com, and in the message, include "subscribe Apple-Net-Servers". If you want to subscribe to the digest version of the list, include "subscribe Apple-Net-Servers-digest".

Apple-Network-Assistant

Apple provides this list for users of Apple Network Assistant. Apple Network Assistant is software that helps you "manage Mac OS workstations on a network and work with other users on the network." To subscribe, send email to majordomo@public.lists.apple.com, and in the message, include "subscribe Apple-Network-Assistant". If you want to subscribe to the digest version of the list, include "subscribe Apple-Network-Assistant-digest".

Apple-Workgroup-Servers

This list discusses the use of Apple servers and bundled software. To subscribe, send email to majordomo@public.lists.apple.com. In the message, include "subscribe Apple-Workgroup-Servers". If you want to subscribe to the digest version of the list, include "subscribe Apple-Workgroup-Servers-digest".

AppleNews Belgium

This daily newsletter contains items related to the world of Apple. To subscribe, send email to applenews_belgium@eurolist.euro.apple.com. In the subject field of your email message, include "subscribe" or "subscribe digest".

AppleScript SIG (German)

To subscribe in German, send email to sigapplescript@udena.ch. In the subject line, include the word "subscribe".

AppleScript-Implementors

According to Apple, this list serves developers creating "AppleScript-savvy applications." To subscribe, send email to majordomo@public.lists.apple.com, and in the message, include "subscribe AppleScript-Implementors". If you want to subscribe to the digest version of the list, include "subscribe AppleScript-Implementors-digest".

AppleScript-Users

Apple says this list serves users of "AppleScript and scriptable applications to discuss writing scripts in the language, interfacing with scriptable applications, and general usage of the language." To subscribe, send email to majordomo@public.lists.apple.com, and in the message, include "subscribe AppleScript-Users". If you want to subscribe to the digest version of the list, include "subscribe AppleScript-Users-digest".

Never, Ever Use A List For Spamming

If you have a product to sell or promote, do not abuse your privilege of belonging to a list by thinking everyone wants to hear about it.

AppleShareIP

According to Apple, this list lets AppleShare users communicate with each other. To subscribe, send email to majordomo@public.lists.apple.com, and in the message, include "subscribe AppleShareIP". If you want to subscribe to the digest version of the list, include "subscribe AppleShareIP-digest".

Apple Users Group Bulletin

This list is for "user group leaders and is used to distribute Apple's User Group Bulletin (AUGB), an electronic newsletter reporting Apple news, user group updates, and events to user groups around the world. This is an announcement list only and there are 2-3 postings per month." To subscribe, send email to majordomo@public.lists.apple.com, and in the message, include "subscribe AUGB". If you want to subscribe to the digest version of the list, include "subscribe AUGB-digest".

Archive Site

This list informs you of software updates. To subscribe, send email to majordomo@cc.rochester.edu, and in the message, include "subscribe archive_site".

ASK-ABOUT-BE

This list is a help desk of answers and solutions to BeOS questions, primarily for those who installed BeOS on a Mac. To subscribe, send email to majordomo@bear-buys.com, and in the message, include "subscribe ask-about-be".

BBEdit-Talk

This list is for users of Bare Bones Software's text editor, BBEdit. To subscribe, send email to bbedit-talk-on@lists.barebones.com. In the subject line or message, include "subscribe".

TIP

Save It For A Rainy Day

After you subscribe to a list and receive the confirmation, cut and paste the instructions on how to unsubscribe into your electronic address book, if you have one, or to the scrapbook under the Apple menu (far left). This step will save you aggravation later when you want to unsubscribe from the list.

BlueWorld Software Lists

BlueWorld, maker of the program Lasso, produces the following mailing lists:

- Adobe Acrobat
- Adobe PageMill
- Claris HomePage
- Claris Organizer
- FileMaker Pro
- FileMaker Pro CGI
- Lasso

To subscribe to any of them, visit **www2.blueworld.com/lists/subscribe/subscribe.lasso**.

Classic Macs Digest

If you own some of the old Macs, here is a good discussion list. To subscribe, send email to majordomo@hitznet.com. In the message, include "subscribe classics."

Cocoa-Users

According to Apple, this list is for "kids, teachers, parents, and others who are using Apple's Cocoa application to produce simulations, games, and other interactive multimedia on the Mac." To subscribe, send email to majordomo@public.lists.apple.com, and in the message, include "subscribe Cocoa-Users". If you want to subscribe to the digest version of the list, include "subscribe Cocoa-Users-digest".

Colorsync-Dev

Apple says this list lets ColorSync developers share technical information. To subscribe, send email to majordomo@public.lists.apple.com, and in the message, include "subscribe Colorsync-Dev". If you want to subscribe to the digest version of the list, include "subscribe Colorsync-Dev-digest".

Colorsync-Users

Apple says this list serves users who are implementing ColorSync color management workflow. To subscribe, send email to majordomo@public.lists.apple.com, and in the message, include "subscribe Colorsync-Users". If you want to subscribe to the digest version of the list, include "subscribe Colorsync-Users-digest".

CorelDraw

This list discusses issues related to CorelDraw for Macintosh. To subscribe, visit **www.r8ix.com/lists.html**.

Cyberstudio-Talk

This list serves users of GoLive's Web site creation software, CyberStudio, one of the best HTML editors. To subscribe, send email to requests@cool.acc-inc.com. In the message, include "info CyberStudioTalk".

Danger, Danger Will Robinson

Do not post a commercial announcement unless it is approved by the list administrator. Otherwise, doing so will get you banned from the list.

Dantz News

This announcement list concerns Dantz products. To subscribe, visit **www.dantz.com/news/news_form.html**.

Daw-mac

This list deals with Macintosh digital audio workstations. To subscribe, send email to daw-mac-request@lists.best.com, and in the message, include "subscribe".

Director (Macromind)

This list serves programmers for the multimedia software program Macromind Director. To subscribe, send email to LISTSERV@uafsysb.uark.edu, and in the message, include "subscribe DIRECT-L *Your Name*".

eMac Daily

A relatively new list, eMac Daily is a daily news service for the Macintosh community that provides late-breaking industry news, including new product announcements, software updates, and special deals. This list is produced by MacDirectory in conjunction with MacCentral. (Both sites are described later in this chapter.) Subscribe by sending email to eMac-Daily@macdirectory.com, and in the subject of the message, include "subscribe".

E.g. (extended guarantee)-Announce

This list will provide announcements about e.g. from Apple. To subscribe, send email to majordomo@public.lists.apple.com, and in the message, include "subscribe eg-announce". If you want to subscribe to the digest version of the list, include "subscribe eg-announce-digest".

E.g. (extended guarantee)-Users

This list is for discussion and mutual support for users of e.g. To subscribe, send email to majordomo@public.lists.apple.com. In the message, include "subscribe eg-users". If you want to subscribe to the digest version of the list, include "subscribe eg-users-digest".

EmailTools-Talk

This list is the official mailing list for EmailTools, hosted by WestCode Software. The list provides a place to discuss EmailTools, a powerful automation and toolbar add-on utility for Macintosh email clients. To subscribe, send email to lists@westcodesoft.com. In the message, include "subscribe EmailTools-Talk".

Eudora-mac

This list serves those who use the email program Eudora Pro and Eudora Light for the Macintosh. To subscribe, send email to majordomo@wso.williams.edu, and in the message, include "subscribe eudora-mac".

4D

This list serves users and developers of ACI's 4th Dimension RDBMS (relational and Web database environment for Macintosh and Windows). To subscribe, send email to requests@lists.foresight.com, and in the message, include "subscribe 4d-nug". To subscribe to the digest, in your message, include "subscribe digest 4d-nug".

FMPRO-L

This list contains discussions on everything about the FileMaker Pro database development environment. To subscribe, send email to LISTSERV@LISTSERV.DARTMOUTH.EDU, and in the message, include "subscribe fmpro-l".

The EvangeList

The EvangeList is a must-have list for finding out what is going on in the Mac community. The list membership (about 40,000+) has been known to send fear through the hearts of many a third-party company who decided not to port a Mac version of their product or some uninformed journalist who didn't quite "get it" when writing about Apple and the Mac.

Started by the first Mac evangelist and Apple legend Guy Kawasaki, the EvangeList is now a three-person effort. Guy still posts but is busy starting up new companies, including his own, at garage.com. Chuq Von Rospach, the man who handles Apple's mailing list machines, makes sure this list gets out, and John J. Halbig, a k a the Digital Guy, is the editor-in-chief who oversees the list content.

When John took over in January 1997, he faced a 60-hour a week job, but now, he has it down to 10 hours. John is no stranger to the Mac because he was a network administrator for the now defunct *MacUser* magazine in 1988 and a tech support engineer at SuperMac (where they kept him even after he insulted a Disney executive). At Apple, John worked on the Mac TV (the black all-in-one computer), the 630 series (the first one with decent integrated video and TV, he says), a CD-ROM project, Copeland, and OpenDoc. If you subscribe to only one list, this is it. To subscribe, send email to majordomo@public.lists.apple.com. In the message, include "subscribe EvangeList". If you want to subscribe to the digest version of the list, include "subscribe EvangeList-digest".

FMP-Web

This list addresses FileMaker Pro 4.0 database Web server issues. To subscribe, send email to majordomo@filemakermagazine.com, and in the message, include "subscribe fmweb-talk".

Future Apple Systems Technologies

According to Apple, this list discusses future Apple technologies such as revisions of the Mac OS operating system, QuickTime upgrades, new logic boards, cache designs, and the like. To subscribe, send email to lyris@clio.lyris.net, and in the message, include "subscribe fast *Your Name*".

Frontier Scripting

This is a list for users of the Frontier scripting language. Visit **www.scripting.com/frontier/admin/mail.html**, and sign up for one of three lists:

1. Frontier Beginner's
2. Stanford's Frontier-Webmaster
3. UserLand's Frontier-Central

Games-L

This list discusses all computer games, including those on the Macintosh. This list also mirrors to the Usenet newsgroup **bit.listserv.games-l**. To subscribe, send email to listserv@brownvm.brown.edu, and in the message, include "subscribe GAMES-L".

Gestalt Selectors List

According to Apple, this list is for "programmers who use the Gestalt Manager with their software." To subscribe, send email to gestalt-selectors-list-request@bio.vu.nl. In the subject line, include "subscribe".

Greebles

Hosted by Stairways Software, this list discusses the game Greebles. You can subscribe to the list by visiting **www.stairways.com/mailinglists/**.

H-Mac (Macintosh Users In The Humanities And Social Sciences)

This list of the History and Macintosh Society deals with the use of Macs in the social sciences. To subscribe, send email to LISTSERV@H-NET.MSU.EDU, and in the message, include "SUB H-Mac *First Name Last Name Affiliation*".

HyperCard

This list discusses Apple's HyperCard multimedia software. To subscribe to the list, send email to hypercard-request@lists.best.com. In the message, include "subsingle" to subscribe to the full list or "subscribe" to receive a daily digest.

Ie-mac

This list downloads the latest version of Microsoft Internet Explorer Web browser for Power PC and 68K machines. To subscribe, send email to microsoft-request@microsoft.nwnet.com, and in the message, include "subscribe ie-mac".

Info-Mac

Info-Mac is the oldest Macintosh discussion list. It is only available as a digest and is moderated. To subscribe, send email to info-mac@starnine.com. In the subject line, include "subscribe".

IO-MUG

This list serves the International Online Macintosh User Group. To subscribe, send email to LISTSERV@LISTSERV.UTA.EDU, and in the message, include "subscribe IO-MUG *Your Name*".

Internet Config

Hosted by Stairways Software, this list discusses issues related to programming a Macintosh using Internet Config. You can subscribe to the list by visiting **www.stairways.com/mailinglists/**.

JAVA-MAC

This list discusses software development using Sun Microsystem's Java language on the Macintosh. To subscribe, send email to majordomo@natural.com, and in the message, include "subscribe JAVA-MAC *Your Email Address*".

ListSTAR-Talk

This list provides general discussions on ListSTAR. To subscribe, visit **www.starnine.com/support/mailinglists/mailinglist.html**.

MACAPPLI

This moderated list discusses Macintosh applications from third-party vendors. To subscribe, send email to LISTSERV@LISTSERV. DARTMOUTH.EDU, and in the message, include "subscribe MACAPPLI".

Mac-Attorney

This list serves legal professionals who use the Macintosh. To subscribe, send email to majordomo@comitia2.uoregon.edu, and in the message, include "subscribe macattorney-digest".

Mac-Audio-Dev

This private list is open to all current third-party developers working on digital audio and MIDI solutions for the Mac OS and Power PC. To subscribe, send email to majordomo@public.lists.apple.com, and in the message, include "subscribe Mac-Audio-Dev". To subscribe to the digest version of the list, include "subscribe Mac-Audio-Dev-digest".

Mac-Chat

Mac Chat is a spinoff from the Mac-L list for those members who tend to take discussions a bit off-track from the discussions on the Mac-L list. To subscribe, send email to lyris@clio.lyris.net, and in the message, include "subscribe Mac-Chat *Your Name*".

Mac-Games-Dev

This Apple-sponsored list serves people who write, code, design, and create games for the Mac OS. To subscribe, send email to majordomo@public.lists.apple.com, and in the message, include "subscribe Mac-Games-Dev". To subscribe to the digest version of the list, include "subscribe Mac-Games-Dev-digest".

MAC-HELP-NEWSLETTER

This monthly list or newsletter contains the latest news of the Macintosh Help Forum on America Online. To subscribe, send email to listserv@ listserv.aol.com, and in the message, include "subscribe MAC-HELP-NEWSLETTER".

Create Your Own Mailing List

You simply might not find a mailing list out there that caters to your specific iMac needs. Start one! Several services online will provide you with a free mailing list. You might have to allow some advertising banners to pop up or be embedded in your mailing, but that is a small price to pay for an otherwise free mailing list.

- Listbot—**www.listbot.com**—This free service by LinkExchange gives you the choice of an announcement, open, or moderated list. With this free list comes a free home page for every list, sign up forms for your existing Web site, and the option to ask demographic questions of your subscribers. You also get a free Web archive of messages sent to your list, automatic handling of bounced messages, and unlimited messages, subscribers, and lists. Can't find a mailing list on your topic? Create one free using ListBot's form on its Web site, as shown in Figure 5.1.

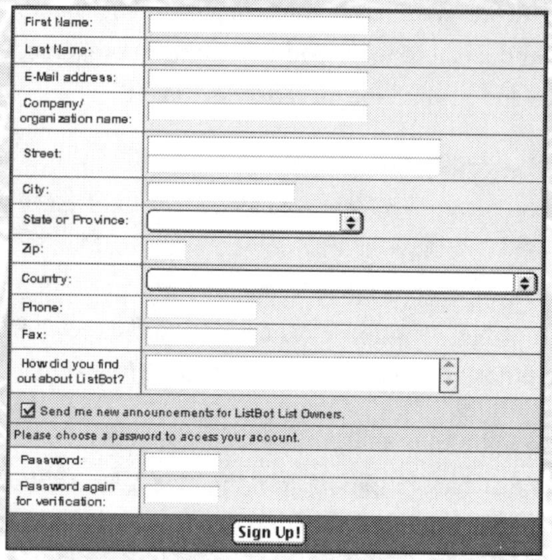

Figure 5.1
ListBot's mailing list form.

- eGroups—**www.egroups.com**—eGroups offers free mailings lists called eGroups. You get a Web interface to manage the group and the choice of a moderated or unmoderated, private, or public list. The service claims to be spam free. Messages are readable through email, the Web, or digests and are fully searchable.
- OneList—**www.onelist.com**—On OneList, you can search for mailing lists, view archives, subscribe to mailing lists, and create new mailing lists.

Some of the online services offer digest and normal subscriptions, a user center where you can view the lists you have subscribed to and the ones you moderate, automatic email alias support to guard against spam, members-only posting, and email notification so you know when people subscribe or unsubscribe from your lists.

You can have multiple moderators, which can ease the workload. You can create a custom welcome letter. You have the option to make your list completely private so it does not show up in an online service search database. You get a lot of service here for free.

MACHRDWR

This moderated list posts alerts about hardware problems and repairs for Macintosh equipment and peripherals from other vendors. To subscribe, send email to listserv@LISTSERV.DARTMOUTH.EDU, and in the message, include "subscribe machrdwr *Your Name*".

Macissues

This list discusses all Mac-related issues. To subscribe, send email to listproc@listproc.bgsu.edu, and in the message, include "subscribe macissues *Your Name*".

Mac-L

This list includes discussions in technical issues for the average and advanced user involving the Mac OS and related hardware issues. To subscribe, send email to lyris@clio.lyris.net, and in the message, include "subscribe Mac-L *Your Name*".

Macintosh-Managers

The Macintosh-Managers list is just what the title says, discussions for those managing Macs. To subscribe, send email to majordomo@lists.cerf.net, and in the message, include "subscribe mac-mgrs".

MacAccounting

This list deals with all Mac accounting software products and issues. To subscribe, send email to subscribeMAL@southgaylord.com.

MACcounting-TALK

This list serves users of business and accounting software on the Mac. To subscribe, send a message to requests@maccounting.com, and in the message, include "subscribe maccounting-talk".

MACAV-L

This list was created to discuss topics relating to Macintosh Quadra audio-visual systems. To subscribe, send email to listserv@UAFSYSB.UARK.EDU, and in the message, include "subscribe macav-l".

Mac8500-L

This list serves users of Power Macintosh 8500/8600 computers. To subscribe, send email to majordomo@cybercom.net, and in the message, include "subscribe mac8500-l". To subscribe to the digest, include "subscribe mac8500-digest".

MACDEV-1

Operated by *MacTech* Magazine, this list serves those interested in developing for the Mac platform. To subscribe, send email to listserv@listmail.xplain.com. In the subject line, include "subscribe MACDEV-1".

MacGamer

This list serves diehard Mac game fanatics. Sign up for news, downloads, demos, editorials, letters, and good discussion. It is published twice a month. To subscribe, send email to andrewsgreg@hotmail.com. In the subject line, include "Show me Mac Gamer".

Mactcl

This list is for topics relating to Tcl on the Macintosh such as Tcl ports to the Mac (MacTcl), file I/O, porting Tk to the Mac, and any issues concerning Tcl-based applications such as Alpha and Tickle. To subscribe, send email to listproc@sunlabs.Eng.Sun.com, and in the message, include "subscribe mactcl *Your Name*".

Macintosh Human Interface Discussions

According to Apple, this list is "for people who are involved in designing great human interfaces for Macintosh and related computers. Topics might include specific design problems, testing issues, technological directions, cross-platform interface challenges, and multimedia development." To subscribe, send email to majordomo@public.lists.apple.com, and in the message, include "subscribe Apple-HI-Developers". If you want to subscribe to the digest version of the list, include "subscribe Apple-HI-Developers-digest".

Read First, Post Later

After you subscribe to a list, and before you jump into a discussion, read a week's worth of postings to make sure the list is right for you.

Mac Lab Manager

This list is hosted by Stairways Software for discussion of issues related to running a Macintosh lab. You can subscribe to the list by visiting **www.stairways.com/mailinglists/**.

Mac Pascal

Hosted by Stairways Software, this list discusses issues on programming a Macintosh using Pascal. You can subscribe to the list by visiting **www.stairways.com/mailinglists/**.

MacPerl

This list discusses MacPerl, a scripting program. To subscribe, send email to mpw-perl-request@iis.ee.ethz.ch.

MacPrint

This list serves Macintosh and newspaper professionals (if your work is printed on a newspaper, magazine, or sheet-fed press). To subscribe automatically, send an email message to macprint-on@beloit-kansas.com.

MacTalk

"Newbies" are discouraged from this list for more complex problems. It is hosted by Radix Consulting Ltd., a Macintosh-oriented computer consulting firm specializing in database design and Internet connectivity. You can subscribe by visiting **www.r8ix.com/lists.html** or by sending email to majordomo@r8ix.com, and in the message, include "subscribe MacTalk *Your Name*".

MacMarines MailCall

MacMarines is a moderated list about Mac issues. To subscribe, send email to Requests@MacMarines.com, and in the message, include "subscribe Mailcall" or "subscribe Digest Mailcall". MacMarines also has a Web site at **www.macmarines.com**. Figure 5.2 is an example of how to subscribe to a mailing list when you only need to insert information in the body of the message. You can leave the "Subject" field blank or insert anything you want, e.g. subscribe, name of the list, etc.

MacMavens

This list is advertised as "the Virtual Community for the Serious Macintosh Enthusiast." To get more information on how to subscribe, send email to requests@connecticutlawyers.net, and in the message, include "info MacMavens".

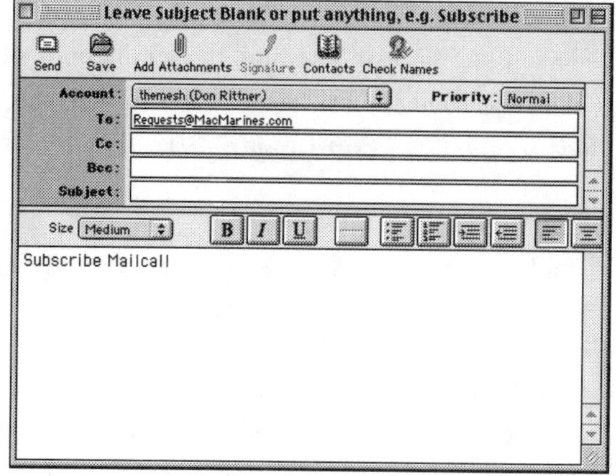

Figure 5.2

Mailing list subscription—body of message text.

MacScrpt

MacScrpt is a list for discussing scripting on the Mac. To subscribe, send an email message to listserv@dartmouth.edu, and in the message, include "subscribe macscrpt *Your Name*".

MACSYSTM

This list discusses the Mac system software and everything that deals with it such as inits and control panels. To subscribe, send email to LISTSERV@LISTSERV.DARTMOUTH.EDU, and in the message, include "subscribe MACSYSTM".

Mac USB Talk List

This list is for Macintosh users to discuss the Universal Serial Bus and the Macintosh. To subscribe, send an email to majordomo@themacintoshguy.com, and in the message, include "subscribe MacUSBTalk *Your Name*".

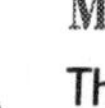

Be Safe, Not Sorry

Reread Chapter 4. Read it until you get it.

Mac Virus

This list announces viruses on the Mac. To subscribe, send email to listproc@listproc.bgsu.edu, and in the message, include "subscribe mac-virus-announce *Your Name*".

Mac Webmasters

This list serves those running Mac Web servers. To subscribe, send email to lists@reformed.net, and in the message, include "subscribe

Webmasters *Your Name*". To subscribe to the daily digest, send email to lists@reformed.net, and in the message, include "set Webmasters digest".

MAE-Users (Macintosh Application Environment)

This list is for discussing the Macintosh Application Environment. To subscribe, send email to majordomo@public.lists.apple.com, and in the message, include "subscribe MAE-Users". If you want to subscribe to the digest version of the list, include "subscribe MAE-Users-digest".

MEKaLISTA

This is a Yugoslavia Mac user group mailing list. To subscribe, send email to listserver@ppc.psc.ac.yu, and in the message, include "subscribe mekalista".

MacOnCall Information Services

This list serves Mac users who want important Apple-specific information in the industry. It delivers three emails each week with top industry news and headlines. To subscribe, visit **www.maconcall.com/mis/**.

MkLinux-Advocacy

This list discusses the MkLinux operating system. To subscribe, send email to majordomo@public.lists.apple.com, and in the message, include "subscribe MkLinux-Advocacy". If you want to subscribe to the digest version of the list, include "subscribe MkLinux-Advocacy-digest".

MkLinux-Announce

This is an announcement list about MkLinux. To subscribe, send email to majordomo@public.lists.apple.com, and in the message, include "subscribe MkLinux-Announce".

MkLinux-Development-Apps

This list concerns application development on MkLinux. To subscribe, send email to majordomo@public.lists.apple.com, and in the message, include "subscribe MkLinux-Development-Apps". If you want to subscribe to the digest version of the list, include "subscribe MkLinux-Development-Apps-digest".

MkLinux-Hardware

This list discusses hardware issues with MkLinux. To subscribe, send email to majordomo@public.lists.apple.com, and in the message, include "subscribe MkLinux-Hardware". If you want to subscribe to the digest version of the list, include "subscribe MkLinux-Hardware-digest".

MkLinux-Misc

This list discusses MkLinux issues that don't fit the other lists. To subscribe, send email to majordomo@public.lists.apple.com, and in the message, include "subscribe MkLinux-Misc". If you want to subscribe to the digest version of the list, in the email, include "subscribe MkLinux-Misc-digest".

MkLinux-Networking

This list discusses networking issues involving MkLinux. To subscribe, send email to majordomo@public.lists.apple.com, and in the message, include "subscribe MkLinux-Networking". If you want to subscribe to the digest version of the list, include "subscribe MkLinux-Networking-digest".

Look Before You Leap

Do not post virus warnings, FCC warnings, or other scare warnings to a mail list unless they are verified. Some of these warnings are actually urban legends. You can verify a virus warning or hoax at the Computer Incident Advisory Committee's (CIAC) Web site: **http://ciac.llnl.gov/ciac/CIACHoaxes.html**.

MkLinux-Setup

This list concerns installation issues involving MkLinux. To subscribe, send email to majordomo@public.lists.apple.com, and in the message, include "subscribe MkLinux-Setup". If you want to subscribe to the digest version of the list, include "subscribe MkLinux-Setup-digest".

MkLinux-X

This list discusses the X Window system as it relates to MkLinux. To subscribe, send email to majordomo@public.lists.apple.com, and in the message, include "subscribe MkLinux-X". If you want to subscribe to the digest version of the list, include "subscribe MkLinux-X-digest".

MMDEVX

This list serves people interested in cross-platform multimedia development tools in general and Apple Media Kit (AMK) and Kaleida ScriptX in particular. To subscribe, send email to Mail-Server@knex.mind.org, and in the message, include "subscribe MMDEVX *Your Name*".

MPW-Dev

This list provides discussions about the MPW environment. To subscribe, send email to majordomo@public.lists.apple.com, and in the message, include "subscribe MPW-Dev". If you want to subscribe to the digest version of the list, include "subscribe MPW-Dev-digest".

MRJ-Announce

This list from Apple makes announcements relating to Mac OS Runtime for Java. To subscribe, send email to majordomo@public.lists.apple.com, and in the message, include "subscribe MRJ-Announce".

MRJ-Dev

This list discusses Mac OS Runtime for Java. To subscribe, send email to majordomo@public.lists.apple.com, and in the message, include "subscribe MRJ-Dev". If you want to subscribe to the digest version of the list, include "subscribe MRJ-Dev-digest".

MUS Info Line (German)

This list comes from the Macintosh users of Switzerland. To subscribe, send email to musinfoline@udena.ch.

NetPresenz

Hosted by Stairways Software, this list discusses NetPresenz and related software. You can subscribe to the list by visiting **www.stairways.com/mailinglists/**.

NetProLive

Co-sponsored by *NetProfessional* magazine and the Depot, this list serves the Web developer and network administrator community. To subscribe, send email to listserv@listmail.xplain.com. In the subject line of the message, include "subscribe NetProLive". To subscribe to the digest version, include "subscribe DIGEST NetProLive" in the subject line of the message.

OneClick-Talk

This official OneClick mailing list from WestCode Software provides a place to discuss OneClick, a powerful automation and toolbar utility for the Macintosh. To subscribe, send email to lists@westcodesoft.com, and in the message, include "subscribe OneClick-Talk".

PageMaker

This list discusses desktop publishing with an emphasis on the use of Aldus Pagemaker. To subscribe, send email to LISTSERV@LISTSERV.IUPUI.EDU, and in the message, include "SUB PAGEMAKR *Your Name*".

Open Transport

Hosted by Stairways Software, this list discusses issues related to programming a Macintosh using Open Transport. You can subscribe to the list by visiting **www.stairways.com/mailinglists/**.

POSIM-Users

This list serves users of Ensign Systems' POSIM (Point of Sale and Inventory Management) program for the Mac and Windows. To subscribe, send email to listproc@lists.unh.edu, and in the message, include "subscribe posim.users *Your Name*".

PowerBooks

This list discusses PowerBooks and other Mac portables. To subscribe, send email to lists@reformed.net, and in the message, include "subscribe PowerBooks *Your Name*". (*Your Name* is optional.) To subscribe to a daily digest, send email to lists@reformed.net, and in the message, include "set PowerBooks digest".

Power Macintosh Bulletin

This list is a special mailing from Apple devoted to the Power Macintosh. It notifies you of the latest product news and information, as well as changes to the Power Macintosh Web site. To subscribe, send email to requests@thing1.info.apple.com. In the subject line, include "subscribe powermacintosh".

PowerMacs

This list serves as a discussion vehicle for users of PowerPC-based Macintoshes. To subscribe, send email to lists@reformed.net, and in the message, include "subscribe PowerMacs *Your Name*". (*Your Name* is optional.) To subscribe to a daily digest, send email to lists@reformed.net, and in the message, include "set PowerMacs digest".

PSHOP

This list discusses Adobe Photoshop software. To subscribe, send email to listserv@sobeavi.com, and in the message, include "subscribe PSHOP *Your Name*". Leave the subject line blank.

Quadlist

Quadlist serves users of 68040-based and 68LC040-based Mac OS computers and includes the Quadra, Centris, some Performas and LCs, 500-series Macs, and several PowerBook models. To subscribe, send email to lists@reformed.net, and in the message, include "subscribe Quadlist *Your Name*".

QuickDraw-3D

This list discusses the QuickDraw-3D technology. To subscribe, send email with an empty subject field to quickdraw-3d-request@seo.apple.com. Include the word "help" in the email.

QuicKeys

This list discusses QuicKeys and macros on the Macintosh. (You'll find a special offer for QuicKeys at the back of this book.) To subscribe, send email to LISTSERV@LISTSERV.DARTMOUTH.EDU, and in the message, include "subscribe QUICKEYS".

QuickTime-Announce

This list announces QuickTime products. To subscribe, send email to majordomo@public.lists.apple.com, and in the message, include "subscribe QuickTime-Announce".

Digest It If You Can

Always subscribe to a digest version if the list offers one. With the digest version, you won't clutter your email box or miss an important posting, and the messages are easier to archive.

QuickTime-Dev

This list discusses QuickTime development. To subscribe, send email to majordomo@public.lists.apple.com, and in the message, include "subscribe QuickTime-Dev". If you want to subscribe to the digest version of the list, include "subscribe QuickTime-Dev-digest".

QuickTime-VR

This list discusses and promotes QuickTime-VR. To subscribe, send email to majordomo@public.lists.apple.com, and in the message, include "subscribe QuickTime-VR". If you want to subscribe to the digest version of the list, include "subscribe QuickTime-VR-digest".

QuickTime-VR Issues

This list discusses non-technical QuickTime-VR issues. To subscribe, send email to list-request@navmark.com, and in the message, include "subscribe vr-issues AS *Your Email Address Your Name*".

Ray Dream Design

This list discusses 3D modeling and rendering, graphics design and editing, and related topics, focusing on products developed by Ray Dream, Inc. To subscribe, send email to listserv@cornell.edu, and in the message, include "subscribe raydream-l *Your Name*".

REALbasic-Talk

This list discusses the REALbasic product from REAL Software. To subscribe, send an email to requests@lists.realsoftware.com, and in the message, include "subscribe realbasic-nug". To subscribe to the digest version of the list, and in the message, include "subscribe digest realbasic-nug".

Retro-talk

This list discusses Retrospect backup software issues. To subscribe, send email to retro-talk-on@latchkey.com.

RumorMill

Hosted by Stairways Software, this list discusses RumorMill and related software. You can subscribe to the list by visiting **www.stairways.com/mailinglists/**.

Sermac (Italian)

This list serves Italian Mac users. To subscribe, send email to sermac-on@freedom.geonet.it.

Stairways Announcements

This list announces new or updated products from Stairways. To subscribe, visit **www.stairways.com/mailinglists/action.shtml?announce**.

SuperMacs

A list for users of UMAX SuperMac computers. To subscribe, send email to lists@reformed.net, and in the message, include "subscribe SuperMacs

Your Name". (*Your Name* is optional.) To subscribe to a daily digest, send email to lists@reformed.net, and in the message, include "set SuperMacs digest".

The Information Alley

This compilation of new and updated tech info library articles is sent daily by service and support engineers and writers. To subscribe, send email to listproc@listproc.info.apple.com, and in the message, include "subscribe infoalley *Your Name*".

TidBITS

TidBITS is an excellent Mac electronic newsletter/list. To subscribe to TidBITS, send email to tidbits-on@tidbits.com. No special subject or message is necessary.

TidBITS Talk

This is a moderated list for readers of TidBITS. To subscribe, send email to tidbits-talk-on@tidbits.com. To subscribe to a digest, send email to tidbits-talk-digest@tidbits.com.

USB Development

This list serves developers of USB technologies for the Macintosh. To subscribe, send email to usb@isg.apple.com.

Vintage-Macs

This list hosts users of 68000-, 68020-, and 68030-based Macintosh computers, which includes the original Macintosh, all the other compact models, the entire Mac II series, and several LCs and Performas. To subscribe, send email to lists@reformed.net, and in the message, include "subscribe VintageMacs *Your Name*". (*Your Name* is optional.) To subscribe to a daily digest, send email to lists@reformed.net, and in the message, include "set VintageMacs digest".

WebSTAR-Talk

This list discusses Starnine's WebSTAR Web server software. To subscribe, visit **www.starnine.com/support/mailinglists/mailinglist.html**. You can subscribe to the next three lists about the following Starnine products all from the same location.

WebSTAR-Dev

This list features programming and development discussions on WebSTAR for the Macintosh. To subscribe, visit **www.starnine.com/support/mailinglists/mailinglist.html**.

WebSTAR-API

This list provides discussion of the WebSTAR API standard for plug-in developers and server implementers. To subscribe, visit **www.starnine.com/support/mailinglists/mailinglist.html**.

WebCollage-Talk

This list features general discussions on WebCollage. To subscribe, visit **www.starnine.com/support/mailinglists/mailinglist.html**.

WestCode Announce

This list provides news, tips, and announcements for WestCode Software. To subscribe, send email to lists@westcodesoft.com, and in the message, include "subscribe announce".

WinMac

This is a list for Windows 95/98/NT and Macintosh integration issues. To subscribe, send email to winmac-on@xerxes.frit.utexas.edu. To subscribe to the digest, send email to winmac-digest@xerxes.frit.utexas.edu.

Post Wisely

Be sure to post to the right address. Do not post to the administrative address (the one you use to subscribe to the list). Learn the difference between the administrative address and the list address.

WP-L

Hosted by Radix Consulting Ltd., this list provides a forum for discussing issues related to Corel's WordPerfect for Macintosh. To subscribe, visit **www.r8ix.com/lists.html**, send email to majordomo@r8ix.com, and in the message, include "subscribe WP-L *Your Name*".

XTension Discussion List

According to Apple, this list discusses "all aspects of using the XTension S/W package for home automation, applying industry-standard X10 modules." X-10 modules let you turn your lights on or off from anywhere in the house or even remotely over the Net.

To subscribe, send email to XTension_Discussion@lists.bzzzzzz.com. In the subject line, include "subscribe". To subscribe to the digest, send email to XTension_Discussion@lists.bzzzzzz.com. In the subject line, include "subscribe digest". Figure 5.3 is an example of how to subscribe to a mailing list when you only need to insert information into the Subject line and not the body of the message.

ZDTips—Netscape Tip Of The Week

This lists gives you weekly tips on how to get the most from your Netscape browser. To subscribe, send email to listproc@zdtips.com, and in the message, include "subscribe inntips *Your Name* ListsNet".

ZDTips—PageMaker Tip Of The Week

If you use PageMaker, get this free tip each week. To subscribe, send email to listproc@zdtips.com, and in the message, include "subscribe ipmtips *Your Name* ListsNet".

Text Only Please

Do not attach files to mailing list postings unless the mailing list allows it. This includes text or binary files, electronic business cards such as vcard.vcf, smime.p7s, or other email attachments.

ZDTips—Photoshop Tip Of The Week

If you use Photoshop, get this free tip each week. To subscribe, send email to listproc@zdtips.com, and in the message, include "subscribe ipstips *Your Name* ListsNet".

ZDTips—Quark Tip Of The Week

If you use Quark, get this free tip once a week. To subscribe, send email to listproc@zdtips.com, and in the message, include "subscribe quarktips *Your Name* ListsNet".

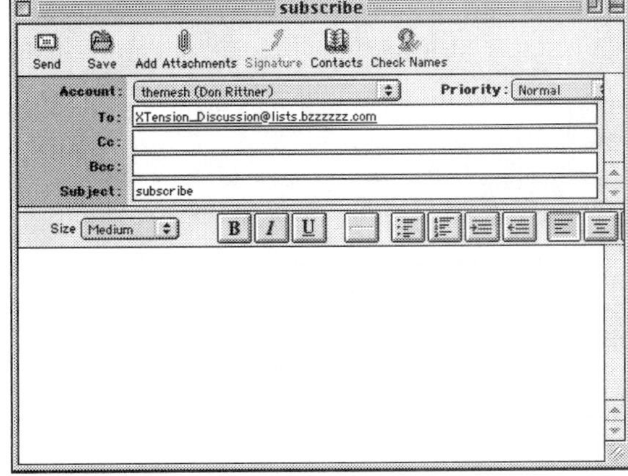

Figure 5.3
Mailing list subscription—subject line text.

Finding More Mailing Lists

New mailing lists are created everyday. You can find the latest and greatest mailing list about any topic by visiting several Web-based databases that let you search by keyword for new and existing mailing lists. Use your Web browser to visit the following sites:

- Publicly Accessible Mailings Lists—**www.neosoft.com/internet/paml/**—This is the Internet's oldest list of lists, online since 1994. Managed by Stephanie da Silva, it is one of the more reliable search engines. Type your keyword, or browse the alphabetical or category index. The search results give you a contact address, a summary of the list, how to subscribe or unsubscribe, what listserv software is used, a Web address if there is one, a list of keywords used for categorizing the list, and the last time information was updated. You can find almost any mailing list by searching by name or subject, or searchable database, on the Publicly Accessible Mailing List Web site, as shown in Figure 5.4.

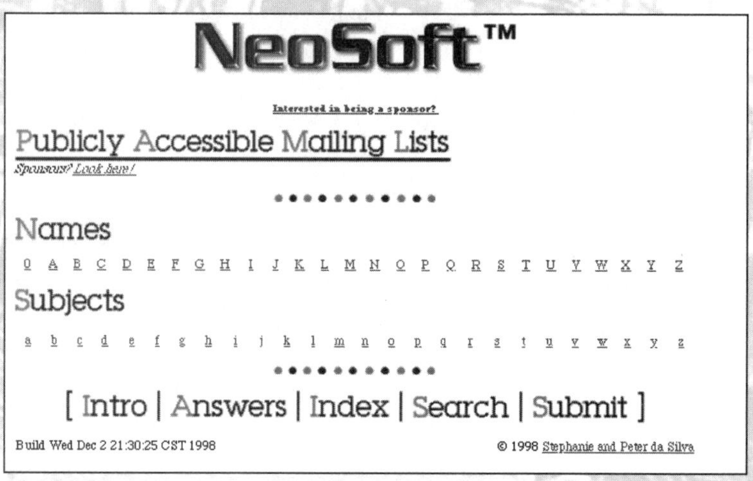

Figure 5.4
Searching a mailing list by name or subject.

- ListsNet—**www.listsnet.com**—This Web site groups mailing lists by categories and lets you search by keyword for a particular list. Other features of the site include a hot pick and an email alert feature that lets you know when a new list is added or deleted in the database.

  Search results give you a great deal of information including a contact address, a summary, how to subscribe and unsubscribe, which listserv software is used, a Web address if there is one, other categories that might be similar in nature, the name of the sponsoring organization, and even the routing address that appears in a list mailing.

- Liszt: The Mailing List Directory—**www.liszt.com**—This database contains more than 90,000 mailing lists. It is searchable by specifying keywords, browsing categories (with the ability to filter out junk), or using advanced methods. Liszt also has gateways to other search engines, so if you don't find what you're looking for, you can easily search a few other search engines automatically. You can submit a list if you like.

(continued)

Finding More Mailing Lists *(continued)*.

The search results list the number of hits by categories. Each list contains the info file on the purpose of the list if it has one. You can also request the info file by email. Finally, you're given instructions on how to subscribe (you can do it from Liszt) or unsubscribe.

- Tile.Net—**http://tile.net/listserv/**—Tile.Net allows you to search by keyword for mailings lists, FTP sites, vendors, Usenet newsgroups, and more, as shown in Figure 5.5. The search results give you the basic information on how to subscribe, the maintainer of the list, and the country of origin.

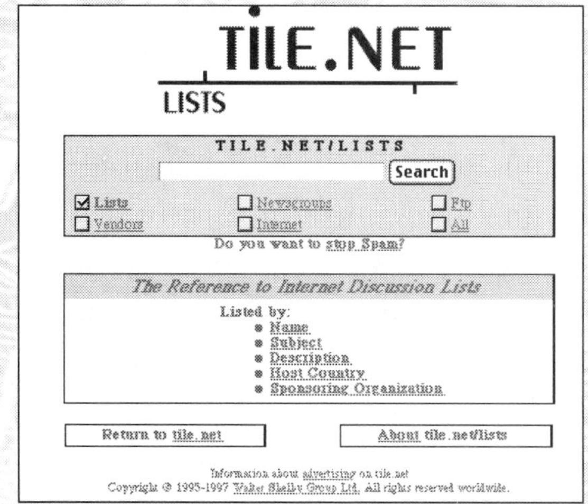

Figure 5.5
Tile.Net search engine.

- Pitsco—**www.pitsco.com/p/listinfo.html**—This is one of the most interesting education companies on the Net. This Web site lists almost every link in the world that deals with mailing lists, so it's a great place to start your search. It also has sites that tell you how to subscribe and discuss basic tutorials and other related issues.

6 iMac Resources: Ezines, Web Sites, News, And Chat

Rittner's Computer Law: i=m+a+c (iMac equals Most Awesome Computer).

In the previous chapter, you learned how to connect with fellow iMac users around the world through the use of Internet mailings lists and electronic newsletters. Many Macintosh evangelists also publish comprehensive magazines, design Web sites filled with the latest and greatest Mac content, produce radio shows, and host realtime chat sessions in text, audio, and even video format. Quite frankly, Mac users will use every possible online technology to share information about their favorite computer.

The capability of the Web in providing low-cost or virtually free distribution to a potential audience of more than 70 million people has caused an explosion of alternative media on the Net. Literally thousands of electronic magazines on the Net cover every conceivable (and some unbelievable) subject. Many of these electronic publications, such as Salon Magazine (**www.salonmagazine.com**), or even the Drudge Report (**www.drudgereport.com**), to name two, are forces to reckon with and have developed legions of followers, not to mention the envy of the mainstream media (and the fear of politicians).

If you have a good idea, a little resourcefulness, and make an effort, you can succeed on the Net in areas that, until a few years ago, seemed unreachable unless you were bank-rolled or had a Ph.D. or other "professional" training experience. Naturally, it helps if the information you are publishing is accurate and presented in an organized fashion.

The other obvious advantage of a World Wide Web site is that it provides a multimedia interface for displaying content. You have the ability to integrate and display text, video, graphics, animation, and links to resources from around the world, all on one page. It's a great way to organize information about your favorite subject—the Macintosh computer, in our case.

Humans are gregarious. They like to interact with each other in realtime. Interactive chat rooms, Net radio shows, and online interactive video (TV) conferencing satisfy that part of the online population. Moreover, you can do it all with a few simple clicks of your mouse.

This chapter will guide you to many of the free electronic magazines, Mac-oriented Web sites, and chat and video-conferencing sites on the Net. You, too, can obtain late-breaking and daily news; read articles, features, columns, reviews, and rumors; grab the latest software updates and shareware; talk to fellow iMac users; and generally become informed about everything related to your iMac.

Forget The Period!

When typing an email address or URL (Web address) from this book, be sure NOT to include the period or comma that may appear after it. This inclusion of a period or comma is for following the rules of convention in typesetting and editorial decisions in the publishing world and is NOT part of the address.

Electronic Magazines (Ezines)

Ezines, or electronic magazines, are magazines that contain news, articles, features, columns, and everything else you expect in a printed magazine, including in some cases, beautiful graphics and cool covers. Like the printed versions, many ezines are delivered to your mailbox (electronic in this case) weekly, monthly, or whatever the frequency happens to be. Some ezines you pick up at your virtual newsstand, usually the publisher's own Web site.

Most ezines are simply formatted text files. Others are produced with special programs such as DocMaker or a desktop software program such as QuarkXPress and saved in Adobe Acrobat format (called PDF or Portable Document Format). The advantage of the latter format is that a magazine looks exactly like a printed magazine except it's easy to turn the pages online. The obvious disadvantage is you can't curl up in bed with it!

The bottom line is that some ezines you simply read as text files and some you must download and double-click on the application to read. I should also point out that many ezines are actually electronic newsletters and vice versa. It really depends on what the publisher wants to call it. Often, the distinction is blurred. Regardless of what they get called, they're free and chock full of useful information.

Getting an ezine is as easy as pointing your Web browser to a Web site, or subscribing to it via email.

You will find that ezines are produced and written entirely by one person or a whole staff (usually volunteers). Some are provided as a courtesy, incentive, or bonus by a company that offers services such as Web design, marketing, or other computer- or Net-related business as a way to get you to its site.

Nonetheless, when you do find a useful piece of information from any of these sites, be sure to send a thank you and let them know you appreciate their hard work. Let's face it: If an individual or group of volunteers spends a great deal of time and effort to provide you with free and useful information, thanking them is the least you can do. It's true that civility is only a passenger on the information superhighway, but Mac users Think Different.

The following ezines will keep you current on your quest to be iMac proficient and in the know.

MacZines—Electronic Magazines

The following electronic magazines all provide excellent features, tutorials, and news. If you read a few every month you will stay informed and up to date about all issues relating to your iMac.

1984 Online

www.1984-online.com

This is not an Orwellian site trying to take control of your mind. The title honors the first Macintosh released in 1984. You have two choices for the contents of 1984 Online: You can download a PDF (Adobe Acrobat file) or DocMaker file. Reviews and commentary are in the Mac user section. You can subscribe to a mailing list to keep current, and there are links to other sites.

Apple Wizards

http://applewizards.net/

Apple Wizards is published in DocMaker and PDF format. Started by Erik J. Barzeski, this site contains news, reviews, tips and tricks, humor, tutorials, history, and commentary. He now has a staff of about 12 volunteers helping out. Erik says that what's important to each member of Apple Wizards is to express their love for Macs. "Giving back to the community," is a common phrase from the staff members, and they take it to heart. It shows.

You can subscribe to an announcement list so you know when to visit and download the latest issue. Previous issues are also available for downloading.

A Special Area contains Shop Talk, a column that discusses technology terms. If you are unsure about the meaning of a term, you can submit it and you might see it defined in one of the issues. Medicine Man is a help desk where you can send a question about your iMac. Finally, you can download some software—not a lot, but some choice packages picked by the Apple Wizards staff.

BigSky MacEzine

www.imt.net/~bgskymac/BigSky_MacEzine.html

This ezine is the official publication of the Big Sky Macintosh users group in Billings, Montana. At one time, there were more than 2,500 Apple user groups; there are less than half that number now. You can read the current and back issues of the *BigSky* publication on its Web site. The site contains reviews, software to download, opinion, and news.

MacAddict

www.macaddict.com

MacAddict is primarily a printed magazine and an excellent one at that. It also includes a monthly CD-ROM crammed with goodies. This Web site allows you to communicate with the staff, to go to some links, and to look through its index, but you cannot read the articles from the printed magazine. On the other hand, this is one magazine that you should get in hard-copy form. The CD-ROM is worth the price all by itself. Subscription is about $30 a year for 12 issues.

MacTech

www.mactech.com

Interested in developing on the iMac? *MacTech* has been the premier magazine for Mac developers since 1984. This Web site makes all the past archives available to you, or you can purchase a CD-ROM or subscribe to the printed version. MacTech has regular columns, industry news, reports, reviews, shortcuts and insider secrets, and even full source-code listings.

MacWeek Headlines

www.tipworld.com/cgi-bin/sub.cgi/macworld

A daily email magazine that features breaking Mac industry news headlines from MacWeek.com. *MacWeek* was a long-time printed weekly with controlled circulation (most people would lie through their teeth to get a subscription). It was abandoned and replaced with *eMediaWeekly*, which seems to cover more Windows material than Mac material. It's not even close to the quality of *MacWeek*.

MacWorld Online

http://macworld.zdnet.com

MacWorld is one of the few Mac-specific magazines published in hard-copy form. It's also one of the oldest Mac mags. The online version contains much of the same features, columns, and news that appear in the print version. A big advantage of the online version is that you can download reviewed programs and demos. Many of the best features written in *MacWorld* come from my friend, Dr. Franklin Tessler, who has been writing for the magazine since 1985. You can also access *MacWeek* and *eMediaWeekly* (the former print version of *MacWeek*) from this site. Message boards, buying guides, and the ability to search previous issues round out this site.

MacWorld also publishes a few newsletters and mailing lists that are geared for specific segments of the Mac market. By going to **www.tipworld.com/cgi-bin/sub.cgi/macworld**, you can subscribe to the following:

- Daily Tip—*MacWorld* sends a daily tip or trick for your Mac five days a week.
- Express—Check out *MacWorld* Online's biweekly coverage of what is happening on its Web site.
- Homepage Direct—This delivers the HTML version of *MacWorld*'s home page to your email box five days a week.

- HotDeals—Every other week, get special offerings and product updates from mail order firms such as MacWarehouse, ClubMac, and others.
- Macshopper—Pick up some demos, downloads, and other things from *MacWorld* Online, including special deals from advertisers.

MacWorld UK

http://uk.macworld.com

This is the real "English" version of *MacWorld* magazine. It contains features, reviews, and opinion like the American counterpart, and it has a special iMac section. You must register to get access to most areas, but it's free. The site was being revamped as of this writing.

Mac Today

www.mactoday.com

Download a PDF version (Adobe Acrobat), or visit this nicely laid-out Web site. *Mac Today* provides features, reviews, regular columnists such as Don Crabb, and various departments such as letters to the editor, a calendar of events, and more. If you like to curl up with a print mag once in a while, this one costs only $15 for 6 issues.

My Mac Online

www.mymac.com

You have two ways to read *My Mac:* You can download a stand-alone version in DocMaker format or read it off the Web site. If you subscribe to its mailing list, you receive a message every month letting you know when the next issue is ready.

My Mac Online contains features, columns, reviews, tutorials, and software to download. The great cover art comes from Mike Gorman and Alan Dingman. A "best of" section contains previous articles, columns, and top-10 software.

Tim Robertson started *My Mac* in June 1995 as a way to share his views on shareware, basic tutorials, and other Mac stuff to a local group of Mac users in Battle Creek, Michigan. When people started downloading off America Online and the now-defunct *eWorld*, Tim got more serious and recruited writers and artists to make it even higher quality. He's produced more than 50 issues.

The iMac Ring—For iMacs Only!

A Web ring is a group of Web sites, usually related in some way by topic, that are linked in such a fashion that you can visit all of them from each of the participating sites. The iMac Ring consists of several Web sites (still growing) for iMac users:

- iMac Central—**www.imaccentral.com**—Produced by MacCentral, this Web site links to other iMac-related sites on the Net and produces news and reviews about the iMac. It also includes iMac secrets.
- iMac Currents—**www.currents.net/advisor/mactips/imac/index.html**—This iMac page produced by *Computer Currents* magazine has news and links.
- iMac Info—**http://imac.macguys.com**—Here is a Web site that produces daily iMac news. An iMac FAQ (Frequently Asked Questions) is available. You can search for and read archived news. A section that lists iMac peripherals, their cost, and a link to the manufacturer's Web site rounds out the site. You'll also find a good tutorial on adding RAM.
- iMacOnline—**www.imaconline.com**—Lots and lots of iMac news will take away the blues. This site features headline news as well as links from other sites and a few cool sites selected by the staff. News is updated 12 times a day, every day.
- iMac Support Center—**http://macsupport.miningco.com/blcenter.htm**—This is a great support site that can answer any of your questions or problems. It includes links to all kinds of iMac issues, problems, upgrades, news, and even weekly live chat sessions.
- iMacWatch— **www.imacwatch.com**—News, press releases, updates, and archives appear on this site.
- iMac2Day—**www.iMac2Day.com**—Here, you'll find a lot of good technical information, updates, news, and features.
- The iMac Channel—**www.mactimes.com/imac/**—This page is produced by MacTimes and contains the latest iMac news, opinion, and links to other iMac sites.
- The iMac.com—**www.theimac.com**—Find iMac columns, news, features, live chat, and pricing information all on one page.
- The iMac List—**www.mactimes.com/imac/list.shtml**—This is the Web site of the Internet mailing list for iMac users. Past discussions are archived here.
- The iMac News Page—**www.mactimes.com/newspage/**—Also from MacTimes, this site provides a lot of news and links to iMac resources.

ZDNET Mac

www5.zdnet.com/mac/

Ziff-Davis is the parent company of *MacWorld*, *MacWeek*, and other publications. This Web site has links to those online mags as well as news, reviews, features, daily tips, and downloads.

Finding Ezines

New ezines come online almost daily. You can make sure you don't miss a new Mac-related ezine by periodically checking the following three online databases devoted to ezine culture:

- EzineSearch—**http://homeincome.com**—You can search this database by more than 80 categories. (The number of ezines in each category appears in parentheses.) It also has a pretty comprehensive search function.
- Ezines—The Ultimate Magazine Database—**www.dominis.com/Zines/**—Search through more than 40 categories or use the built-in search engine and find your topic by keyword. You can also check out the monthly top-5 zines, 100 hot zines, and 100 popular zines with the click of a mouse.
- John Labovitz's E-zine List—**www.meer.net/~johnl/e-zine-list/**—Since 1993, John has been keeping this site, as shown in Figure 6.1, which contains one of the most accurate ezine listings. He constantly checks and updates the list, which contains almost 3,000 zines. You can check his update page for the latest additions, browse by keyword, or check out the list by title if you know what you are looking for.

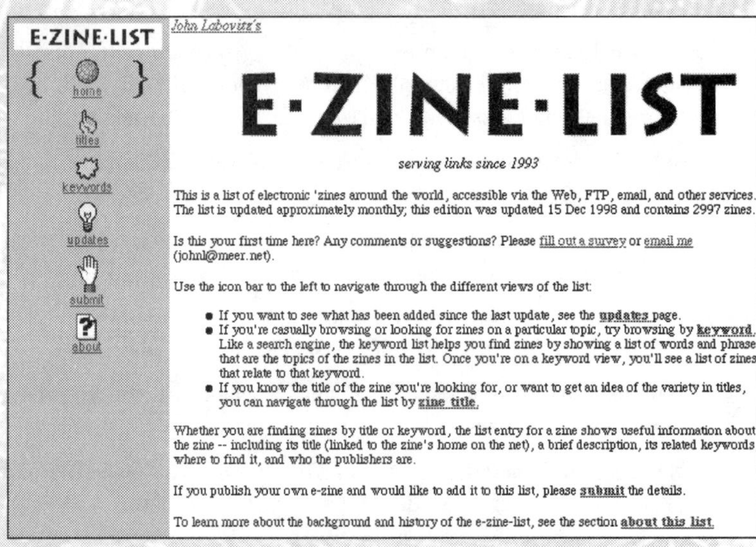

Figure 6.1
John Labovitz's E-ZINE List.

MacWeb—Mac Sites On The Web

The World Wide Web is a great place to acquire information about the iMac and Apple Computer. Many excellent Web sites provide software and hardware reviews, the latest news, software downloads, discussions, and almost anything you want to know about your iMac. Some Web sites are devoted to all things Macintosh. Some are devoted only to the iMac specifically. Many are topic-specific Web sites devoted to games, software updates, or news and reviews about the latest software or hardware peripheral. Some Web sites have hundreds of links to other Mac-related Web sites.

Surf to the following Web sites, which are the cream of the crop, for daily information about your iMac.

RAM Upgrade

iMac Info (**http://imac.macguys.com**) and iMac Support Center (**http://macsupport.miningco.com/blcenter.htm**) both offer good RAM upgrade tutorials.

Always Apple

www.alwaysapple.co.uk/

Promoted as the number-one Web site in the United Kingdom, this is a great site to get a different perspective on your Mac. You can download the latest software upgrades and shareware. The site also contains classified ads, links to other Mac sites, and a daily version tracker so you know which software versions are the latest. The site also has an online help section where you can send email if you are having problems and a message bulletin board where you can discuss Mac issues. You can subscribe to the Always Apple Newsletter online to keep up to date with U.K. Macintosh software releases and Apple Technical News.

Ambrosia Café

http://cafe.AmbrosiaSW.com

Ambrosia Café, organized by Ambrosia Software, Inc., is a Web site that links more than a dozen sites that deal with games, technical issues, programming, multimedia, and more. Ambrosia produces great games for the Mac. The following sites are included:

- **alt.sources.mac**: A Usenet newsgroup for Macintosh programmers.
- Ambrosia Software, Inc.: Games and productivity software.
- An Apple a Day: Come here for the Web site of the day.
- **comp.sys.mac.games** FAQ: The most Frequently Asked Questions from the **comp.sys.mac.games** Usenet newsgroups.
- GUI Central: Just about anything you want to do with your graphical user interface.
- Mac Files: One-stop shopping for game demos.
- Mac Game Resources on the Internet: An alphabetical guide to the game FAQs, sites, and other Mac game resources on the Net.

- Macintosh C: Program on the Mac in C.
- Macintosh Pascal: Calling all Pascal programmers.
- Max Joy: Do you want to see the creative and artistic side?
- Networkable Mac Games: Play games with people around the world.
- ShareTheMac Users Group: An online help site.
- The Mac Pruning Pages: A technical help site that explains what each control panel and extension does.

EveryMac.com

www.everymac.com

Whether you are brand-new to the Mac community or an old-timer, this Web site is a complete guide of every Macintosh and Mac OS-compatible in the world with detailed technical, configuration, and pricing information. This information includes the former clone makers and even companies of the past that are no longer around. You can also find the latest news and a book and application of the month.

EveryMac.com was started by Brock Kyle in April 1996 and was launched officially on July 2, 1996. Since then, Brock has enlarged and enhanced EveryMac.com, and if you browse through his What's New pages, you get a detailed listing of the updates.

Brock created the site originally because he wanted to find out the RAM type for a Macintosh IIci and couldn't find the information anywhere. He figured others would be interested in similar information that now includes every Mac system you can imagine. You can find information in four ways: manufacturer, processor, case type, or currently shipping. If you are in a hurry, use the searchable database. There is an excellent iMac FAQ (Frequently Asked Questions) document. You can sign up for a mailing list that will let you know when Brock updates the list.

Mac Update

www.macupdate.com

Looking for the latest update to a game, shareware program, or commercial product? Looking for a good demo? This site probably has it.

Not sure what a product does? Read the review, and then download it. You can search by title, programmer, size, and even date as well as subscribe to the newsletter to make sure you are kept informed of the latest offerings. Software titles are neatly categorized (business, development, education, games, home and personal, Internet, multimedia and design, utilities, and updates), making it easy to find the files you need.

Macinsites

www.macinsites.com

There are more than 200 links to Mac-related sites here arranged in several categories, including one for the iMac.

Mac OS Daily

www.macosdaily.com

According to the publisher, Matthew Linton, Mac OS Daily is not a site about news but rather thought-provoking, heavy-hitting editorial and opinion. Throw in some investigative reporting, and this site is bound to make you think about issues relating to the Mac—pro or con. You can find features, several regular columns, and hardware and software reviews. Mac OS Daily has also launched Vertigo—The Ultimate in Macintosh Gaming, an ezine devoted to games on the Mac (see Chapter 10).

Mac OS Rumors

www.macosrumors.com

This site provides just what the title says: reports on things it hears through the grapevine, rumors on hardware, software, the industry, and other Mac-related issues. You can chat in realtime on IRC chat. You need the software chat program Ircle for chatting, but you can download it on this site.

MacSense

www.macsense.com

Visiting MacSense is common sense if you are a digital artist. MacSense reviews new products, offers tutorials, provides links to other Mac sites, and highlights news for digital artists.

Site Link

www.sitelink.net/

If you are looking for a one-stop Web site from which to visit most Mac Web sites, this is the one. Site Link is the mother of links to news sites, references, resources, software, ezines, directories, and a great deal more.

The Mac Orchard

www.macorchard.com

If you are looking for any Internet application that runs on a Mac, start at this Web site. Along with software, the site links other Net-related resources and reviews. The site has 16 Net categories (chat, FTP, Usenet, and so on). A built-in search engine lets you find the exact file you are looking for with a few simple keywords. Each file is reviewed, and you can download it immediately.

theImac.com

www.theiMac.com

Robert Aldridge and George Cole are the brains behind theimac.com. Robert is the Webmaster and George is the marketing guy. Robert has plenty of experience in printing and in Web and graphic design, and George works for a major online retailer, so both know how to serve the public, and theimac.com does just that–serves the iMac public. You can find well-written features, daily news, columns, and tutorials. A weekly live chat on beginner's guides, upgrade tutorials, software updates, technical support, and a great deal more fill this site. You can participate in public chats Tuesdays at 12 P.M. CST and Thursdays at 7 P.M. CST. I check this site daily; so should you.

All The News For The Bondi Blues

A great deal of news comes out of Apple Computer, third-party companies, and the computer industry in general every day. New advances, new software, or updates of current software, new hardware, and tons of stories about the industry are released. How do you keep up with all this news? It's easy; simply visit the following Web sites that specialize in bringing you a daily dose of Apple and company news.

AppleLinks

www.AppleLinks.com

On the AppleLinks front page, you will find reviews, regular features such as the Farr Site and Business Mac Forum, daily Mac news, other technology news, software upgrades, and software by category or title. A forum area lets you discuss topics of the day.

If you're busy, get AppleLinks and several other mailing lists delivered to your email box with a free subscription. Looking to buy a Mac-related item? AppleLinks has an online shopping center. Its search engine queries companies so you can get the best possible prices.

MacCentral

www.maccentral.com

MacCentral reminds me of the AP (Associated Press) wire. You see daily news stories written and published as they happen along with their time stamp. Old-time Mac writers like Don Crabb and others provide columns and features. Message and tip forums allow you to post and read. Also available are special reports and a free subscription to the electronic newsletter MacCentral Direct, a daily newsletter with content indexed in HTML format. MacCentral also publishes iMac Daily and iMac Central.

MacCentric

www.maccentric.com/index.shtml

MacCentric provides news about the Mac but also has areas for the old Apple Newton, users groups, some shareware, search engines, and other links. The site also has a feature called "Mail a Mac" that lets you email a virtual Mac with a custom message to friends, family, or anyone else.

Greg Nye started MacCentric in August 1997, to promote the Macintosh platform. MacCentric includes links to many other Macintosh-, Net-, and computer-related sites, tips, shareware, and search engines. The site began as Greg's personal home page. According to Greg, it quickly began to take on a pro-Mac quality because of the many Macintosh links that he added and the fact that he began using it as an outlet for some of his Macintosh shareware titles.

MacInTouch

www.macintouch.com

MacInTouch is one site you should visit daily, as shown in Figure 6.2. Ric Ford has been writing about the technical issues of the Macintosh as far back as the dawn of time (Mac time, that is). MacInTouch is where you find out the latest hardware or software problems, upgrades, software updates, and general Apple news. You can count on solid information from this Web site. A special iMacInTouch section also produces daily iMac information.

Mac Mania

www.mac-mania.com

Brian Breslin is the founder of infiniMedia, the company that runs Mac Mania, iMacOnline, the former GUI Mania, and several other Web sites. Brian is one of the youngest Web site owners in the Mac community. Mac Mania has news, features, game info, an iMac section, features, and many links.

MacMarines

www.macmarines.com

The few. The proud. The MacMarines. Its mission is clear: According to its preamble, it "...formulates ideas and strategies to counter the misperception by many in the media, industry, education, and general public that Apple is dead, that the Mac is not a serious computer

Figure 6.2
MacInTouch Home Page.

platform, and that we Mac loyalists are a bunch of crazy-eyed fanatics clinging to a sinking ship."

This Web site complements the mailing list mentioned in Chapter 5. You can read current and back news. A great feature of this site is the lists of various news outlets and writers and their email addresses so you can "strike," uh, write, when you need to correct a negative article or comment about the Mac. The Ammo area gives readers plenty of punch to use in fighting back or responding to non-Mac or Mac-challenged opponents.

Macnews.net

http://macnews.net/

Updated every 24 hours, MacNews provides about 25 stories a day. An archive with a keyword search engine lets you search previous news. MacNews is available in English, Spanish, German, French, and Italian.

MaCNN, The Macintosh News Network

www.macnn.com

Daily news, software updates (on the home page), reviews, and opinions all make this site a worthy visit. A great list of links to Mac resources and a searchable database of previous news and software round out this site.

Macresource Page

www.macresource.com

This is a no-nonsense daily news page relating to Mac subjects. RAMWatch (find the best prices) and Mac OS Watch (software updates) are part of this site. The site has a search engine that gives you access to the last three years' worth of news. You can also download selected software and browse an organized section of links to other Mac sites.

MacTimes Network (MTN)

www.mactimes.com

You'll find a lot of current news on this site. Dig through features, editorials, links to other Mac Web sites, financial information, recent software updates that you can download, top stories, software and hardware reviews, and even a section for older Macs. There's not much you can't get from this site. The MacHound channel grabs other interesting Mac-related stories from around the Web and other Mac sites. MTN breaks its sections into channels, and you navigate through the channels from the channel guide.

The Mac Report

www.macreport.com

Here's another excellent news source for Mac information such as features, reviews, columns, and archives. You can download a Mac Report plug-in for Sherlock, the Apple Internet search finder.

File Not Found

Sometimes a Web page is moved or renamed, and you get the error message "File Not Found" when trying to connect. Delete the part of the address on the right-most end of a Web address, and work your way back to the left, one slash (/) at a time. You might find the moved page through that process.

Mac Directories And Databases

These Web sites offer a complete one-stop solution for finding answers to many of your iMac questions.

MacDirectory

www.macdirectory.com

MacDirectory is a comprehensive site of searchable databases, providing daily news, reviews, job opportunities, listings of events and seminars, and an online dictionary. Its software download pages let you search for programs via keyword or category. Each product is reviewed and linked to the publisher if it has a Web site. Looking for a consultant?

MacDirectory has a searchable database. Simply type a keyword in a form of company name, city, state, ZIP code, or country. Other searchable databases include hardware, software, services, and events. Looking to upgrade? A searchable database will tell you how much RAM you need and where to buy it, although at the time of this writing, the iMac was not listed.

Macinsearch

http://macinsearch.com/index.html/

Macinsearch is a search engine for Mac-specific information. It's a database of Mac-related information that you can search by keyword. If you are interested in grabbing some shareware, you can search more than 20 predefined categories from arts to virus. You can grab news (in five languages), visit listed Web sites, and more.

MacTemps

www.mactemps.com

MacTemps is a temporary hiring agency that specializes in placing Mac proficient users into the workplace.

The Ultimate Mac

http://users.aol.com/myee/umac.html

Michael Yee is one busy guy. He is responsible for this site, and it's one of the most complete Web sites on the Net for all aspects of the Mac. This page has more links than a sausage factory. Michael started this site when he was working for Sun Microsystems in May 1995 to help Mac users find the best Mac-oriented Web sites. Since 1995, the site has had more than 3.5 million hits and has won numerous awards, including *MacWorld*'s Best of Mac Web sites for two years in a row.

The bonanza includes news, software archives, hints and tips, troubleshooting, graphics, sound, desktop publishing, graphic arts and design, music and audio, software and hardware reviews, software, programming, buying and selling, non-English sites, publications, games, and so much more. You can spend days visiting this site.

TIP

Download With Caution

Before you download any programs off the Net, be sure to have a working virus detector. Download files to a Zip disk or Superdisk, not to your hard drive. Then, scan your downloads for viruses before you launch them.

Video And Audio Streaming

The Internet is getting closer to the day when it will become a true multimedia engine, driving all forms of communication via text, audio, and video on demand. The day when anonymity is the choice rather than the rule is quickly disappearing as real full-motion video is getting closer to reality. It's only a matter of time until you will download your favorite motion picture for viewing in one corner of your monitor, have your local news broadcasting in the other corner, or chat with your overseas friend or relative on the other. In the meantime, check out the following audio and video offerings that are possible right now.

CU-SeeMe

http://cu-seeme.cornell.edu/ (Cornell), www.wpine.com (White Pine Software)

Many people give Tim Dorcey and CU-SeeMe credit for starting public video conferencing on the Net. A team of students led by Dorcey created CU-SeeMe video software while at Cornell. Tim has moved on to create his own video program, Ivisit, but CU-SeeMe is still available as a free program from Cornell, or you may purchase an enhanced commercial version from White Pine Software which has added some bells.

CU-SeeMe works by connecting you to a "reflector," a server that connects 10 to 20 people at a time. However, you can only view eight users at a time (your choice on which eight). There are thousands of private and public reflectors. Private reflectors usually require a password to enter, although some of the public ones do as well to restrict who can enter the chat. You can also connect one-to-one with other CU-SeeMe users. Basically, you can see people and chat with them by typing into a chat box.

You don't need a video camera to participate, although you should have one; otherwise, why join a conference designed for video conferencing? Some reflectors just won't let you in without a camera. Some don't care. You're called a lurker if you can't be seen. Video cameras are inexpensive these days with some available for less than $100 each.

There are many adult-only reflectors. If you are allowing your children to surf and use CU-SeeMe or any other video connection, be aware of this. Not every adult site can be screened out by name alone.

Here are a few good reflectors to get you started:

- 128.2.230.10, Carnegie-Mellon University
- 128.158.1.154, NASA Marshall Space Flight Center
- 129.186.112.242, Iowa State University
- 131.123.5.1, Kent State University
- 139.88.27.43, NASA Lewis Research Center
- 198.69.121.50, Global 2000
- 204.249.164.2, Internet Cafe

Be Safe, Not Sorry

Never use your real name or location when surfing the Net, chatting, or video conferencing. There are 5,000 great people for every jerk on the Net, but that is still a lot of jerks. Never give out your phone number, addresses, or other personal information to strangers.

For a longer list, go to **http://ask.simplenet.com/cu/helpref.htm**, which also contains a good help page. White Pine Software (**www.wpine.com**) has a demo of its commercial version of CU-SeeMe on its Web site.

Ivisit

www.ivisit.com

If you own a QuickCam or other video device, Ivisit lets you "see" whoever you're talking to, along the same lines as CU-SeeMe. Ivisit lets you join conferences by connecting to the Ivisit server automatically when you start the software, but if you know the Internet address (IP number) of the person you want to talk to, you can connect one-to-one (called peer-to-peer).

Aside from viewing the person at a rate of about 15 frames per second (not quite ready for realtime), you can type into a chat box and carry on conversation. You can also hold down the Control key on your keyboard, talk into your built-in microphone on the iMac, and have a two-way, realtime conversation with the other person. The quality of the audio is very good. (Can you say videophone?) You can play back QuickTime movies as well. The software is in beta and available for free.

Ivisit was created by Tim Dorcey from Internet Excellence, ixl, (formerly Boxtop Interactive), the same fellow who created CU-SeeMe.

The Mac Channel

www.macchannel.com

The Mac Channel is an Internet broadcast network that delivers news and information to Mac users around the world using its NewsFire media-streaming technology and a free client program that you download from its Web site. By connecting to the site, you get daily news and info feeds about the Mac industry. You may also download a user guide. Once you select what you want to hear and when, the software will grab it and play it back for you. The content is delivered in zones and includes Daily Mac News, Software-To-Go, WebFlash, Bit Shift, The Bookstore, AudioBeat, and AudioNews. You need to download the software that links into your browser.

iMac FAQ

iMac Info (**http://imac.macguys.com**) and EveryMac.com (**www.everymac.com**) both have great FAQs on the iMac.

Radio Shows On The Net

More than 1,700 radio stations broadcast over the Net using various audio-streaming technologies. This includes 899 stations in the United States and Canada, 631 international stations, 132 Internet-only broadcasters, and 46 radio networks.

Besides listening to your favorite rock-and-roll music or NPR news, you can also listen to talk radio—about the Net, of course. Download the RealMedia Player from **www.realaudio.com** to listen to the following live or archived shows. RealMedia software from RealNetworks (formerly Progressive Networks) is the most popular audio format at the present time.

Inside The Net

www.themesh.com/netradio

This weekly radio show broadcasts from Albany, NY, the capital of New York, on WROW 590AM, every Saturday from noon to 1:00 P.M. EST. Incidentally, I'm the producer and host of the show.

Each week, I interview Net celebs and everyday people who are using the Net for progressive issues and discuss education, entertainment, and every other issue important to humanity. A weekly PC tip and Web site of the week is provided by Roger Gibbs from The Learning Factory, a unique education center in Albany (**www.themesh.com/learnfact.html**). In addition, Dr. Franklin Tessler, a long-time contributing editor of *MacWorld Magazine*, gives the rundown on the world of Apple Computer and the Mac each week. Although the show is geared toward Net activities and people, all three participants are Mac users (fanatics).

You can listen to the show in RealAudio format, participate in a live chat room, or receive an email newsletter. We give away software and other goodies each week. You can call toll free at 800-WROW-590. I started the Net show as Internet FM, more than three years ago on WRPI, 91.5 FM, a college radio station in Troy, New York, before moving to a commercial station. The show is broadcast live using Ivisit video software and RealAudio.

Point And Click Radio

www.kzyx.org/pc/

Point And Click Radio airs from Mendocino County, California, and is the only regularly scheduled call-in computer radio show in the area. Bob Laughton hosts the show, along with Jim Heid, co-host, special correspondent, writer, and author.

Point And Click Radio airs every Wednesday evening from 7:00 to 8:00 P.M. PST on KZYX (90.7 FM, Philo), KZYZ (91.5 FM, Ukiah and Willits), or K202BE (88.3 FM, Fort Bragg). The show is live, and you can call in locally at 707-895-2448 or tollfree at 800-499-7117 within California. You can subscribe to the mailing list as well. Can't tune in? Archives are available in RealAudio format so you can listen any time you choose.

The Mac Show

www.ttalk.com/mactalk/

This is a live radio show in RealAudio format over the Net. There are two hosts. Shawn King is a Macintosh and Internet consultant in Vancouver, BC, Canada, with 15 years of experience in computers and the Macintosh. He and his co-host, Adam Clark, have been doing The Mac Show in various iterations for almost three years.

The show is a RealAudio broadcast of exclusively Apple and Macintosh content. It's broadcast every Wednesday evening from 9:00 to 11:00 P.M. EST. The show is unscripted and unrehearsed, giving it a chaotic feel. Shawn and Adam do the usual news of the week, give out tips and tricks, weigh in with their own opinions, and share the opinion of others. One of the odd bits of the show is the "Bozo of the Week," where Shawn picks on a columnist or two who have said something particularly stupid (in his mind) about Apple or Macintosh.

The guys occasionally goof when reading the news (and you can listen to their bloopers) and sometimes have no idea what they are going to say next, but the chemistry between the two hosts makes up for their occasional lack of professionalism. As neither of the hosts are "real" radio experts, they don't know what they're doing wrong. The show has interviews with folks both inside and outside the Macintosh community. Shawn has interviewed Mac luminaries along with many Mac folks from Apple, Microsoft, Blizzard, Imation, IXMICRO, and others.

As in a typical radio show, they take live callers on their tollfree line. They also have a live and active Internet Relay Chat (IRC) room on the **irc.dal.net** server at **#macshow** where listeners can comment, ask questions of guests, and interact with each other. The hosts also accept email questions during the show.

Chatterboxes, Unite! Chat, Chat, Chat

If you're the kind of person who likes to talk, debate, or share your knowledge with a lot of people, then Internet Relay Chat (IRC) is for you. IRC lets you "talk" to people around the world as though you were sitting in the same room with them.

IRC has been around since the early days of the Net; however, using it in the old days required a great deal of patience and perseverance. You had to memorize cryptic commands. You had to know whether the person you wanted to communicate with actually was online at the same time. That wasn't fun if you were trying to find someone in another country, halfway around the world where it might be 3:00 A.M. or even the next day. Finally, you could type only one line at a time, and it often took what seemed to be eons to get a reply.

Finding More Net Radio On The Web

- First Music—**www.firstmusic.com/radio/**—Looking for radio? First Music lets you choose by country or by state in the U.S., and a simple click on the link takes you to the site. If it is streaming its audio on the Net, you can also tune in and listen.
- Gebbie Press—**www.gebbieinc.com/radintro.htm**—Gebbie Press has a complete list of almost 4,000 radio stations listed alphabetically. You can hop to the station's Web site if it has one and even send email. You can find talk-only stations from the list.
- Iradio—**www.iradio.com**—Interactive Radio is a Web site and newsletter about the online radio industry. Subscribe to its newsletter for free.
- BRS Media Web-Radio— **www.web-radio.com**—You can jump right to this list of all Net radio shows, which is advertised as the most comprehensive Web directory of radio stations. You can choose news and talk format to find other Net-related shows.

Times certainly have changed. Realtime chat is now one of the most popular pastimes on the Net. Chat rooms are almost everywhere: on Net search engines, Web sites, commercial online services, and even private bulletin boards. Some programs even work like a one-to-one pager so you can talk to your buddy.

Realtime chat works like this: You usually log onto a server that is connected to an IRC network, create a nickname, sign in, find the conference you're interested in (called a channel on IRC), and start typing. Hundreds of IRC channels are available, and several cater specifically to the Mac community. There are several large IRC networks: EFnet (**www.efnet.net/**), UnderNET (**http://servers.undernet.org/**), DALnet (**www.dal.net/**), and IRCnet (no Web page yet) make up the big four. Others such as ChatNet (**www.chatnet.org/**) and GalaxyNet (**www.galaxynet.org/**) are smaller IRC networks but are still very active. Go to **www.irchelp.org/irchelp/networks/nets/** for a more complete list of IRC networks.

The other way to chat is to connect to various chat rooms offered by the commercial online services or Web search engines, or to use the pager type of chat program where you locate and chat on a peer-to-peer basis or via a small personal group that you select.

Let me issue a warning. Many public chat rooms are pretty boring, childish, and time-consuming unless you want to talk about sex, politics, or other topics that are guaranteed to raise your blood pressure. Stay away from the public chat rooms that cater to this kind of nonsense. On the other hand, chat is a great feature if you want to carry on help sessions, educational discussions, or classes, have monthly business or hobby meetings, or even work with people around the world. The great thing about chat is the ability to create private chat rooms that are password-protected so only the people you want to talk to can enter your virtual room.

Not all chat programs are created equally. Some are pretty easy and straightforward to set up. A few need to be tweaked. Overall, most of the versions for the Mac are easy. You can set up and chat with someone in a matter of minutes.

Several varieties of chat programs are available. Some are standalone applications, and some are plug-ins for your Web browser. Some chat programs are called buddy lists, pagers, or private chats. These programs let you create lists or groups of people you want to talk to. When your "buddies" log on to the Internet, the program lets you know they're online and you can page them. You have the option to chat one-to-one or in small groups.

Public chat programs let you enter small or large chat rooms and talk to many people at the same time. They often have the ability to let you send a private instant message to someone in the room. They also have options such as being able to block someone who is obnoxious, highlight a chat member, participate in multiple chat rooms, and more. Public chat sites are more common.

Additionally, special chat programs incorporate 3D effects and cool graphics or even combine video and chat (such as CU-SeeMe or Ivisit). You better have a fast Net connection for these.

Finally, commercial online services such as America Online or CompuServe have built-in chat features using their proprietary software. Several third-party companies have developed chat servers, and your own local Internet Service Provider may be using one. All you need to do is to select the chat room and to start typing.

If you are new to online chat, it may not be easy to actually find a chat room that interests you. Online search engines such as Excite (**www.excite.com**) attempt to make it easy by organizing chat rooms by themes: age, interest, geography, and so on. Some folks who are really into chat publish lists of channels and times on their Web sites.

The best way to find a chat room is to visit the Web site of the developer of the chat program you're using. It often has links to channels, rooms, the latest version of the chat client for downloading, and even a FAQ document. A good FAQ on IRC is available at ChatNet's home page (**www.chatnet.org/**). Remember, online etiquette applies in chat sessions as well as any other public discussion on the Net.

What Flavor Chat Would You Like?

Depending on your needs, the following free, shareware, beta, or demo chat clients will serve you well.

Politeness Counts

Be sure to reread Chapter 4 before you chat.

Private, Pager, and Buddy Chat Programs

By using any of the software programs below, you can stay in immediate touch with friends, colleagues, or family when you are online.

AbbottChat

www.abbottsystems.com

AbbottChat, originally known as AtChat, enables you to conduct one-on-one or group chat. Because the program is free (it has an advertising banner), all you need to do is to make sure your friends have a copy. Like other similar programs, AbbottChat lets you know whether your buddies are online. There is no server to connect to, so your connection is fast. You can even move a person to a private chat while you are in a group discussion. I like the interface of this program. It's organized in a logical manner that makes it easy to use. A cool feature is the ability to send alerts to an individual or group even if you are not chatting with them. You can send files while you are chatting as well, so this program is good for collaborative efforts. Instant Chat programs like AbbottChat, as shown in Figure 6.3, lets you talk live to people while you are online.

Ahoy

www.quicomm2.com/AHOY/ahoy.html

Ahoy is another peer-to-peer chat program—no need for a central server. Ahoy allows you to have listed and unlisted numbers so only people you want to talk to can find you. Ahoy has a search function that will find the IP address of your friend, a good feature because most people have dynamic IP addresses. (Your Internet Service Provider gives you a different IP address every time you sign on. If you have your own Net connection at work, you most likely have a static IP, an address that never changes.)

Another cool feature is the ability to share URLs. If you are looking at a great Web site, just click the browser button, and your connected buddy's browser will open to the same Web page.

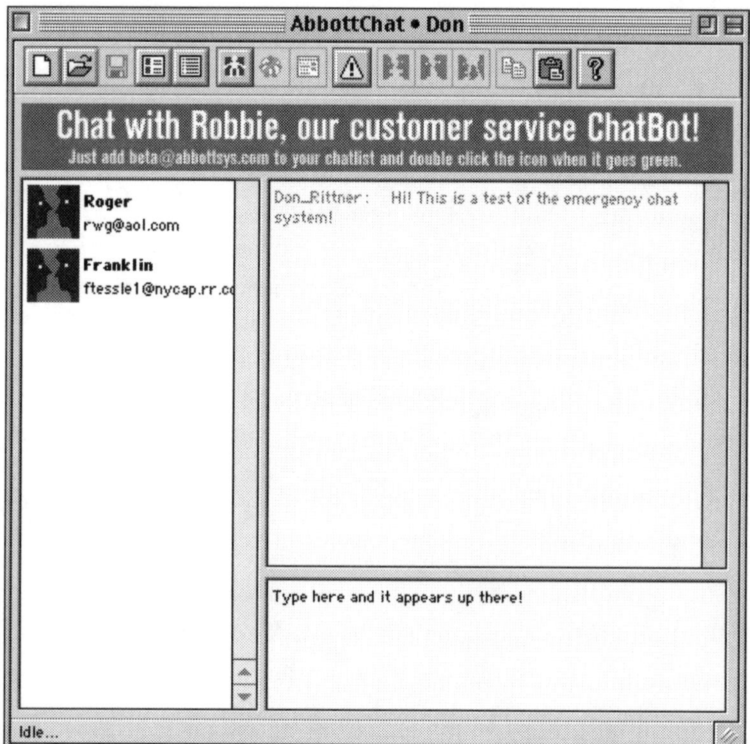

Figure 6.3
AbbottChat.

You can leave a message if the person is busy or not online—sort of a caller ID—and you can upload fully encrypted BBEdit documents at the click of a button.

AOL Instant Messenger (America Online)

www.aol.com

As much as I dislike America Online, its Instant Messenger is quite nice, and you don't have to be a member of the service to use it. You create buddy lists or individual listings, and when a member of your list signs on to the Net, you know it. You can then choose to send an instant message. You can talk one-to-one or in a group.

Excite PAL (Personal Access List)

www.excite.com

Excite PAL is a free chat program that you download from this excellent search engine and that ties into your Web browser. It reminds me somewhat of AOL's Instant Messenger, but it has a cool feature that lets you link into its search engine, email lookup, or the PAL directories. The Excite home page has rooms arranged by categories.

ichat Pager

www.acuity.com/ichat/index.html

What doesn't ichat Pager do? You can create buddy lists and know whether your buddies are online or away from the computer or even search for them. You can send instant messages, create private rooms, and even send a file via FTP to your friend by dropping it on his ID or send him a Web link. If you use RealPlayer for video or audio playback, you can send your friends a link, and ichat Pager will launch it automatically.

You can send ichat pages to initiate Microsoft NetMeeting or Netscape Conference sessions as well. The client software lets you enter chat rooms already built into the software and organized into several categories.

ICQ (I Seek You)

www.icq.com

ICQ is a phenomenon. Go to its Web page, and you will see what I mean. ICQ allows you to chat, to send messages and files, and to play games. When you sign up, you get your own unique identifier number. You can create lists of associates that you can page when they go online. (Their ID turns red when they are online.) ICQ has a floating palette that lets you know when there is an incoming message.

PeopleLink

www.peoplelink.com

PeopleLink is a chat program that lets you chat one-on-one or conference style. You have the option to let people see whether you are online. PeopleLink lets you find people that share your interests. Just fill out the template and mark off choices; PeopleLink will give you a list of people who match your criteria. You can then add them to your buddy list, send them email, or ask to chat if they are online. You can join and chat with a number of PeopleLink communities on its home page.

Public Chat

Use the following chat programs if you like to talk to more than one person at a time.

ChatNet

www.elsinc.com/chatnet.html

If you are accustomed to chatting on services such as America Online, ChatNet will be familiar to you. ChatNet offers two modes for chat. By using the AppleTalk mode, multiple Macintosh computers running ChatNet can chat or send files on a local area network, with or without a server—great for the office environment. The IRC mode allows you to chat and send files through an IRC server. Both private and public chats are available. ChatNet is a commercial program, so it is not free.

Excite Virtual Places

www.excite.com

Excite VP is a free download from the Excite search engine that lets you log on to its chat rooms, which span the world. Double-click the Talk application and start chatting. You can go to a room based on peers, subject, location, or even interest level.

Ircle

www.ircle.com

Ircle is a shareware client that is probably the most widely used program for IRC talk. It has most of the widely used commands and is easy to use.

MacIRC

www.macirc.com

MacIRC is probably the second most popular chat client. Although it is still in beta, it is free to download.

ShadowIRC

www.netlink.co.uk/~greghl/dshadow/shadowirc

ShadowIRC is a new and fast IRC client for the Mac, which is expandable through the use of plug-ins.

Snak

www.kagi.com/kent/Snak.html

A relatively new chat client, Snak has impressive features. It has an address book so you can keep track of information, a guardian feature that can help control what channels you can visit (good for children and students), multiple connections and channels per connection, and more.

Video 3D And Fancy Stuff

If you like more than just text, the following chat programs will bring some interactivity and visually appealing features to your chat session.

Chat TV

www.chattv.com

Here is real interactive TV. Do you watch TV talk shows and wish you could share the jokes or comments made by Dave Letterman, Jay Leno, or Bill Mahr? If you're watching TV while chatting, then Chat TV could be fun for you. Using your ichat Pager or any major browser software, you can chat with others while the show is going on and make comments or discuss the show you're watching. Once you log on, you are connected to a TV guide with rooms. Just select the room, enter, and chat.

The Palace (Palace Inc.)

www.thepalace.com

The Palace is a three-dimensional world with rooms and sounds. Chat users can create their own customized worlds by selecting from a collection of prepared images. It's an interesting way to chat, but you need a good Net connection and a fast computer.

7 Using Your iMac For Research

Rittner's Computer Law: Never argue with people who write with digital ink and pay by the kilowatt-hour.

Research And The iMac? Elementary, Sherlock

The Internet and your iMac are a powerful combination for conducting research. The iMac is fast and easy to use and has the right tools to search the Internet, the world's online information library. There are literally millions of documents, software, and data in this digital library waiting for you. With your iMac, you can:

- Conduct bibliographical searches of entire library catalogs and magazine and newspaper databases.
- Conduct research on existing businesses throughout the world, track stocks and other business information, and even learn how to create your own business and incorporate online.
- Sift through thousands of pages of encyclopedias for your children's schoolwork and access online multilanguage dictionaries, thesauri, and other collections.
- Conduct scientific research with access to scientific collections such as NASA's star catalogs, Hubbell Telescope images, botanical herbarium, U.S. census data, and even medical databanks.

Your access to this wealth of information—your virtual library card—is your Web browser. As the Internet grew, it became clear to many that there had to be some way to access this vast collection of information—a way to quickly find related information that was scattered over millions of computer systems around the world. As you learned in Chapter 2, early attempts to organize information with search tools such as Archie and Gopher helped but were more a la carte in their implementation. It wasn't until 1989 that Tim Berners-Lee from CERN, the European Laboratory for Particle Physics in Switzerland, came up with the idea of the World Wide Web. His idea was that knowledge in its many forms—text, graphics, animation, video, and sound—should be accessed from one central starting point, known as a hypertext approach. You can read his original proposal online (**www.w3.org/History/1989/proposal.html**).

The rest is history, as they say. The Web today encompasses more than 100 million people in 170 countries. It is fast becoming the global electronic communication MESH (Berners-Lee's first name for the Web). Within five years, anyone not online will have made a conscious choice not to connect, like a Luddite who resists technological change. This chapter will give you a head start on conducting research on the Net by pointing you to some of the great searching tools and databases available for free.

Net Search Engines

An Internet search engine is similar in many ways to your local library. You make a visit, check the card catalog, and access the information you need. With a search engine on the Net, the offerings are a bit more extensive because the bookshelves are worldwide and are more up to date by far. Some search engines continually update their databanks. No library could afford to purchase that many books.

Many search engines are available to you. Although they all do similar things—index information on the Net—not all are created equal. Search engines work on two principles. You are interested in finding a lot of information on a particular subject and want to access it regardless of whether that information is on a Web, FTP, or Gopher site and where it is geographically. Several of the best search engines are described later in the chapter.

Most Net search engines allow you to perform detailed searching using various techniques. You can search combinations of words with what is known as Boolean logic, using connector words such as AND, OR, and BUT (named after George Boole, the British mathematician who invented it). You can simply search by typing words or phrases separated by commas. You can even search on a specific phrase by enclosing it in quotes. For example, if we are looking for any information on New York State libraries, our search terms would be

```
libraries new york state
```

A search engine searches on every word: libraries, new, york, and state. Obviously, you get a large number of returns (called hits), and many are not usable. However, if you type

```
libraries "new york state"
```

you get a completely different number of hits. The engine searches for all occurrences of the word libraries and the phrase "new york state," not three separate words.

Let's use the search engine WebCrawler (**www.webcrawler.com**) on the preceding example. After searching for all four words without quotes, WebCrawler returns 209,685 hits. When I put "New York State" in quotes, the number of hits is reduced to a little less than 16,000. When I add the Boolean delimiter AND (libraries AND "new york state"), the number of hits is down to a manageable 238.

You can see that there is a big difference in the number of hits returned, based on the way you ask for the information. In this case, the Boolean approach is the more reasonable one. However, sometimes, you simply want to throw a term out to the wind and see what turns up. It's similar to thumbing through a card catalog at the library. The bottom line is that before you start searching, narrow your search terms and tailor them to get the best possible return for your search.

Not all search engines process their information the same way. You need to try them all and see which engine gives you satisfactory results. Much of the way information is displayed is subjective. Pick the format that suits you. Search engines such as Savvy Search (**www.savvysearch.com**) actually search several other search engines (Lycos, Excite, HotBot, WebCrawler, Google, Galaxy, Alta Vista, Thunderstone, National Directory, Infoseek, Direct Hit, and so on) at the same time for you. This is known as a metasearch engine, and I describe several of them later in this chapter.

Today's Net search engines are more than just searchable databases. Many of them offer you the latest news, shopping, travel information, free email accounts, and other information. A few of them let you customize the home page so you see information tailored to your interests each time you log on to the site. They all give you the tools to search the Net (and some have access to Usenet and other online databases). Search engines that offer all these services are called "Portals."

Sherlock To The Rescue

Until the introduction of the iMac and System 8.5, the only way to search the Net was to visit a search engine or a Web site that listed several search engines. I often thought I was missing important information if I couldn't search them all, but that was time-consuming. Apple has taken care of that problem with Sherlock, a search tool that makes searching on the Net elementary.

When Apple released System 8.5, it included a new version of the old Find desk accessory, a simple search application that allows you to search your hard drive or any storage device attached to your Mac. Find

Free Email Has Its Price

The free email accounts offered by search engines are useful if you do a lot of traveling because you can access your email anywhere in the world as long as you can log on. Unfortunately, many of the early spammers used these free email accounts to spam the Net community, so many folks have filters to reject email from these free sites. I for one refuse any email from Hotmail and Juno because of all the junk mail I've received from them. America Online is the biggest problem. Its persistence in flooding the world with free disks containing hours of free time gives spammers ample opportunity to exploit the system. I would drop my AOL account in a second, but I was a beta tester and ran several online forums in the early days, and therefore, my AOL user ID has been my primary business account for years. The majority of the spam I get comes from AOL. In its defense, it has sued many of the spammers, but spamming still happens enough to be offensive. It isn't the fault of the Internet Service Providers that unscrupulous people abuse the privilege, yet I grow tired of having to deal with it.

If you can afford to get a local Internet account, then pay for it. If you do obtain one of the free email accounts from a search engine, do not use it as your everyday or business account. Use it for friends and family who write occasionally, for going out of town, or as a receptacle for mailing lists.

has a few options such as finding a file by date, size, or type. Sherlock, on the other hand, allows you to search your disks and their contents, as shown in Figure 7.1, but also the entire Net, in effect serving as a search engine of search engines.

If a Web site has a Sherlock plug-in, you simply drop the plug-in in your Internet Search Sites folder in the System folder. When you launch Sherlock (Command+F), you have the option of searching on all sites or any combination of sites that are in the folder. Sherlock initially came with a set of plug-ins for the major search engines, but new Sherlock plug-ins are made available almost every day.

Be sure to give Sherlock plenty of memory if you plan to use a lot of plug-ins. You can do this by finding Sherlock in your Apple menu folder, which is located in the System folder. Highlight it by clicking it once, access the File menu (or hit Command+I), and select Get Info. Notice under the icon and Sherlock's name a box called Show: General Information. Click in the box, and hold it down until you see Memory. The area called Memory Requirements shows a suggested, minimum, and preferred size. Increase the preferred size to prevent memory problems, as shown in Figure 7.2. (Mine is set at 3,000K.)

When Sherlock searches the Net, it keeps track of whether the search engines need updating and will ask whether you want to update your plug-in. Be sure to click OK.

Sherlock returns a list of all sites it finds, along with a relevance factor, and the address of the site. The total number of sites (hits) found is

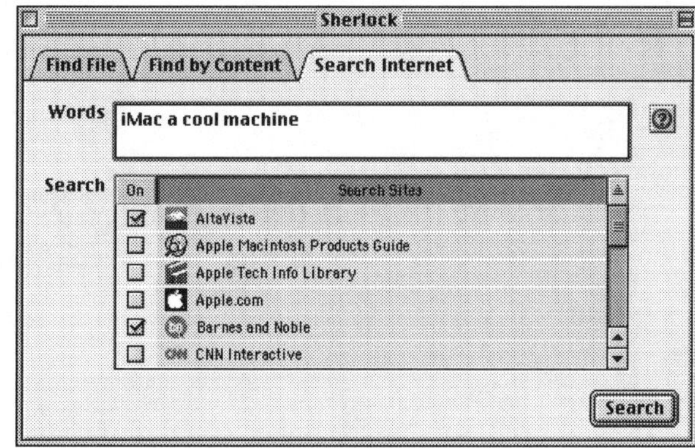

Figure 7.1
Sherlock is Apple's Internet search tool.

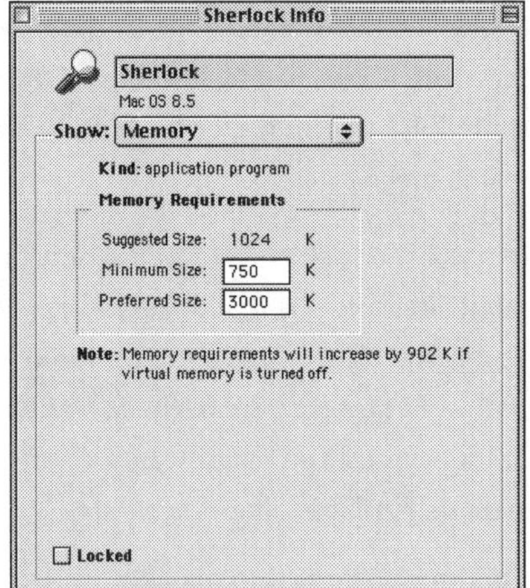

Figure 7.2
Giving Sherlock more memory.

indicated at the top. When you select a site in the list, more information about the site displays in the bottom half of Sherlock (along with some banner advertising). This gives you the relevance factor in a percentage, the title of the site as a link, the URL, and a summary if there is one, as show in Figure 7.3.

You can go directly to the site by clicking the title or by clicking the name in the listing above it. Either way, Sherlock launches your browser if it is not open and takes you to the site.

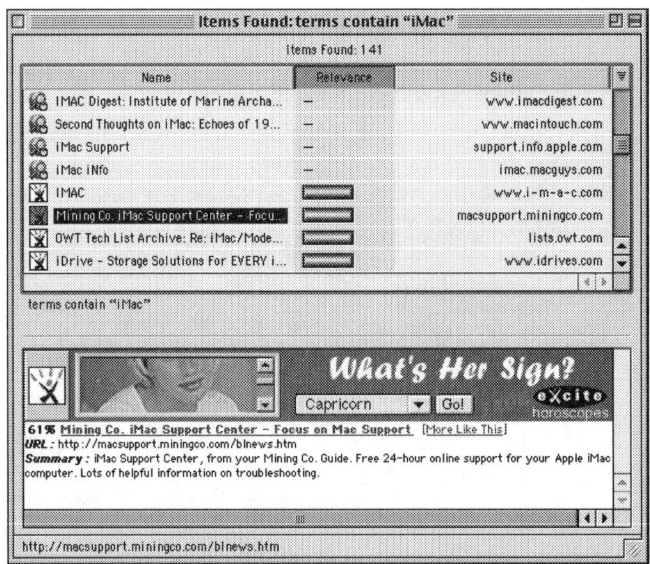

Figure 7.3
Sherlock's Items Found list.

Multiple Searches

Sherlock lets you perform multiple searches and saves each listing. Even better is the fact that you can save the search terms for later use. After you conduct a search with Sherlock, access the File menu, select Save Search Criteria (Command+S). This will save your search terms on your hard drive. Later, select Open Search Criteria, find the one you want to use on the hard drive, and Sherlock will leap into action. If you are not online and you select the search criteria, Sherlock will force your Mac to dial your Internet Service Provider (ISP).

Sherlock Shortcuts

If you have already saved a Sherlock search criteria shortcut, you can open it for searching in your Microsoft Internet Explorer browser. Choose Open File and select the file (called Terms containing "xxxx"), and Sherlock will open and perform an updated search. Interestingly, this feature does not work on Netscape Navigator.

More About Sherlock

If you are spending the day researching and you want to start collecting all the URLs you are finding, you can copy and paste the Sherlock lists into a text file. When Sherlock is done surfing, click the window of the lists, choose Select All under the Edit menu, or Command+A, copy and paste the lists into a word processor, and save the document as a text file. The file will not include the names of the sites—only the URLs—but that's okay.

You can turn that text file into a browser-ready document, one where you can simply click the URLs and go surfing. I import the text file into an email message using Outlook Express and send it to myself. Within seconds, I receive the lists as an email message with all the URLs in clickable form.

There's even an easier way to make your Sherlock list a Web document. Download the great shareware program HTML Markup by Scott J. Kleper (**www.printerport.com/klephacks/**). Prepare HTML Markup by double-clicking it (make sure you pay the shareware fee), and select the options "End all lines with break" and "Convert URLs into links", as shown in Figure 7.4.

After HTML Markup is prepared, choose Convert File. Select the text document that contains the URLs, and it will be saved with the same name you gave it with the .html extension. Now, you can open it with your Web browser, and the links are Web ready. Both Netscape and Microsoft browsers will work with your new document. You can create many clickable documents this way, as shown in Figure 7.5.

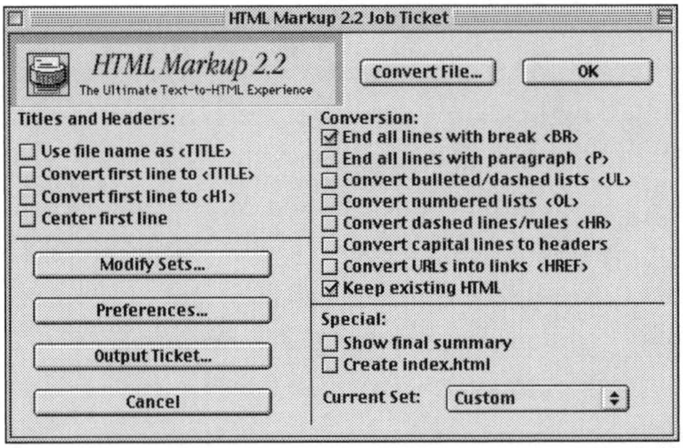

Figure 7.4
HTML Markup.

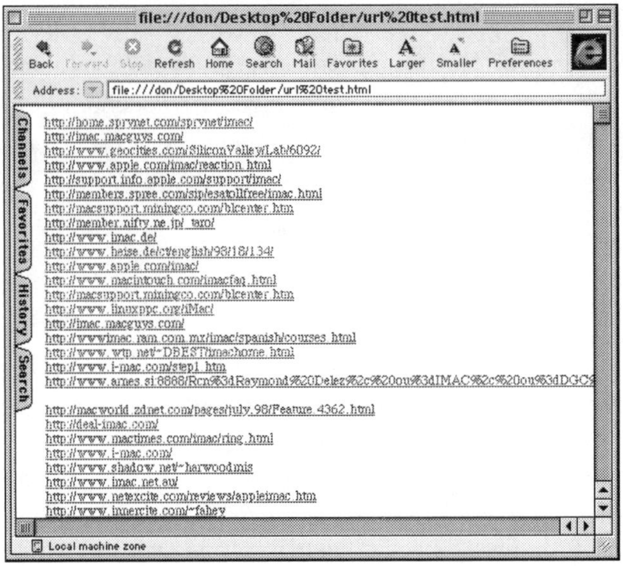

Figure 7.5
By importing the URL list into Internet Explorer, you're ready to surf the Net.

Search Engines

Here are several of the best search engines on the Net that will guide you to worldwide resources.

Alta Vista

www.altavista.com

Alta Vista is a multicultural search engine. You can type your keywords in more than a dozen languages. Alta Vista lets you search special categories such as automotive, hobbies, and the like. It also has search engines for Usenet and for finding people, travel, entertainment products, and

Too Many Open Windows Can Give You A Freeze

Do not make the mistake of selecting Open Search Criteria after you select all the hits (Command+A, or Select All from the Edit menu) because this will attempt to open every URL listed in a new browser window, and you will run out of memory.

other consumer-oriented sites. Alta Vista has ABC news summaries and other highlights and offers a free email account.

When you conduct a search on Alta Vista, you receive 10 hits at a time. Each hit has a title linked to the site, a one-sentence summary or description, the URL, the date last modified, the page size, and the ability to translate the page into another language, which is a great tool.

Dejanews

www.dejanews.com

Dejanews is the premier search engine for Usenet newsgroups. Type a keyword or phrase, and you get a list of 25 articles at a time, all posted on the subject you indicated, along with the name of the newsgroup, the author, the date, and the subject heading.

You can click the title of the post and read it, and you can get a profile of the person whose posts you read. Dejanews might remind you of *1984*, but it does list every post you send, grouped by newsgroup. Be careful what you say on Usenet because your mother or the FBI will know about it.

Dejanews is a great service if you are interested in checking Usenet once in a while and you don't want to go to the trouble of actually subscribing to newsgroups. You can reply to any article publicly or privately (through email), although you still have to join by giving your email address and the newsgroup name you want to reply to.

Search No Further

The Search Engine Report **(http://searchenginewatch.com)** is a monthly newsletter that covers the latest developments with search engines. If you do a lot of research, this is a good site to frequent and mailing list to join.

Dejanews actually has five engines. You can search the standard edition or complete archives and search only for jobs, the for-sale lists, and adult posts. If you want to find out what is being discussed on any given subject, Dejanews is the place to start.

Excite

www.excite.com

Excite is the search engine that comes preconfigured as your home page on your iMac. Excite is a great search tool that lets you personalize the home page.

Excite is a search engine, but when you type your keyword or phrase, you get a lot more than a list of hits. On the results page, you are offered a choice of additional search terms, Web sites on your topic, news articles, and Usenet newsgroups.

The hits based on your search criteria are listed 10 at a time. Each hit gives the title in clickable form, a summary, and the URL for the site. A nice feature on each hit is the ability to search for more matching sites. If one of the hits looks like something you want, the search engine will try to find more sites just like it.

Excite displays searchable topics arranged in predefined categories and top news stories that include technology, sports, and business news. You have the ability to configure Excite to find news stories that interest you, making you the publisher of your own newspaper.

You can find your horoscope, check local weather by typing your ZIP code, participate in live chat sessions, and even check the sports scores.

A personalization manager lets you configure Excite right down to what color you want displayed on your monitor. Excite has engines in the following languages: English, Chinese, French, German, Italian, Japanese, Dutch, and Swedish.

Galaxy

www.einet.net/index.html

Galaxy lets you search by keyword or phrase, and like most other search engines, it offers advanced search techniques.

Galaxy presents its home page as a directory of categories that include business and commerce, community, engineering and technology, government, humanities, law, leisure and recreation, medicine, reference, science, and social science. Subcategories follow supercategories.

When you select a category's subcategory, you see a choice of articles to read, collections to view, directory listings, non-profit organizations, periodicals, and other categories if appropriate. You have a choice to type your own keyword if none of the selections suit you.

Galaxy is a nice way to start a search because it presents information to you in an organized approach, a way that might get you thinking about other avenues for searching.

Google

www.google.com

Google is an interesting search engine. It claims to conduct a complicated mathematical analysis of more than one billion hyperlinks on the Web and then return a high-quality search. A section called "I feel lucky" will take you right to the pages it finds.

The red bars you see in the search results are Google's estimation of the quality or importance of the Web page, based on the billion or more hyperlinks Google has downloaded. The basic idea is that Web pages are ranked highly if other highly ranked Web pages link to them. This circular logic means that computing the rankings is complicated. Google also looks carefully at the text of all the links on the Web to improve your search results.

HotBot

www.hotbot.com

HotBot gives you many search options up front, such as the ability to search on parts of words or phrases in several languages, use Boolean terms, the title of a Web page, or even on a link. You also have the option to search based on how far back you want to search, from "unlimited" or only the last two years. You can order the hits to appear in groups of 10 to 100 and decide whether you want full descriptions, summaries, or just the URLs. You can insist that pages include images, audio, video, or JavaScript.

HotBot has news, sports, and reference items and consumer-oriented areas for automobiles, real estate, travel, and shopping. A section on technology lets you read reviews of software and hardware and download software, including tools for working on your Web page. There is a link to HotWired, the online version of *Wired* magazine.

With HotBot, you can also search Usenet and the Yellow and White Pages and look for email addresses or domain names, jobs and résumés, classifieds, homes and loans, stocks, downloads, music, and even road maps. You'll find a lot of choices to control your searches.

Infoseek

www.infoseek.com

Infoseek is one of my favorite search engines. The newly designed Infoseek presents categories and subcategories for quick searching, or you can use its keyword or phrase search engine. The four search categories are Web sites, news, companies (business), and Usenet newsgroups.

Your search results page gives you a list of directory topics that are also searchable and a group of 10 hits with a clickable title, summary date, size, and URL. You can also find similar pages and grouped results. Suppose a Web site has a number of related links. Instead of trying to find each one, Infoseek presents them all on a page, one Web site at a time.

Interested in the day's news? You can read the headlines and stories and personalize Infoseek to deliver the type of news stories you want. There are several news categories to choose, from headlines to world news.

Infoseek has a program called Quickseek that you can download (**www.infoseek.com/iseek?pg=quickseek/Download,.html**). It installs an Infoseek button directly on your browser. No matter where you are on the Web, Infoseek's engine is right there to do the searching for you. Infoseek is available in other languages as well.

Lycos

http://lycos11.lycos.cs.cmu.edu

Lycos is organized as "Web guides" on its home page. Select a category, and you see links to resources pertaining to that category.

Lycos has a free email service with an option to Hotmail, another free email service. Like Excite, you can create a personalized home page to Lycos. It's free. Get news and stock quotes and even maintain a daytimer (very cool), participate in chat and forums, play games, and find people. There are a shopping area and an advanced search section that lets you access Yellow and White Pages, email lookup, road maps, and more. You can search by keyword or phrases.

Magellan

http://magellan.excite.com

Magellan is a search engine similar to others in that it's arranged as Web guides, categories of frequently sought after information (autos, shopping, business, education, and so on). Other features include classifieds, free email, map makings, people finder, stocks, weather, and Yellow Pages.

You can keyword or phrase search the entire Web or a green light sites only. Green light sites are reviewed and contain no adult content at the time of review.

Your search results are returned by relevance (more relevant at the top) and present 10 at a time with summaries. Both the title and URL are clickable. You have the option to find similar pages for any hit.

Open Text (LiveLink Pinstripe)

http://index.opentext.com/indexb.html

This search engine is designed specifically for business users and is updated every two weeks. A great deal of information here is organized in an easy-to-use way. The search page, called "Slice Search," is organized into business categories, and you can selectively search one or more of them or all of them.

Search results are listed 10 hits at a time, and each hit has the title (which is clickable), summary, and URL. You can refine the search using Boolean operators and other advanced search techniques.

There are other ways to search on LiveLink. A Quick Search function lets you search current events, national jobs, newsgroups, and companies online. Just type your keyword or phrase. The Powersearch function lets you use several Boolean operators and other attributes to get better results in your search. There are also search engines to look for financial information such as stock quotes, investor services, portfolio services, company research, and other stock-related resources.

Looking for business news? Search *Fortune, Forbes, Financial Times, San Jose Mercury News, Investor's Business Daily, Business Week, Bloomberg, USA Today, Worth,* and *Toronto Star*, singularly or in total. You can look for jobs nationally or by region and even submit your résumé and find job placement firms. Several headhunters and career services are available as well. If you are trying to find people, several telephone directories, an email lookup, and tollfree numbers are available. Looking to book your airline flights? Yup, that's there, too, along with links to the major airlines. Finally, there is a link to Dejanews for newsgroup lookup, and you can read the thoughts of several business columnists. This is a great business site.

Snap

http://home.snap.com

Snap is a search engine that has searchable categories on its home page like several of the other search engines. It provides services such as email lookup, White and Yellow Pages, stock quotes, chat and message boards, and software downloads. Similar to other search engines, it offers a free email service.

A great feature of Snap is localizing your page. Just type your ZIP code, and presto, you see local weather, personals, news, movies, TV listings, and maps. It has links to local Web sites and more.

Finally, you can sign up for free and customize Snap, what it calls My Snap, which lets you arrange what kind of news you want to read and even track lottery numbers.

Starting Point

www.stpt.com

Starting Point is a search engine that lets you search by keyword on any topic. You also have a choice to search other engines, Yellow Pages, and other guides. It has arranged categories into channels that you can select, or you can select each category and do a keyword search.

A great feature is the ability to view new submissions in all categories in realtime. You can get a free email account, and you can personalize the search page to reflect the categories you are more often likely to use. You are allowed four more choices in the drop-down menu under the Search function. Starting Point also features services such as weather, stock quotes, news, maps and directions, a people finder, and telephone lookup.

WebCrawler

www.webcrawler.com

WebCrawler organizes its home page into categories called channels (from arts and crafts to travel topics). Headline news and daily features round out the page. You can search by keyword or phrase on the whole database or each channel, but unlike the other search engines, the resulting list of 25 hits gives you only the title of the site, which is linked. This arrangement is good if you know exactly what you are searching for. I like to use WebCrawler when I know exactly what I'm looking for, such as a specific Web site or topic. It's fast.

You do have the option to obtain summaries of the hits, which gives you the title, summary, and URL, and the option to search for similar pages. A shortcuts section lists newsgroups based on your topics and also gives you options for checking Web sites that it guesses you might be interested in. Additionally, it gives you a list of news stories based on your search topic.

Yes, you can personalize your own page, giving you news, local sports, weather, horoscopes, stocks, and other information, and you can get a free email account. I like the fact that you can get a TV listing for your home area so you can make sure you don't miss a show.

Yahoo!

www.yahoo.com

Yahoo!'s home page provides several organized subject categories from arts to culture, ready for exploring. You can search by keyword or phrase, and several advanced search techniques are available. Besides the usual links to shopping, Yellow Pages, people searches, maps, travel agents, classifieds, chat, news, weather, and so on, Yahoo! has a pager section that lets you find and communicate with friends online. You don't have to download it; it works with your browser.

When you search for a topic, in addition to giving you a list of 10 or more hits like the other search engines, Yahoo! instead gives you a list of categories that has your keyword highlighted. By selecting a category, you hop to another page that has a list of sites with title and summary. The title is clickable. You have the option to search more of Yahoo! or just the category you are in. Personally, I don't like this arrangement, but you might. You need to choose which search engine fits your tastes.

Yahoo! lets you personalize some of the categories on its home page to provide you with more useful information that is tailored to your interests. If you enter your ZIP code, you get a list of local weather, news, a local Web directory, and more.

Yahoo! provides an area called clubs. These are virtual communities centered about their subject categories. Each club has chat, messages, and even a calendar of events. If there isn't a club dealing with your interest, you can create one. There is a search capability on the clubs as well.

Want to keep track of your appointments online? Yahoo! provides you with a calendar that is great for appointments and birthdays and sends email reminders. You can synchronize it with Microsoft Outlook and the Palm Pilot. This is a great feature. You can also get a free email account with Yahoo!.

Learn The Advanced Search Techniques

Most search engines have advanced search techniques. If basic keyword searching is not doing the job for you, become familiar with your favorite search engine's advanced search features and use them.

Metasearch Engines And Groups

Metasearch engines are sites that bring together, under one roof, more than one search engine or the ability to search more than one search engine at a time. Like single search engines, they offer a wide range of other services such as links to other databases or sites, shopping, entertainment, news, and so on. The following sites are good starting points to do multiple searching.

All In One

www.albany.net/allinone/all1www.html

This site contains more than 400 links to search engines and other data collections on one page. Just find the one you want to search, type your keywords, and press the Enter key.

Cyber411

www.cyber411.com

This metasearch engine checks 16 other search engines at the same time for your keywords. It also has advanced search functions.

Mamma

www.mamma.com

Mamma is a metasearch engine (although I could not tell how many search engines it covers), and you can search the Web, Usenet, news, stocks, and other categories. Options on searching are available. It contains other databases for reverse lookup, telephone directories, maps, and so on.

Savvy Search

www.savvysearch.com

Savvy Search checks more than 150 search engines, guides, auctions, storefronts, Usenet archives, news archives, and shareware libraries at once. You'll find several language varieties, as well as specialty areas on the home page.

The Ultimate Internet Search Index

www.geocities.com/SiliconValley/Heights/5296/index.html

This site has several categories of search engines available from mainstream engines to email address lookup, shopping, newsgroups, mailing lists, software files, and much more.

Specialized Databases And Collections

Although Net search engines are trying their best to create online communities, they are still search engines and therefore are seen as jumping-off points, not places to mill around. The best scenario for an online user, regardless of whether she is a scientist, business person, or mom, is to find people and resources who share a similar interest. We are always looking to increase our circles of friends and workmates—in this case, creating a virtual community of peers.

Fortunately, many people and organizations on the Net create supersites that contain hundreds and even thousands of links on a particular subject. If you are an archeologist or zoologist or you're simply looking for a good Web page on bead making, it's much easier to go to a site devoted to that topic. The site is usually updated with new material on a regular basis, and you will find knowledgeable people "hanging" around. Supersites also tend to attract those specialists in the discipline, and a virtual community thereby grows.

To give you a head start on finding your connection, the following supersites cover almost all the major disciplines I can think of. Remember also that every supersite will link you to hundreds of other sites, and those, in turn, link to hundreds of other sites. Once you find the supersite that caters to your interest, you will have enough links to last a lifetime.

World Wide Web Supersites

All Engineering Resources On The Net (EELS)

www.ub2.lu.se/eel/ae/

More than 1,000 selected engineering resources are available on this site. You can find information by keyword search or criteria such as pages sorted by domain or country, pages sorted alphabetically by title, the most cited individual engineering URLs, or a hot list of the most cited engineering file directories.

Anthropology Resources On The Net

www.nitehawk.com/alleycat/anth-faq.html

This site contains hundreds of links to anthropology resources, including Web sites, newsgroups, and mailing lists, all on one page.

ArchNet

http://archnet.uconn.edu/

This site is for the archeologist. It contains archeological resources. The site is organized by subject area and is broken down by geographic regions. It lists museums, academics, journals, and more. This is a top-rated site.

Astroweb Database

www.cv.nrao.edu/fits/www/yp_protoname.html

This site features hundreds of links listed alphabetically of almost every astronomy-based Web site in the world.

Campus Newspapers On The Internet

http://beacon-www.asa.utk.edu/resources/papers.html

This site lists many of the online newspapers published by colleges and universities across the world. Daily or less frequent publications are listed.

Chemical Elements On The Internet

http://chemicalelements.com

This site started out as an eighth-grade project, but it is now one of the best stops to get information about any of the elements on the atomic table.

Chemistry Collection Of Infostead Australia

www.zip.com.au/~sswans/chemistry-2.html

This excellent site contains hundreds of links in eight sections to every aspect of the field of chemistry. You can get a Ph.D. worth of education on this site. It even features a music intro.

Companies Online

www.companiesonline.com

Want the goods on companies that have Web sites? This site purports to have data on more than 100,000 private and public companies. Browse by industry or search by keyword.

Consumer World

www.consumerworld.org/pages/resource.htm

Never buy a car without visiting this site first. It offers a lot of great consumer-related information in several categories from autos to health.

Cyndi's List Of Genealogy Sites On The Internet

www.cyndislist.com

Looking for your roots? This site boasts more than 39,250 links, categorized and cross-referenced, in more than 90 categories.

Dictionary, Thesaurus, Science Library, And Reference-Related Sites

www.initium.demon.co.uk/indsci3.htm

This site by Paul Steward is geared toward the science minded. It has links to several dictionaries and thesauri, including a NASA thesaurus. There are eight technical dictionaries.

It covers topics such as biotechnology, chemistry and computing, scientific quotations, law, and more. There are links to several libraries, including the British library and Gutenburg Project. Finally, the site provides links to other resources such as societies, institutes, agencies, patents, journals, magazines, and publishers, and even scientific software.

Directory Of Public Relations Agencies And Resources

www.webcom.com/impulse/prlist.html

If you need a public relations firm, check out this site. You can locate them by regions in the U.S. but also visit links to worldwide firms.

EcoLinking

www.themesh.com

More than 1,000 environmentally related Web sites are linked here on my environment site. EcoLinking was the first Net book designed to link the worldwide environmental community.

EducationWorld

www.education-world.com

This site maintains a searchable database of educational sites on the Net, including lesson plans, book reviews, and resources for school administrators. It is mostly designed for educators but provides a great source for more than 50,000 education sites.

Fedstats

www.fedstats.gov/index.html

Looking for statistics? Fedstats has linked just about every federal agency (more than 70) that compiles statistics into one nice searchable engine. You can also limit your search to a few selected agencies or look at regional info. If you want to search a specific agency, you can scroll the alphabetical listing.

Guide To Philosophy On The Internet

www.earlham.edu/~peters/philinks.htm

As the title implies, the site links to various philosophy-related Web sites, mailing lists and newsgroups, and more.

Historical Map Web Sites

www.lib.utexas.edu/Libs/PCL/Map_collection/Map_collection.html

If you are into maps and cartography, visit this site, which is linked to every map site in the world. The site is also part of a larger map site that includes sections on city, state, and country maps, weather maps, and more.

IBM Patent Server

http://patent.womplex.ibm.com/index.html

This site by IBM lets you search more than 26 years of U.S. Patent and Trademark Office (USPTO) patent descriptions as well as the last 17 years of images. The first entries date back to January 5, 1971. You can search, retrieve, and study more than two million patents. For some humor, check out the Gallery of Obscure Patents.

Internet Biodiversity Service

http://ibs.uel.ac.uk/ibs/

Learn the animal or plant kingdom and even make bio maps on this site. You'll find a lot of information on the fossil record.

Information Resources For Biology

www.library.ucsb.edu/subj/biol.html

You'll find a lot of links to biology resources, but this site also has sections on other sciences.

Internet Ancient History Sourcebook

www.fordham.edu/halsall/ancient/asbook.html

This is an intensively loaded site of ancient history links that cover the ancient Near East, Greece, and Rome, and much more. Tons of great sources are here for the scholar or anyone interested in the subject. Many of the sites let you view or read ancient text. This site is an education in itself.

Internet Directory Of Botany

www.botany.net/IDB/

You can find everything you want to know about botany here. Check out hundreds of links on every aspect of botany, arranged alphabetically or by subject.

Internet Guide To Electronics

http://webhome.idirect.com/~jadams/electronics/

This is a great beginner's site for learning the ins and outs of basic electronics.

Internet Guide To Mental Health Resources

www.med.nyu.edu/Psych/src.psych.html#index

Find hundreds of links to mental health resources on one page.

Internet Resources For Non-Profits

www.window.state.tx.us/tba/nonprof.html

This site contains several links to resources in grant making and other non-profit issues.

Internet TV Resource Guide

www.specialweb.com/tv/

Check out TV-related books, Web sites, shows, actors, commercial magazines, newsgroups, and networks.

LibWeb: Library Servers Via WWW

http://sunsite.berkeley.edu/Libweb/

There are thousands of libraries online—public, private, and academic. Using Telnet and other online catalog software, you can search card catalogs, request books through interlibrary loan, and even read full-text documents. LibWeb has links to libraries in more than 70 countries. The site is arranged by geographic location but also has a keyword-searchable engine. There are links to related library sites, too.

Mailing List And Other Internet Resources For Historians

www.hist.unt.edu/09-ml.htm

As the title says, this site is an eclectic array of resources for historians: FAQs, mailing lists, Web sites, and guides.

Mathematical Resources On The Internet

www.math.ufl.edu/math/math-web.html

This is a pretty substantial page full of math resources.

MedWeb Plus—Medical Resources

www.medwebplus.com

This is a complete biomedical site covering most medical areas. You can keyword search or browse a master list of 744 topics. A location list is also available. Check out medical information in 132 countries. All sites are rated.

Movie Sites

www.internetdatabase.com/movie.htm

Movie Sites is actually a page that lets you download a guide to more than 100 movie and cinema-related sites on the Net. It covers the Web, mailing lists and newsgroups, Gopher and FTP sites, and Telnet. You need a special program, IRD—Reader Notebook, to view the document. You can download it from the site, although it only works on Windows. If you have Virtual PC or SoftWindows, you should have no problem.

Newslink

http://ajr.newslink.org/

Newslink covers the mainstream media through analysis, features, and stories but has links to more than 9,000 newspapers, magazines, broadcasters, and news services around the world.

Neuroscience On The Internet

www.neuroguide.com

This is a dedicated site on the field of neuroscience. It contains links to labs, software, databases, guides, journals, clinical departments, and much more. The site is keyword searchable.

Online Reference Materials

www.web-savvy.com/reference.html

This site has links to various dictionaries, thesauri, and encyclopedias but also has a nice section on people directories: phone, address, and email locators. Related ZIP code and area code directories are also here. If you need cartographic information, seven linked sites allow you to create and find maps and locations.

OSHA Public Safety Internet Site

www.osha.gov/safelinks.html

This government site lists a number of organizations and sites dealing with occupational safety.

PC Industry URL List

http://members.aol.com/rbakerpc/ref/url.htm

This site offers an alphabetical list of computing and related companies that have Web sites. It contains more than 29,000 companies and 80,000 products.

Pharmacy Resources On The Net

www.pharm.su.oz.au/resources/

Here, you'll find links to Web sites, discussion groups, newsgroups, colleges, journals, and other pharmacy-related information.

Physics Resources (And Other Sciences)

www.sussex.ac.uk/library/pier/subjects.dir/sci.dir/physics.html

This site includes sciences in general, agriculture astronomy, biology and botany, chemistry, computing, electronics, engineering, environmental, genetics, geography, linguistics and language, math, medicine, psychology, and zoology.

Political Science Resources

http://libraries.rutgers.edu/rulib/socsci/polsci/polsci.html

If you are a political scientist or want to be, this site from the Rutgers University Library contains hundreds of links to poly sci sites. It features a lot of good sites with statistics and demographic material.

Preservation Internet Resources

www.ncptt.nps.gov/pir/

This site for the historic preservationist contains information and links to any kind of site on the Net that contains preservation material in archeology, architecture, historic landscapes, history, materials, and related topics. You can search by terms or phrases.

Resources In Science Studies

http://sshl.ucsd.edu/science_studies/

Find links to the history of science, technology, and medicine and other collections and bibliographies.

RxList—The Internet Drug Index

www.rxlist.com

Search this database by drug name or imprint code, and get all the information you need on that drug, such as generic and brand names, ingredients, and the category of drugs. Drug categories are explained in detail, along with side effects and reactions if known.

SciCentral

www.scicentral.com

This is a complete site for science news and links to all areas of science. Each large category of science is organized into subdisciplines.

School Libraries On The Web: A Directory

www.voicenet.com/~bertland/libs.html

If you are only interested in k-12 school libraries, or libraries maintained by school districts, visit this site with links in 20 countries. Linda Bertland, the librarian at Stetson Middle School in Philadelphia, Pennsylvania, maintains the site.

St. Joseph County Public Library List Of Public Libraries With WWW Services

http://sjcpl.lib.in.us/homepage/PublicLibraries/PubLibSrvsGpherWWW.html#wwwsrv

This site contains links to more than 570 public libraries around the world.

Statistics And Statistical Graphics Resources

www.math.yorku.ca/SCS/StatResource.html

The odds are great that if you have an interest in statistics, you will visit this page. It has links to hundreds of sites and information relating to all aspects and subdisciplines of statistics.

SynthZone

www.synthzone.com

If you are interested in MIDI sound, music clips, and audio in general, visit this great site. You can download tons of synthesized sounds here.

The Advertising Index

http://advweb.cocomm.utexas.edu/world/

This site links to hundreds of advertising resources from account planning to Web development tools. The site is maintained by the Department of Advertising at the University of Texas at Austin.

The Golden Pages: Links For Musicians On The WWW

www.sun.rhbnc.ac.uk/Music/Links/index.html

This site is for anyone interested in music resources on the Net. There are literally hundreds of links to music-related resources, including all types of music from all periods.

The Internet Public Library

www.ipl.org/about/

It was only a matter of time before some forward-thinking librarians got together and created a virtual library. The idea was an outgrowth of a 1995 graduate seminar from the School of Information and Library Studies at the University of Michigan. It now has a full-time staff.

The library is composed of four sections: Reference, Reading Room, Libraries and Librarians, and Young People. The more than 20,000 "holdings" are carefully selected, screened, and reviewed by a member of the library.

One feature is the Resource of the Week, where librarians review and link a new or outstanding online resource. There is also a special section for librarians. You have the option to browse a section, organized nicely by categories, or search by keyword in each section. Unfortunately, you have to be careful about the quality of the content of most Web sites, but this is one site where you can feel just as comfortable as you do when you visit your local hometown library.

The Law Engine

www.fastsearch.com/law/index.html

Before you hire a lawyer, check this site first. There are tons of legal decisions and case law on federal and state levels, legal references, links to law libraries, law enforcement, and education, and a great deal more.

The Virtual Earth

http://atlas.es.mq.edu.au/users/pingram/v_earth.htm

This site was created as a source of information for anyone interested in the earth sciences. You'll find a good number of links to Web sites, FTP and Gopher, List servers, and Telnet sites.

Thomas

http://thomas.loc.gov/home/thomas2.html

Thomas (named after Jefferson) is the Federal government's search engine for the people. If you want to keep track of bills or any kind of legislative matter in the House, Senate, or government agencies, this is the place to start looking. You can search bills by number or words and phrases. You can look up basic information about your legislators. You can read some historical documents such as the Declaration of Independence, the *Federalist Papers*, and more.

U.S. Geological Survey

www.usgs.gov

Learn all about the geology, biology, mapping, and hydrology of the United States. This site has a great education section that lets you download and make paper models of earthquakes, volcanoes, and more.

U.S. Library Of Congress

http://lcweb.loc.gov/

Perhaps the world's biggest library, the U.S. Library of Congress lets you search its many catalogs using a variety of criteria from simple word to complex searching. You can browse its catalog, looking for books published as early as 1898. Look through some specialized databases such as the Historic American Building Survey files, which document achievements in architecture, engineering, and design in the United States.

Voice Of The Shuttle: General Humanities Resources Page

http://humanitas.ucsb.edu/shuttle/general.html

Alan Liu has put on one page hundreds of links in the humanities. In addition to those links is information on broader issues such as copyright, critical thinking, style, and links to software downloads. There are some good tutorials on Web searching.

WebEc—World Wide Web Resources In Economics

www.helsinki.fi/WebEc/

If you want to learn about economics, this Finnish site has hundreds of links covering theory to economic history and much more. You can select large categories or visit subcategories, but most links are annotated.

WJB's Architecture Resources

www.ionet.net/~usarch/WTB-Service/Architecture/WTB-Architecture.html

This site doesn't seem to be updated regularly, but it has tons of links to architectural resources on the Net. It's a good place to start looking.

Women's Studies Information Sources

www.york.ac.uk/services/library/subjects/womenint.htm

This is a complete collection of women's studies material from the University of York. You can find links to Web sites, mailing lists and newsgroups, journals, bibliographies, and more. You'll also find a section listing women who have made contributions in various disciplines such as science and technology, writing, and the like.

Writing And Language Sources

www.waterboro.lib.me.us/writing.htm

If you want to be a writer, this site contains links to many sources that can help you with writing. There are links to style guides, language use studies, journals, copyright issues, grammar, forums, various English and foreign dictionaries, glossaries, and many other resources.

People Finders And Telephone Directories

Looking for anyone in the world? Chances are you can find them because many of the countries of the world have made their telephone directories available online. Some 50 countries are represented here:

Argentina

- Telecom Argentina White Pages—**www.telefonica.com.ar/**
- Telefonica—**www.telefonica.com.ar/GUIAS/Paginas.htm**
- The Argentine Business Exchange—**www.externa.com.ar**

Australia

- Telstra White Pages—**www.whitepages.com.au**
- The Australian Yellow Pages on the Internet—**www.yellowpages.com.au**

Austria

- Austrian Telephone Directory—**www.herold.co.at/herold/**

Belgium

- Belgian Yellow Pages—**www.advalvas.be/yellow/**
- Infobel 97—**www.infobel.be**
- The Belgian White Pages—**www.advalvas.be/white/**

Bermuda

- Bermuda Yellow Pages—**www.bermudayp.com**

Bulgaria

- Sofia Directory—**www.cit.net/services/phone.html**

Canada

- BCTel Yellow Pages (British Columbia)—**http://bcyellowpages.com**
- Canada 411—**www.canada411.sympatico.ca/**
- Electric Fingers (Alberta)—**www.alberta.com**
- Gold Pages—**www.goldguide.com**
- Infospace—**www.infospace.com**
- MTS Internet Yellow Pages (Manitoba)—**www.mtsdirectory.com**
- QCTel Yellow Pages (Quebec)—**www.pagesjaunesqctel.com**
- Sask Yellow Pages—**www.saskyellowpages.com**
- World W.I.D.E. Internet Directory—**http://wideinc.com/index.html?**

Chile

- Chile Electronic Yellow Pages—**www.chilnet.cl**

China

- China Internet Yellow Pages—**http://china.webshop.net**

Denmark

- Denmark Online—**www.krak.dk/**

Egypt

- Egypt Company Profiles—**http://163.121.10.42/amman/company/**

Finland

- Finland Yellow Pages—**www.keltaisetsivut.fi**

France

- France's Minitel—**www.epita.fr:5000/11/english.html**

Germany

- German Telephone—**www.gelbe-seiten.de**
- TeleAusKunft 1188 Online—**www.teleauskunft.de/**

Greece

- Hellenic Telephone Directories—**www.hellasyellow.gr**

Holland

- Dutch Yellow Pages—**www.markt.nl/dyp/info/inschrijven.html**

Hong Kong

- Hong Kong Internet Directory—**www.internet-directory.com**
- The Official Yellow Pages Business Directory—**www.yp.com.hk/eng/main.html**

Hungary

- Hungary Online Directory—**www.hungary.com/hudir**

Indonesia

- Indonesia Yellow Pages—**www.yellowpages.co.id**

Ireland

- Green Pages (Ireland)—**www.paddynet.ie/pages/**
- Kompass Ireland—**www.kompass.ie**

Israel

- Israel White Pages—**www.yellowpages.co.il/cgi-bin/w_main.pl**
- Yellow Pages—**www.yellowpages.co.il/?WELCOME**

Italy

- Italian Yellow Pages—**www.paginegialle.it/**
- Pagine Gialle On Line—**www.paginegialle.it/fe-docs/ricerca/index.htm**

Japan

- TownPage (English Directory in Japan)—**http://english.townpage.isp.ntt.co.jp/**

Korea

- Korea Directory—**http://korea.directory.co.kr/**

Latvia

- Business in the Baltic States—**www.binet.lv/english/database/select.htm**

Luxembourg

- Giel Säiten (Luxembourg Yellow Pages)—**www.editus.lu/html/gs.html**
- Wäiss Säiten (Luxembourg White Pages)—**www.editus.lu/html/ws.html**

Malaysia

- Telekom Yellow Pages (Malaysia)—**www.tpsb.com.my**

Mexico

- MexSearch Yellow Pages (Mexico)—**www.yellow.com.mx**

Netherlands

- Dutch Yellow Pages—**www.goudengids.nl**
- Faxguids—**www.faxgids.nl/**
- Telefoongids—**www.telefoongids.ptt-telecom.nl/index2.html**

New Zealand

- Telecom NZ Directory—**http://tdl.tols.co.nz**
- Yellow Pages—**www.yellowpages.co.nz**
- New Zealand Quick Reference—**www.Q.co.nz**

Norway

- Telnor Gulesider—**www.gulesider.no**

Pakistan

- Jamal's Yellow Pages—**www.jamal.com**

Paraguay

- Guitel Digital—**www.uninet.com.py/GUITEL/**

Poland

- The Business and Visitors Phone Book—**http://kasia.wonet.com.pl/samples/database/**

Portugal

- GUIANet in English—**www.guiao.pt/english/**
- GUIANet in Portuguese—**www.guiao.pt**
- Portugal Telecom—**www.telecom.pt/**

Romania

- Romanian Yellow Pages—**www.romanianyellowpages.com/~mozaic/**

Russia

- St. Petersburg Directory—**www.presscom.spb.ru/ind.asp**
- The Traveler's Yellow Pages Online—**www.infoservices.com**

Singapore

- SingaporeConnect—**http://sgconnect.asia1.com.sg/**
- Singapore Phone Book—**www.asiapages.com.sg/PhoneBook.htm**

Slovenia

- PIRS—**www.slo-knjiga.si**
- Telefonski imenik Slovenije—**http://s15.bigyellow.com/g_slovenia.html**

South Africa

- EasyInfo—**www.easyinfo.co.za/**
- South African Internet Directory—**http://os2.iafrica.com/w3/bus_dir.htm**

Spain

- Páginas Amarillas Multimedia—**www.paginas-amarillas.es**

Sri Lanka

- Lanka Business Web—**www.lanka.net/lisl2/yellow/**

Sweden

- Gula Sidorna—**www.gulasidorna.se/e_gula.html**
- Lexivision Company Information—**www.lexivision.se/eng/company/default2.htm**
- Svensk företagsinformation—**www.netg.se/Resources/Company/index.html.se?**

Switzerland

- Swiss FirmIndex Online—**www.firmindex.ch/scripts/firmindex/d/index.idc**

Taiwan

- Taiwan Online—**www.twn-online.com.tw**
- Taiwan Yellow Pages—**http://yellowpage.com.tw/main.htm**

Thailand

- Thailand Yellow Pages—**http://207.158.204.20/**

United Arab Emirates

- Kompass UAE—**www.kompass-uae.com**
- UAE Yellow Pages—**http://uae-ypages.com/html/1.htm**

United Kingdom

- Electronic Yellow Pages—**www.eyp.co.uk**
- Freepages—**www.freepages.co.uk**
- InBusiness—**www.inbusiness.co.uk**
- YELL!—**www.yell.co.uk**

United States Of America

- AT&T Toll Free Internet Directory—**www.att.net/dir800/**
- BigBook—**www.bigbook.com**
- BigYellow—**http://s16.bigyellow.com**
- Database America—**www.databaseamerica.com**
- GTE Superpages—**http://superpages.gte.com**
- Infospace—**www.infospace.com**
- Lookup USA—**www.lookupusa.com**
- Onvillage Yellow Pages—**www.onvillage.com**
- Pc411—**www.pc411.com/pc411v2.html**
- Switchboard USA White Pages—**www.switchboard.com**
- The Internet 800 Directory—**http://inter800.com**
- True Yellow—**www.trueyellow.com**

- US West—**http://yp.uswest.com**
- WhoWhere—**www.whowhere.com/phone.html**
- Worldwide Business Directories—**www.procom.it/import_export/wwdir_e.html**
- Yahoo People Search—**www.yahoo.com/search/people/**
- YellowNet—**www.yellownet.com**
- Yellow Pages on the Internet—**www.ypi.net**
- Zip2—**www.zip2.com**

Yugoslavia

- Yugoslavia.com—**www.yugoslavia.com/Phonebook/default.htm**

8 Feed Your iMac: How To Get Tons Of Free, Not So Free, And Commercial Software

Rittner's Computer Law: Most computer users don't think about backing up their software until the day they lose it.

You probably heard over the years from non-Mac users or PC zealots that there is no software for the Macintosh platform. There are also people who believe the Earth is flat and we never landed on the moon. In other words, an awful lot of people are not well informed.

Here are some facts to consider. Media Metrix (PC Meter) of New York recently published the 50 most used home software applications on the Wintel platform (computers running Windows software). Twenty four of the titles are cross-platform (they run on the Mac, too), and nineteen titles have similar software on the Mac side. As it turns out, 43 of 50 of the leading software titles that run on PCs with Windows also run on the Mac.

Further consider that with a PC software emulator such as Virtual PC or SoftWindows, you can run almost every Windows-based program on your iMac. Add that to the fact that there are more than 50 software emulators for your iMac, covering every operating system from CP/M to Nintendo 64. Finally, there are close to 2,000 software titles that only run on your Mac and not on any PC platform.

Now you know the real truth. You can run more software titles on the Mac than any personal computer. You get the picture. In this chapter, you are going to learn where to get all the Mac software you can ever use, much of it for free.

If you're a previous PC user, then Figure 8.1 will look familiar. By using Connectix Virtual PC software you can play just about any PC game or software program on your iMac.

Figure 8.1
Solitaire.

Software Flavors

Three types of software are available for your iMac:

- *Commercial software*—This is software you pay for that may cost anywhere from a few dollars to thousands of dollars.
- *Shareware*—Shareware is software you use for a given period of time and then pay for if you decide to keep it.
- *Freeware*—Freeware doesn't cost you a thing unless you want to make a donation to the author.

Commercial

Commercial software is generally software you buy in a box, although purchasing it over the Net is becoming popular. A recent study by NPD's SofTrends, a company that tracks consumer purchasing and behavior, revealed that 11 million online subscribers have acquired software through the Internet, accounting for 55 percent of total households online.

Commercial software usually comes packaged (sometimes over-packaged) and includes printed manuals. The software is usually in the form of floppy disks, or more likely a CD-ROM. Often, the manuals are on the CD-ROM in text or Adobe Acrobat format instead of printed and bound. From an environmental standpoint, that's good. From a curl-up-on-the-couch-and-read standpoint, that's bad.

Commercial software comes with some form of warranty, and depending on where you buy it, you might not be able to return it. A commercial software purchase usually includes a period of technical support via phone, fax, email, or Web access. Good commercial software is constantly updated and revised, and you might have to pay for those updates.

One of the most interesting aspects of the software industry is licensing. Although you have purchased the software with your hard-earned cash, you technically do not own it. You are licensing it from the company. That means you cannot give copies to your friends, which is called pirating. Pirating is illegal, and you don't want to be a pirate unless your name is Blackbeard. Pirating means you're a thief.

There is good reason for not pirating software. It often takes years to develop a good software program, and a company or individual (often both are the same) wants to make some money on that investment. If you give copies to everyone, there is no reward for the developer. They can't feed their kids, or dogs, if they have them. Add to that the months of all-nighters writing code, drinking diet soda, and eating candy bars, not to mention the cost of producing the package, CD-ROMs or disks, manuals, distribution, and support; it's only fair that you pay for the software. Don't pirate. Imagine if you spent two years composing a beautiful painting of your local landmark, only to have your cheesy neighbor make color copies at a local Kinkos and sell them at the mall without your permission. Yeah, I would be mad too.

An old argument for pirating was that software was too expensive, it was buggy, or it didn't do everything it was supposed to do. A lot of those arguments are true. However, today most software companies have full working demos of their product so you can test drive them to see whether you like it before you shell out your cash.

Commercial software tends to be a bit more expensive than shareware, but you often get more for your money (not always).

Shareware

Shareware is an amazing concept. An individual or group of programmers spends months, sometimes years, creating a neat and useful software program. Instead of selling the rights to a commercial company, they put the program on the Internet, or computer bulletin boards, and hope that you will download it, use it, like it, and pay for it. How's that for faith in humanity? About 1 percent of all shareware is paid. Scott Watson of Red Ryder fame (an early Mac telecommunications program) is one of the few shareware developers who made money. The fact that Scott had a new version almost every week may have helped his popularity and bank account. You could count on updates. Some products that started as shareware spun into commercial companies. CE Software is one such case. An early software trio of shareware programs—MockWrite, MockTerminal, and MockPrint—was on the desktops of every Mac Plus in the early 1980s.

Some shareware programs are just plain junk and don't deserve to take up digital space. Shareware is a crap shoot. It may be great, or it may stink. Most of it is good. Some shareware is far superior to any commercial equivalent. Unlike commercial software, shareware does not carry the same warranties as commercial software. Even if you pay for it, you might not get support. You might also get better support from a shareware group than you get from the big commercial corporate companies. Most shareware developers take their products personally and want them to be the best.

One other problem with shareware is reliability and future support. The author might decide to abandon the product because he or she did not make enough profit or changes careers. That can be frightening if you have your entire business data on the program and you can't export it! The version you pay for may never get updated. The software may be so buggy that it doesn't work when a new version of the system comes out for the Mac. Of course, all this could be said about commercial programs as well.

Looking on the positive side, the shareware software might be so good that it continues to work on every new revision of the system software that's released by Apple. McSink, a little text editor desk accessory almost as old as the Mac itself, works to this day, even on a PowerMac. The software hasn't been updated in years.

Perhaps the biggest confusion over shareware is the way it's distributed. If you get a CD-ROM chock full of shareware, such as with a book or from a retail establishment, you did not pay for the software with that purchase. You paid for the book or disk. Shareware developers often give permission to include their work on a CD-ROM or disk that accompanies a book or CD-ROM compilation in the hopes that the wider distribution will allow them to make more money on their work. Remember that if you use shareware for any length of time, you should pay the shareware fee, which is often a fraction of the cost of commercial products.

Freeware

Take everything I said about shareware and include it here with the exception that freeware is just that—free. No strings attached. Of course, there are no warranties either. It may not work. It might do strange things to your computer. Freeware has no support, often not even an email address for complaints. You get what you pay for. However, a great deal of good freeware is in the Mac universe. Being free doesn't mean it isn't good.

Freeware has interesting forms such as beerware, postcardware, and emailware. I like to think of freeware as egoware. It certainly helps the psyche feel good to know that people are using your software program. Download counts are more important than bank accounts for many freeware developers. The bottom line is that you shouldn't expect much from the author of freeware in terms of support. The quality and future of the product is as good as the author wants it to be.

Where Do You Get The Goodies?

In 1985, the entire monthly meeting of my local Mac user group (MECCA in Albany, New York) centered around the first shareware game, Social Climber. We spent hours playing and talking about it and wondering whether there would ever be any more games for the Mac. At that time, there really wasn't any software for the Mac. In those early Mac days, you could count on your local Apple user group to obtain the latest news and copies of shareware or freeware to distribute to hungry members. In fact, that was the only place you could get free software.

Today, there are multiple ways to get software for your iMac. The Internet, user groups, subscription-based services, mail-order companies, magazines, and even local computer stores carry commercial brand software as well as shareware. It's a billion dollar plus industry.

The most convenient way to get software is to download it off the Internet. Downloading is easy. All the sites in this chapter allow you to use your Web browser to download files to your computer. Some sites allow you to use FTP or visit Gopher sites for access. A note of caution: Never download a program, especially shareware or freeware, from the Internet without a virus checker on your computer.

Catching A Virus

No, not you, your iMac. Unfortunately, some malicious programmers want to hurt your computer or mess up your data. They write software programs that will erase your hard drive, delete files, or replicate itself so it bogs down the operation of your computer. These nasty programs go by the names Trojan horse, worm, or virus, but whatever they're called, getting one can give you hours of grief.

Fortunately, not a lot of nasties run around the Mac community. On last count, or so have appeared in the last 15 years, but only one or two are malicious enough to do damage. (There are hundreds on the PC platform.) But have no fear! Several freeware, shareware, and commercial virus detectors and eradicators will do the job of keeping your iMac virus-free.

One of the most popular and free virus killers is Disinfectant by John Norstand. Although this software is no longer under development (John stopped working on it in May 1998), it works on stopping and killing most of the Mac viruses running around prior to 1998. You can download it from most of the sites mentioned later in this chapter. Besides allowing you to scan and disinfect, the program will install a small software program called an init (short for initialization file) to your system folder. Inits are those little icons that run across the bottom of your monitor when you boot up your iMac. This particular init will monitor your hard drive and warn you if it finds anything suspicious.

Commercial virus killers such as SAM or Virex also can do the job nicely. As new bugs enter the community, these commercial companies (and the shareware developers) send out patches or updates to their software to kill them.

Mac viruses fall into four categories: autostart worms, system attackers, macro viruses, and hypercard viruses. They all behave a bit differently, but the end result is the same, to either kill your data or hardware or to harass you.

The excellent Web site MacVirus (**www.macvirus.com**) is a one-stop site that can give you the most information about every Mac virus. You can download free and shareware virus killers and updates from the commercial products there and also read reviews of the various virus-killer software products.

Watch Where You Download

I never download programs from the Net directly to my hard drive. Instead I have a Zip disk that acts as my Net download receiver. After I download the programs to the Zip disk, I run Disinfectant and other checkers on the Zip disk and check for viruses. In 15 years of using a Mac, I have never had a virus (knock on wood).

You should always be cautious. The commercial online services America Online, CompuServe, and others maintain that their software is checked for viruses before they are made available for downloading. This is true for the most part, but even they have been fooled. Recently, *MacAddict*, a great Mac magazine that includes a CD-ROM packed with goodies with each issue had a nasty on the CD-ROM. It can happen to the best of us. Get a virus checker. It's better to be safe than sorry.

Ready, Set, Download

Thousands of software programs are on the Net. In fact, there are so many programs, you will never in your wildest dreams download or use but a fraction of them. The average computer owner uses only three or four programs regularly. A study by Media Metrix in 1997 revealed that PC owners use only 13 percent of the software they own during an average month.

Because you are an iMac user and obviously above average, the following sites will give you hundreds of choices to download.

BrowserWatch

http://browserwatch.internet.com/plug-in/plug-in-mac.html

A plug-in is a little application that helps your Web browser do cool things such as show video, play sounds, and display animation and other multimedia effects. There are hundreds of plug-ins. This site presents all the available plug-ins for your Mac on one easy-to-use page. Just find the plug-in you want, click it, and visit the location for downloading. There is a message area where you can discuss plug-ins as well.

DOWNLOAD.COM For The Mac

www.download.com

This software site maintained by c/net, an excellent overall computer news Web site, contains thousands of files organized by category (and subcategories), or you can type a keyword and it will find the program for you. There are lists for the most popular, top-10, new file titles. The page also includes reviews and news. When you click a category, each topic has a feature story or software pick, a nice touch. Once you find the file, you see the usual information such as size, version, and description. My only complaint is that you have to click too many windows from start to finish (five) to finally download the file.

Emulation.net

http://emulation.net/

Emulation software lets you run other operating systems and the software that was designed for them on your Mac. John Stiles is the king of emulation. He created Emulation.net around four years ago, although it has only been called Emulation.net for a year and a half. John is a college student in Berkeley and started the page so he could learn more about emulation himself, as well as share his collection with anyone interested in emulating other operating systems on the Mac platform. He says he had heard about a lot of emulators but could never find them, so he set out to make a complete emulator collection, if he could. He did. You can find the following emulators on his site: Amstrad CPC, Amstrad PCW, Apple I, Apple II, Apple III, Atari 800, Atari ST, BBC Micro, Commodore 64, Commodore Amiga, CP/M, Edsac, IBM PC, IBM Series 1, Macintosh,

MIPS, R2000, MO5, MSX, Oric, PDP-8/E, SAM Coupé, Sinclair QL, Sinclair ZX81, Sinclair ZX-Spectrum, Thomson TO8, TI99, TRS-80, TRS-80 Color Computer, VAX, VIC-20, Atari 2600, Atari 5200, Colecovision, Intellivision, MESS (multi-console), Nintendo, Nintendo 64, PC Engine/ TurboGrafx, Sega Master System, Sega Genesis, Super Nintendo, TB-303/ TR-808, Z80 Processor, 6502 Processor, 68000 Processor, 6809 Processor, Vector-based, MacMAME, Space Invaders, Atari Lynx, Nintendo Gameboy, Sega Game Gear, HP 48, Magic Cap, PalmPilot, TI Calculators.

Many of the emulators come with software to run. As an example, the TRS-80, one of my first computers (now collecting dust in the attic), has a ton of software you can run, including software for the Model I, II, III, IV, Model 100, Color, and more.

Many of the emulators have versions for both PowerMacs and older Macs, as well as source code. Figure 8.2, **Emulation.net**, proves that you can run more than one operating system on the Mac platform. Next time your PC friends tell you there is no software for the Mac, direct them to this great site.

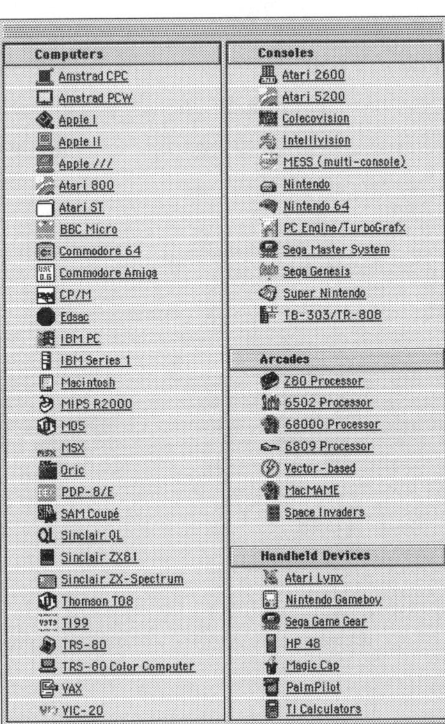

Figure 8.2
Emulation.net
Web page.

Filez

www.filez.com

Filez is a search engine for FTP sites. Similar to a Web search engine, Filez searches more than 7,000 FTP servers weekly giving you a convenient one stop shopping list of more than 75 million files. You can search by categories and even PC files if you need them. The resulting list from your search gives you the links to wherever the files are located for easy downloading.

Info-Mac Archives

http://hyperarchive.lcs.mit.edu/HyperArchive.html

One of the best sites for getting Mac software, Info-Mac is sponsored by MIT's Laboratory for Computer Science. You can keyword search for a file or browse through a list of software categories. You can subscribe to the digest and find out what is posted (see Chapter 5). Walnut Creek Software (**www.cdrom.com**) periodically publishes a three-disc CD-ROM set of the Info-Mac Archives with more than 1,700 files for around $40.

Info-Mac Archives is one of the best free sites to download the latest shareware and freeware for your iMac, as shown in Figure 8.3.

Jumbo

www.jumbo.com

Here is another great site that boasts 300,000 shareware and freeware programs arranged in 18 categories. You can keyword search the whole database or by category. All platforms are supported.

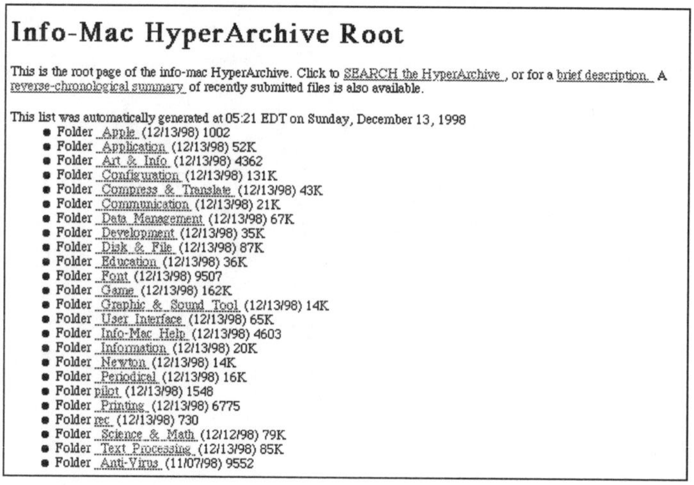

Info-Mac HyperArchive Root

This is the root page of the info-mac HyperArchive. Click to SEARCH the HyperArchive, or for a brief description. A reverse-chronological summary of recently submitted files is also available.

This list was automatically generated at 05:21 EDT on Sunday, December 13, 1998

- Folder Apple (12/13/98) 1002
- Folder Application (12/13/98) 52K
- Folder Art & Info (12/13/98) 4362
- Folder Configuration (12/13/98) 131K
- Folder Compress & Translate (12/13/98) 43K
- Folder Communication (12/13/98) 21K
- Folder Data Management (12/13/98) 67K
- Folder Development (12/13/98) 35K
- Folder Disk & File (12/13/98) 87K
- Folder Education (12/13/98) 36K
- Folder Font (12/13/98) 9507
- Folder Game (12/13/98) 162K
- Folder Graphic & Sound Tool (12/13/98) 14K
- Folder User Interface (12/13/98) 65K
- Folder Info-Mac Help (12/13/98) 4603
- Folder Information (12/13/98) 20K
- Folder Newton (12/13/98) 14K
- Folder Periodical (12/13/98) 16K
- Folder pilot (12/13/98) 1548
- Folder Printing (12/13/98) 6775
- Folder rec (12/13/98) 730
- Folder Science & Math (12/12/98) 79K
- Folder Text Processing (12/13/98) 85K
- Folder Anti-Virus (11/07/98) 9552

Figure 8.3

Info-Mac Archives Web page.

Mac On The Net

www.moxienet.com/macnet/

Because you are going to be spending a lot of time on the Net, check here regularly for the latest versions of Net software for your iMac. Download the latest versions of archivers, email clients, Telnet programs, FTP clients, newsreaders, utilities, audio and video programs, graphic applications, video players, chat clients, helpers, and more. You can find programs by searching an alphabetical listing or by choosing a category listing if you are not sure what a program does.

Mac.org

www.mac.org/

This Web site gives you the following categories to choose from: Audio/Video, Games, Graphics, Internet, System, Utilities, and Updates. Each category lists the files with a short description, but when you select one, you get a full illustrated review. In addition, you get information on how large the downloadable file is, plus the ability to download the selected file. This site doesn't contain thousands of files here, but rather files carefully selected by the site's owner. Both shareware and commercial demos are presented. Finally, sections on Apple and miscellaneous Stuff round out the site.

MacShare.com

www.macshare.com

This site has several categories of files for downloading. Each downloadable file has information such as version number and date, size of file, whether it is freeware, shareware, or a demo, the home page of the developer if one exists, and a description of the file. A mini review follows all of that. Included on the site are a tips page with columns and a resource page that lists Web links, news, graphics resources, and more.

Shareware Author Index

http://mini.net/sax/

The Shareware Author Index (SAX) database contains about 4,500 products by more than 2,000 shareware authors. You can search by platform: Mac, OS2, Windows, and so on. I have one problem with the site. Even though it says there are more than 51 Mac products, it does not allow you to see the rest after the initial hit is presented. You can download a standalone version of the database, and although it only works in Windows, it should work if you are using Virtual PC or SoftWindows.

Shareware.com

www.Shareware.com

Maintained by c/net this site contains more than 250,000 files for most computer platforms, including the Mac. Search the database or click the title of the most popular software archives such as Aminet, CD-Games, Hobbes-OS2, Info-Mac, Linux, Sim-Win95, OS2, Win3, and others.

University Of Michigan (UMICH) Mac Archive

http://www-personal.umich.edu/~sdamask/umich-mirrors/

This site is one of the most popular Mac archives, and several mirror sites have been set up to relieve congestion. You can access the site via the Web, FTP, or Gopher. On sites such as this one and others that have FTP or Gopher access, it is wise to download the index file first so you can get a description of the files.

University Of Texas (utexas) Mac Archive

http://wwwhost.ots.utexas.edu/mac/main.html

This site features another great collection from the University of Texas. Files are organized in categories or search indexes by author, date, or product.

Apple Stuff

You can obtain the latest system software updates for your iMac directly from Apple's own support sites. On the Web, visit **http://til.info.apple.com/swupdates.nsf/search**. When using FTP, log on to **ftp.info.apple.com**.

By visiting the Apple Software Updates Web page periodically, you can make sure you are using the latest versions of Apple software, as shown in Figure 8.4.

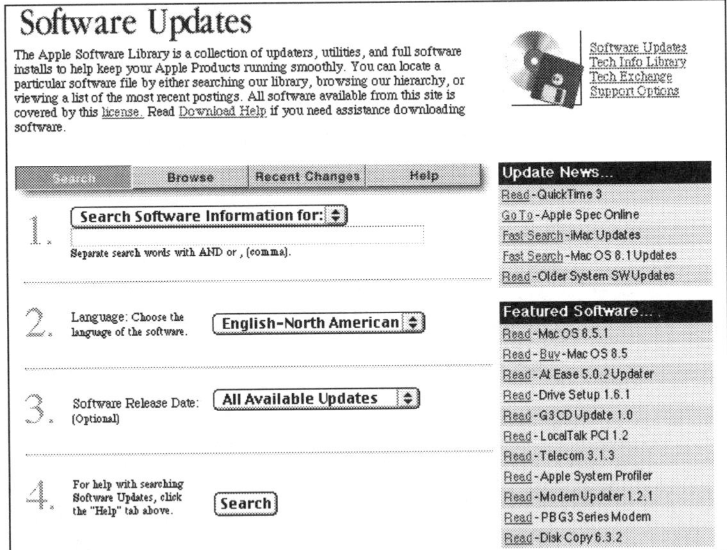

Figure 8.4
Apple Software Updates Web page.

Commercial Software Vendors

Most commercial software and hardware manufacturers have Web sites where you can download the latest software updates, learn about new products, and get technical support. This section lists a few sites that will steer you to the Mac vendor you need.

Companies Online

www.companiesonline.com

You can locate companies with Web sites in the area of wholesale computer equipment, retail computer hardware and software, computer programming services, software publishing, computer system integration, computer data processing, computer information storage and retrieval, computer maintenance and repair, and other computer services. Find them by looking through those categories, or keyword search on title, city, state, URL, and even stock symbol if they have one. Search results give you the Web address, DUN rating (credit rating by Dunn & Bradstreet), phone numbers, and more.

International Manufacturers Of Computer And Communications Products (Hardware And Software)

www.compinfo.co.uk/cmhard.htm

This is one of the most complete lists of software and hardware Web sites on the Net. Lists are in alphabetical order to make searching easy.

Surf Point

www.surfpoint.com/Business--Companies_Industries--Software.html

Surf Point has an alphabetical listing of 242 commercial software companies and their Web sites.

America's Biggest 100 Software Companies

www.best.com/~valley/top100am_vendors.html

Here is an alphabetical list with links to the Web sites of the top-100 vendors. You can also view a list by sales figures.

Confusing Catalogs

A major annoyance of mail-order catalogs is the lack of any real organization in the way they are laid out. Sometimes, it's difficult to find products. Because mail-order companies all have toll-free phone numbers, I simply call them and ask whether they have the product I'm looking for.

Mail-Order Companies Online

I purchase the majority of my hardware and software from mail-order catalogs. With mail order, you can save 20 percent or more on products, you often do not pay for the shipping, and you do not pay for sales tax. The best reason is that some mail-order companies stand behind the product and often go one step further to keep you a satisfied customer. Not all of them will, but most do.

There are a large number of mail-order companies. I recommend only a few, although I have ordered from a good number of them. My recommendations are based on 15 years of trial and error. All of my choices are similar in pricing of both hardware and software, often separated only by pennies, and have good delivery and return policies. Each has a Web site so you can order online, but most are open 24 hours for phone orders. I would rather talk to someone before I order.

Most of these companies also have a PC division; for example, MacConnection has a PCConnection, MacWarehouse has a PCWarehouse, and so on. If you need to purchase PC software, simply ask for that toll-free number.

MacConnection, as shown in Figure 8.5, is one of the best mail-order houses for buying Mac products. As a member of a Mac user group, you get free UPS ground shipping.

Figure 8.5 *MacConnection's Web page.*

Chip Merchant

www.thechipmerchant.com

The Chip Merchant isn't a software company, but it is the best place to buy memory for your iMac. I have always found that Chip Merchant has the best prices overall and stands behind its product for life. Keep your receipt. I once returned a memory module that went bad, and it was more than three years old.

Ask First

When you order a product, be sure to ask whether it is currently in stock. Sometimes, mail-order companies will charge your credit card and not have the item in stock. It may take several weeks before they get a shipment and you get the product. Why should they have your money before you get your product?

ClubMac

www.clubmac.com

ClubMac, another California-based company, also publishes a hard-copy catalog as well as the Web site. Call on the toll-free at (800) 258-2622.

MacConnection

www.macconnection.com

MacConnection was one of the first companies to support the Mac community and has continued to do so for 15 years. Good prices and good support have been its trademark. Although it does not have as large an offering as other companies, it will give you free ground shipping for any product if you are a member of a Mac user group. In 1985, I was the user group editor for the now defunct but not forgotten

MACazine, one of the first national Mac magazines. I approached MacConnection for this special offer for members of Apple user groups. It continues to this day to honor it!

If you don't believe MacConnection is an early supporter of Apple, check out the toll-free number: (800) MAC-5472. MacConnection's catalog averages 75 pages and is mailed monthly, but you are not inundated with multiple copies as you are with some of the other mail-order companies.

MacMall

www.cc-inc.com/home.asp

MacMall is another mail-order company that advertises that it will beat any price on Mac hardware. It often has some good incentive deals. The catalog averages 75 pages. The toll-free number is (800) 222-2808.

MacTreasures

www.mactreasures.com

One thing you probably noticed when you visited a large computer superstore is the lack of Mac software on the shelves. Also, many of the mail-order catalogs do not carry every piece of Mac-related software, especially software that may be geared for a small segment of the population, a specialized industry, and so on.

MacTreasures tries to take up the slack. It specializes in having or getting that software that may not be so easy to find. If it doesn't have what you need, it will try to find it for you.

MacWarehouse

www.warehouse.com/macwarehouse

I find MacWarehouse to be a few pennies more expensive than the rest, but it offers a good assortment of Mac products as well as good support and fast delivery. It does not have a special deal for members of Mac user groups. Actually, the employees aren't sure whether they do or not; it depends on whom you talk to. Some salespeople will give you the free delivery after talking to a supervisor; most will not. They really should develop a policy one way or the other because it is annoying. I have had a few problems in returning some items, but overall, MacWarehouse is an excellent company.

MacWarehouse's catalog averages 100 pages, and once you are on its mailing list, you will get one or two or three of them often. Did I say often? You can call MacWarehouse at (800) 622-6222 and request a copy or visit the Web site.

Other Ways To Get Software

As I mentioned earlier, some computer magazines such as *MacAddict* publish monthly CD-ROMs with their printed magazine that contain new shareware, freeware, and commercial demos. Companies such as Walnut Creek Software (**www.cdrom.com**) produce collections of shareware on CD-ROM for a small fee. Mac user groups often publish a Disk of the Month or CD-ROM collection loaded with new shareware offerings. If you do not belong to a local Mac user group, join now. If you visit many of the Mac-oriented Web sites mentioned throughout this book, you will never be in the position of not having enough software for your iMac.

9 Technical Support And Maintenance For Your iMac

Rittner's Computer Law: Computer prices are guaranteed to drop within two weeks after you purchase your computer.

Nothing in this world is perfect. Human cells mutate, answering machines garble messages, and sometimes, I can't get through to Pizza Hut. Yes, even my iMac sometimes doesn't do what I want it to do. Once in a while, computers simply don't want to work.

Fortunately, most of the problems facing Macintosh users are not fatal. You can usually recover from a system crash or freeze. If your computer crashes, you don't have to back up your entire hard drive and reformat it or lose everything that's on it—most of the time. Even a hard drive failure can often be restored. Of course, if you have a mechanical defect in your hard drive or CD-ROM drive or your monitor blows, it's a different story, but most Mac problems stem from software conflicts.

Macs have a pretty good history of reliability. Only twice in 15 years have I found myself in a situation where I could not recover my data. I had three hard drives crash within minutes of each other during a summer hot spell. Hard drives have a certain temperature tolerance, or intolerance, as I found out.

Theoretically, you should never lose information if you back up your important data on a daily basis. Most people do not back up at all, let alone daily. I don't know why. You brush your teeth every day, don't you?

Your iMac is upgradable. You can add more system or video memory (unless your iMac's video memory is at full capacity) and a bigger hard drive and connect more than 100 peripherals, thanks to the Universal Serial Bus (USB). New third-party products appear every day for your iMac.

In case you ever do need help, especially after the Apple one year warranty, you still have access to a great deal of support, thanks to the wonderful Mac community. Many Web sites are devoted to providing free technical support. The bottom line is you will rarely hear horror stories similar to the tales of the Wintel side that I hear almost daily.

This chapter explains how to troubleshoot problems if you have any, how to fix things when they go zonk, how to perform basic maintenance, and where to go on the Net to get good technical help. This chapter does not replace the emergency handbook that came with your iMac. You should study it thoroughly. The manual offers many great tips; you didn't buy this book to get the exact same information. Also, be sure to visit the Apple Web site (**www.apple.com**), which has a great help section.

No External Bootup

You cannot boot the iMac from an external USB drive.

Screen Freezes, Computer Crashes, And Other Digital Problems!

If your iMac screen freezes, or you get the dreaded dialog box with a System Error and the Bomb, don't panic—at least, not yet. Often, a restart will take care of the problem. By simultaneously pressing the Command+Option+Esc keys, you should quit the program and return to the desktop. If that does not work, you have to force a restart of your computer.

The first release of the iMac, model M6709LL/A (with System 8.1 preinstalled), has a slight problem. Previous models of Macintosh computers allowed you to force a restart by pressing the Command+Control+Keyboard Power Button combo. The emergency manual that came with the iMac tells you to do that, but it doesn't work in the first release of the iMac. They fixed it in the second revision, model M6709LL/B (bundled with OS 8.5).

For the owners of the first model, the Apple-recommended way to restart your computer is to perform surgery, sort of. You insert a paper clip in the reset hole that is located between the modem and Ethernet ports on the right side of your iMac. You need to open the panel door to do that. That's a pain.

The easiest way, for right-handed folks, is simply to take your right hand and pull out the power plug on the right-back side of the computer. Plug it back in, wait 30 seconds, and press the power key on your keyboard. It's a sure bet that you'll lose whatever you were working on by doing this, but I make a habit of pressing the Command+S (Save) keys every few seconds while I'm working as a safety precaution. Even when my Mac freezes once in a while, I hardly ever lose information. Many software programs allow you to set the interval for automatic saving, and some programs actually write a backup file automatically while you work (WordPerfect and Microsoft Word do this).

Never let it be said that entrepreneurship is dead. Shortly after the issue of the reset button became public, two companies offered a solution. Power Port, a Japanese company, has a plastic reset switch that fits over the reset hole, but I cannot find a place to buy it. If you visit **www.imacbutton.com**, you will find an enterprising solution for $10. A disgruntled iMac user designed a clever reset button that attaches over the reset hole.

Most of the common crashes on your iMac are due to faulty software. It can be caused by extension conflicts, incorrect drivers for your hard drive, or a corrupt preference file, to name a few culprits. Software viruses can also be a culprit although in the Mac community there are not a lot of them.

Brownouts Are Not Fun

The August 1998 issue of *iMac iNfo* says that brownouts can put the iMac into a coma. To alleviate this problem, purchase an uninterruptible power supply (UPS).

Preference Files

If you look in your system folder, which is equivalent to looking under the hood of your car, you will see a folder called preferences. It contains many folders and files. These preference files are important for your software to work correctly. Not all preferences are stored there; some applications like to keep their preference files in the same place as the application. I suppose it's like keeping your kids at home.

Preference files keep track of what software programs are supposed to do for you, such as call up the phone numbers for a bulletin board you visit regularly, make sure your desktop is blue, set Charcoal as the font the Finder uses, and so on.

Every time you change a setting, a preference file is updated or a new one is created. Once in a while, these files get corrupted and screw up everything. If you suspect that a preference file is the culprit, just throw it in the trash can and empty it, but make sure the application it belongs to is closed before you try. When you start your software program, a new preference file will be created. You might have to reset your software settings (because the old settings are now in virtual heaven), and you might have to reinstall the original software application itself (but usually not).

Even under the best conditions, there are times when you can't simply move the preference file directly to the trash can. You'll see a dialog box that says the file is in use, and you can't delete it. I've removed the preference file from the system folder altogether, placed it somewhere on the hard drive, and then restarted my Mac. This process also creates a new preference file. (Be sure to throw the old one in the trash.) If that doesn't work, then reinstall the application software.

The trash-can fix won't work with the Finder's own preference file. Because the Finder is always "on," it is difficult to throw its preference file in the trash and empty it. When you reboot, the Finder will go into the preference file, even if it's in the trash can, and look for some of the instructions to use.

A surefire way to work around this limitation is to restart your iMac from the system CD-ROM that comes bundled with your iMac (remember to hold down the C key when booting up) and drag the Finder preference file from the CD-ROM over to your system folder on the hard drive. A dialog box will tell you there is a preexisting file, but just click OK. That should do the trick.

Yank It!

Download Yank (**http://tucows.wau.nl/mac/adnload/dlyankmac.html**), a $15 shareware application that you can use to uninstall an application and all the files created by the application by moving them to the trash. You can also use it to scan your preference folder and to remove old preferences by moving outdated files to the trash.

Who's In The Driver's Seat?

Another common problem Mac users experience comes from not updating your driver software. Every time Apple releases a new update of the system software, there is new software for the hard drive. Your hard drive needs special software instructions that lets it interact correctly with the software and operating system. If you don't update your drivers when you update the system software, you are asking for problems. With Apple's newest Install program, updating the drivers are part of the process, making it easy as pie. Although you can override that part, don't do it!

The only exception to this override rule is if you are using a third-party driver other than Apple's. If you're using a hard drive that is not an Apple hard drive, perhaps, a second external hard drive for backup, then you must use that third-party's driver software. Although it's possible to overwrite it with Apple's drivers (with version 1.3 or better), it's strongly suggested that you don't. You can probably fit a Ford engine into a Mercedes, but will it run perfectly?

A Crowded Highway

One of the greatest features of the Mac operating system is the ability to add mini applications or helper files during startup that make using the Mac fun as well as productive. These files are known as extensions and control panels. Both are automatically installed when you turn on your Mac; that is, they load into memory. Extensions are usually preconfigured; they know what they're supposed to do. Control panels allow you to set certain functions. Some examples of these are virus checkers, drivers that let your Mac recognize a particular scanner, a calculator, and even a screen saver such as After Dark. Like a crowded highway, if you have a lot of extensions, one or two may eventually run into each other and cause a traffic accident. This translates into your computer not starting properly.

This glitch will happen after you install a new software program when the new extension conflicts with a preexisting one (or vice versa), or it may wait until you write the last sentence of your doctoral thesis.

If it happens immediately after installing a new program, that's a clue that the new program's extension may be the culprit, but it's not a sure bet. Restart your iMac, but hold down the Shift key while you reboot. This turns off all extensions, and your iMac should boot up, although some of the functions will be disabled.

Under the Apple menu, in the Control Panels section, select Extensions Manager. This control panel from Apple lets you turn on and off extensions and create special sets of extensions. Figure 9.1 shows you what the Extensions Manager looks like.

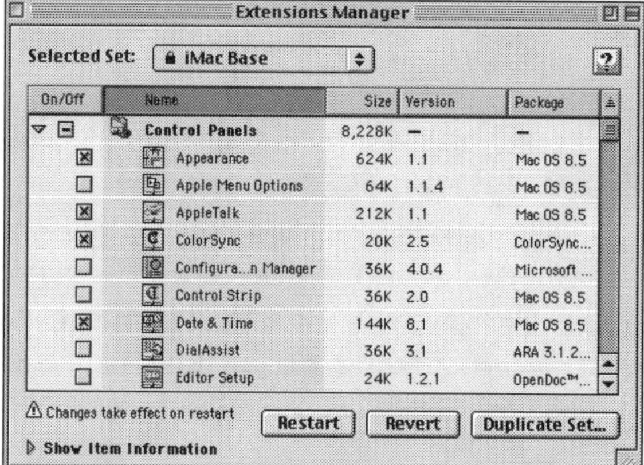

Figure 9.1

The Extensions Manager lets you turn on and off extensions.

Look for the new extension that was just installed, and deselect it by clicking the checkbox to the left. Reboot the machine. If it boots correctly, then the problem is your new extension. If it still does not boot correctly, go back to the Extensions Manager and select the iMac Base option. This is the minimum number of extensions needed to start your machine. If it does not boot after that, you might have to perform a clean install of the system software or conduct a labor-intensive trial-and-error search.

A trial-and-error search includes moving all the extensions out of their folder, adding one or two back at a time to the preexisting folder, and then restarting. You continue to move files in and out until it fails to restart; by then, you know the name of the offending file. Or create a folder called disabled extensions, move all the extensions into it, and move one or two at a time back into the extensions folder, restart, add more, etc., until you find the culprit.

Another possible solution is to hold down the Shift key while restarting the iMac. If your machine continues to start and makes it to the desktop, go into your system folder. Find the extension folder, grab the new extension file, and take it out of the system folder. Restart the machine. If it starts up fine, you know the file was the problem. Because the conflict can come from the way the extensions are loading (they load alphabetically), you can rearrange the order in which they load. Click the new extension to highlight it. You will notice that the area where the name is located blackens, and you can insert a new name, or instead, just place a space, a tilde (~), the letter Z, or other character before the name. Then, restart. If the iMac loads fine, then the problem is solved. If not, you might have to do a clean install of the system software.

If you do indeed have a conflicting extension and you need it for the software to work, contact the software company or visit its Web site to check whether it has a newer version. This step is mandatory if you upgraded your system software to a newer version. The software company might not have had time to release an update or even know it conflicts with the newer system software. It's wise to wait a month or two after a new system software update comes to market. You can read about the problem files from others who did not wait. Avoid the hassles if you can.

Of course, as your Mac experience broadens, you will collect a lot of extensions. There is a great program called Extension Overload (**www.mir.com.my/~cmteng**) that you can download or read online. This program contains a list of all the system extensions and control panels that you can find in the system folder of every Macintosh, including the iMac. The program conveniently lists them by name and explains what they do. This allows you to decide whether to keep a certain control panel or extension. Additionally, Extension Overload lists Mac error codes and gives you Easter eggs (little hidden surprises in the software).

Watch That Resolution

If you have the original iMac with only 2Mb of video RAM, be careful when you switch the resolution on the fly. If you choose millions of colors in the 1024 x 768 mode, your screen will go blank and you will have to restart your iMac. This is not a problem if you have 6Mb of video RAM.

You can avoid a lot of hassles by purchasing Conflict Catcher by Casady and Greene (**www.casadyg.com/products/conflictcatcher/default.html**). This is one of the best Mac software programs on the market. Its sole purpose is to help your computer avoid system conflicts. Conflict Catcher describes and lets you manage thousands (3,900+) of files from everyday startup files to plug-ins and filters. If you do have a problem with your system, it determines which files are causing the problems.

One sure way to raise your blood pressure is to turn on your iMac and spot the dreaded flashing icon and question mark on your monitor. No hard drive appears. Your iMac simply does not start. If you are the kind of person who backs up your data every day religiously (and probably folds your socks), then it's no more than a mere inconvenience. However, if you are like me and the rest of the human race, who can't seem to be that robotic, you let out a scream. A hard drive crash will always happen the day after you failed to back up and you really need that file. It happened to me while writing Chapter 5 of this book!

Most of the time, the problem arises when your system software gets corrupted and a system reinstall will make the fix. Place your iMac Install CD-ROM into the CD-ROM drive, hold down the C key and reboot, and then reinstall the system software. Do a regular, not fresh, install first.

I have taken some shortcuts when in a hurry. If the hard drive appears after I boot up with the CD-ROM, I take the System, Finder, and Finder Preference files from the hard drive's system folder and trash them (empty the trash). Then, I simply take the System, Finder, and Finder Preferences files from the CD-ROM boot-up disk and drag them over to the system folder on the hard drive. That usually works as a temporary fix. If it doesn't, I perform a complete reinstall.

If none of that works, you need to call in a professional—software program, that is. Several programs on the market recover crashed disks and files. One of the most popular recovery programs is Norton Disk Utilities from Symantec (**www.symantec.com**). It can recover hard drives, floppies, Zips, and even separate files by themselves. I recommend it; it's a great program.

Disk First Aid, Apple's recovery system that comes on your iMac, automatically leaps into action if your iMac is turned off without powering down or crashes. You can periodically run the program to keep your hard drive in good working order. I like to give it a spin about once a week.

There are other third-party drive and disk recovery programs. Be sure the product you choose works on the iMac and System 8.1 or better.

Back Up, Back Up, Back Up!

If the crash stories have scared you by now, make it a habit to back up your important files every day or at least once a week. I know I have said this many times in the book, but back up your data! There is really no reason to lose important information other than laziness or living on the edge.

This is what I do: I don't worry about backing up the actual software programs (ClarisWorks, Quicken, and so on). After all, you own the software restore CD-ROM that will reinstall all the software that came with your iMac. However, the files I create are priceless to me. If they are zapped beyond help, that represents hours of work down the drain. Many people recommend the grandfather approach for backing up. You have two backup disks. The first backup disk is called the father. The second one is the grandfather. Each day as you back up, you switch disks so that you are no more than two days out of backup. The grandfather disk becomes the father the next day, the father disk becomes the grandfather, and so on.

It is also wise not to store the backups in the same place. I keep one, the grandfather, at my education center, and the father disk goes home with me. When I am working on something really important such as a chapter of a book, I like to upload a copy to one of my email addresses, just in case. Call me paranoid (I also carry a second set of car keys with me), but I've bought plenty of tissues for a number of friends after they lost a month's work and had no backups.

I like to use Zip disks as my backup disks, but the new Imation Superdisks are superb as well and hold more information.

There are several commercial and shareware backup software programs on the market. Retrospect, DiskFit Direct, and DiskFit Pro, all by Dantz (**www.dantz.com**), are perhaps the best. Retrospect has been available for the Mac for years. If you want to back up a network or any number of Macs, look at the Dantz commercial programs.

For simply backing up the iMac for personal use, I use the drag-and-drop routine. Just grab the files to back up over to the Zip or Superdisk.

This advice may seem like a no-brainer, but never store your backup disks or any disks on top of your computer, on a TV, or near any electrical appliance. The magnetic effects can garble the information on your disks. Store your backups in an area where the temperature does not fluctuate a lot, preferably remaining at room temperature. A friend of mine used to store his backup disks on top of his Mac, right over the power supply. He couldn't figure out why he was always having trouble reading his disks!

Rebuild Your Desktop

You should periodically rebuild your desktop. No, you don't need a hammer. Not only does a rebuild prevent certain problems from occurring (such as files losing their icons or not recognizing their parent applications), but also it helps your iMac keep track of files stored on your hard drive more efficiently.

Rebuilding the desktop is easy. When you start your iMac, hold down the Command and Option keys. A dialog box will ask whether you are sure you want to do this. Click OK. It will take a few minutes if you have a lot of files. Perform this procedure at least once a month.

Reset Parameter RAM

Parameter Random Access Memory (PRAM) is a tiny amount of memory that is always on, continually powered by a small battery in your iMac. PRAM maintains information on things that you don't want to keep setting, such as background color, video settings, network information, and time of day. PRAM can become corrupted and crash your computer.

To ensure this crash does not happen, you can reset the PRAM (affectionately called zapping). However, zapping the PRAM resets the iMac to the factory settings for most of Apple's control panels such as the General Controls, Keyboard, Startup Disk, Mouse, and Map, so you need to reset them to your liking.

To zap the PRAM, choose restart, or when you boot up your iMac, hold the Command+Option+P+R keys and wait till you hear the startup tone. Keep holding it until you hear the tone for the second time, and then release. Return to your control panels and reset them. I zap the PRAM once every six months.

Check Regularly For Viruses

I discussed virus checking in Chapter 8, but I will emphasize it again. It is a good precaution. Viruses, worms, and Trojan horses can bring you a great deal of grief, lost information, downtime, and even hardware failure.

First Things First: Keep Informed!

Subscribe to the Mac Virus mailing list to keep informed of new viruses. This list announces viruses on the Mac. To subscribe, send email to listproc@listproc.bgsu.edu. In the body of the message, type "subscribe mac-virus-announce *YOUR FULL NAME*". (Do not include the quotes when typing the text.)

Get A Virus Checker!

Be sure to have a virus checker such as Disinfectant, Virex (**http://antivirus.miningco.com**), SAM (Symantec AntiVirus for Macintosh) or Norton AntiVirus for Macintosh (which will supersede SAM), both from Symantec (**www.symantec.com**), the French, soon to be English, program Rival (**www.intego.com**), or others. Make sure you install all new updates as they become available. Figure 9.2 shows a scan of my hard drive by Disinfectant. Disinfectant is still the premier free virus checker for all viruses prior to 1998. It does not detect Macro viruses or the new Autostart worm.

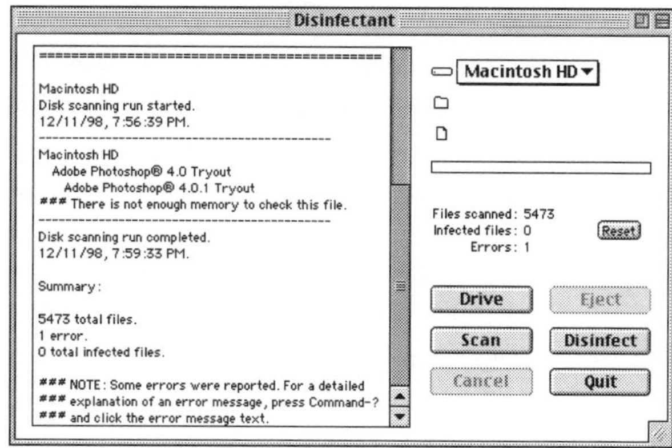

Figure 9.2
Disinfectant virus checker.

Relax

Every so often, look away from the monitor and relax your eyes. Make sure you have good posture when typing. Make sure you brush after every meal.

Watch Where You Download

Never download files from the Internet directly to your hard drive. Instead, download them to a special Zip disk or Superdisk that you have labeled for such purposes. Then, scan the disk after you download files to it.

DOS or Windows viruses do not affect Macintosh computers, but they can affect that part of a Mac using Virtual PC or SoftWindows. You might want to install DOS or Windows virus protection on these partitions because they are not protected by Macintosh virus detection programs.

Although Disinfectant 3.7.1 (**ftp://ftp.nwu.edu/pub/disinfectant/**), the leading and free virus checker, is no longer being supported, it still works on all previous viruses prior to 1998. Get it.

When you get an email about the Good Times email virus, ignore it; it's a hoax, an urban legend that pops up at least once a year. You can learn more about such hoaxes by visiting the Computer Incident Advisory Committee's (CIAC) Web site (**http://ciac.llnl.gov/ciac/CIACHoaxes.html**). Some macro viruses attack Microsoft Word files for Windows and Macintosh, but they can be detected and killed as well.

The new Autostart worms can be killed with Worm Guard (**http://hyperarchive.lcs.mit.edu/cgi-bin/NewSearch?key=WormGuard**) or WormScanner (**http://members.aol.com/jwwalker/pages/worm.html**). There are other viruses to avoid. Be sure to check with Mac Virus (**www.macvirus.com**), one of the best Mac virus Web sites.

Memory Problems

If you upgrade your iMac's memory, as detailed in Chapter 1, you may notice some problems. The iMac may not start, or the Apple menu might indicate it has less memory than it's supposed to have. There are some bad 32MB and 64MB memory modules in the marketplace.

Before you upgrade, check in at the iMacIntouch Web site (**www.macintouch.com/imacramprobs.html**) and read the section on memory problems. It will give you an idea on what brands to avoid and the likely cause of the problems.

I always recommend getting your memory from The Chip Merchant (**www.thechipmerchant.com**) because it is good about returning defective chips.

Initial iMac Updates

Any brand new technology has bugs at first. The iMac was no exception when it first came to market. If you own the first model of iMac, you must install a few software updates, as explained in Chapter 1.

Be sure to download the following five files from Apple's software update site at **ftp://ftp.info.apple.com/Apple_Support_Area/Apple_Software_Updates/US/Macintosh/iMac/**.

iMac_CD_Update_1.0.smi.bin, iMac_CD_Update_1.0_Info.txt

If you place in the drive a CD-ROM that is heavy with graphics on the top, you might notice a loud whirl. The drive is vibrating. The iMac CD Firmware Update reduces the amount of vibration caused by these CDs. The vibration is caused by unbalanced CDs spinning at high speeds in your CD-ROM drive and can cause problems for the drive reading the CD. The iMac CD Firmware Update places new firmware on the CD-ROM drive to reduce the amount of vibration.

iMac_Update_1.0.smi.bin, iMac_Update_1.0_Info.txt, or Mac Update 1.01

This update improved the workings of the Universal Serial Bus (USB).

iMac_v34_Only_Modem_Script.smi.bin,
iMac_v34_Only_Modem_Script_Info.txt

You may be living in an area where the phone line simply stinks and cannot get access to the 56Kbps transfer rate of your modem. In that case, try this iMac Internal 56Kbps (v.34 only) script. It forces the modem to connect at 33.6Kbps or lower speeds. Of course, you could move.

Modem Updater

http://til.info.apple.com/swupdates.nsf/artnum/n10665

The first iMac experienced frequent hang-ups when online at 56Kbps. It didn't seem to handle the speed as well as it should. This software installs the latest Rockwell firmware, based on version 2.2. It has been pretty solid. I still get dumped once in a while but not as frequently as before the update.

Speed Thrills

For faster performance of your iMac, set virtual memory (in your memory control panel) to 64MB if you only have 32MB of real memory.

System Profiler

http://til.info.apple.com/swupdates.nsf/artnum/n10098

Apple System Profiler collects and displays information about the configuration of the iMac This version provides additional information and corrects errors in the initial iMac version.

Keep A Maintenance Schedule

When was the last time you put oil in your car? It's pretty easy to forget to do basic maintenance on your computer as well. I put together a chart and placed it on the wall in front of my iMac. If you do the same and follow it, chances are you will have few problems with your iMac. Table 9.1 shows you my schedule. You are free to copy it and do the same.

Table 9.1 Don's Maintenance Schedule.

Chore	Daily	Weekly	Monthly	3-6 Months	Never
Back up files	x				
Zap PRAM				x	
Rebuild desktop			x		
Virus check	x (on down-loads)	x (overall)			
Check Mac news Sites	x				
Check Mac Web sites	x				
Wash Mac (no hose)		x			
Run Disk First Aid or Norton's		x			
Watch *X-Files*		x			
Vacation					x

No Hub At Startup Time

To boot up your iMac using the keyboard startup key, you must have the keyboard plugged directly into an iMac USB port. It will not work if the keyboard is attached to a hub.

The MacWeb Support Line

Hundreds of Mac users on the Net are brilliant techies who are willing to share their knowledge with everyone for no charge. I have found that whenever a technical problem arises, you can find out about it almost immediately online. You can also be sure that the solution to the problem will be posted, too. The following Web sites cover almost any technical problem, question, or issue relating to the Macintosh platform.

Apple Tech Info Library

http://til.info.apple.com

Apple's technical information library contains more than 14,000 articles that cover product information, technical specifications, and troubleshooting information. The site is updated every day, and a search engine helps you find previously posted material. A section called "Did You Know" highlights information that Apple deems important and current.

Apple Tech Exchange

http://support.info.apple.com/te/te.taf

This Apple site is a combination of information collected from Apple's Tech Info Library, the software update archives, discussion forums, and news. There are several categories to choose, including a special iMac section. Basic troubleshooting, prevention, repair, and common problems are featured. You can also read an online edition of the iMac emergency manual that came with your iMac.

The iMac section offers several categories of information, including some troubleshooting and everything from modems to USB networking.

Focus On Mac Hardware

http://machardware.miningco.com

This Web site has many links to hardware-related sites in several categories from Classic Macs to video cards. Realtime chats occur, and you can read past transcripts. Features and tips are also part of the offerings. Ryan Fass maintains this Mining Company site.

Focus On Mac Support

http://macsupport.miningco.com

This Mining Company site, coordinated by Dave Merten and Shari Shroeder, links to many sites that specialize in Mac support issues from

batteries to virus checkers. You'll find features and tips, as well as chat on Tuesday and Thursday evenings from 8:00 to 11:00 P.M.

Let The Breeze In!

Make sure you have plenty of ventilation around your computer.

Focus On Mac OS

macos.miningco.com

This site covers the Mac operating system and contains links to OS issues, including other operating systems that run on the Mac such as Be or Linux. Features, tips, and chat are also part of the site; however, no one is in charge of the site as of this writing.

iMac2Day

www.imac2day.com

Jeff Keller created this site because he felt iMac users, many of them are first-time Mac users, could use some good tech support. Mark Jarmon helps with the contest and news hunting, and Jim Stoneburner manages the message boards.

iMac2Day features daily news, message boards for discussion, a place to track pricing and availability, a list of iMac-compatible peripherals, reviews, and a great tech support page.

MacFixIt

www.macfixit.com

This is a great site to visit daily to find out about problems in the Mac world and their fixes. An iMac section includes troubleshooting, workarounds, and news. If you missed anything, you can search the archives. A Sherlock Plug-in lets you keyword search MacFixIt.

MacintoshOS.com

www.macintoshos.com

This site is a good reference site for System 8 and beyond. Learn some tips and shortcuts on using System 8, read news, and find out about updates.

Mac Pruning Pages

http://cafe.AmbrosiaSW.com/DEF/index.html

This site is dedicated to make sure you have the "cleanest" Mac operating system around. If you want to know what a particular control panel

Watch The Lighting

Make sure you have backlighting toward the computer. If you have a computer in front of a window, close the shades; you don't need stray light on your eyes. Use a desktop color scheme with good contrast.

or extension does, you can find out here. Often, you will collect a bunch of extensions and control panels that you really no longer need. Find out if you need them and what you can do to get rid of them if you don't. Dan Frakes, who runs this site, is the author of InformINIT (**http://cafe.AmbrosiaSW.com/DEF/InformINIT.html**), a great database of information primarily on system INITs but also on system folder contents, control panels, and other system-related files. This is a must read.

Mac Tips

www.themacintoshguy.com

Mac Tips is brought to you by The Macintosh Guy (Eric Prentice) and MacCNN. The site contains many great tips on using your Mac, an archive of back material, and an area for getting Apple software updates for version 8.1 and after. A mailing list will inform you when the page is updated.

MacVirus

www.macvirus.com

Maintained by Susan Lesch, MacVirus is the one-stop Web site for learning all about Mac viruses. You can find answers to the most commonly asked virus questions, including how to prevent an infection. There are current news and warnings, a complete reference area, and, best of all, an archive of the best virus killer software you can download.

Mining Co. iMac Support Center

http://macsupport.miningco.com/blcenter.htm

Here is another 24-hour iMac service station at your fingertips. You'll find a lot of great links to help sites, FAQs, and answers to your questions about anything iMac related. News and features are also on the site.

No Wonder! Internet Technical Assistance Center

www.nowonder.com

If you don't believe in volunteers, check out this site. More than 350 volunteers from around the world have been giving free technical support to anyone who asks for the past 2 years. According to the Web site, they have answered about 30,000 questions in 1998.

Ask a question and get an answer within 24-28 hours. Want to discuss it with others? Join the message boards, or participate in live chat.

The Complete Conflict Compendium

www.mac-conflicts.com

Are you interested in all the possible conflicts that can happen to your iMac? You can download them from this site, or visit frequently and read them online. According to the Web site, the Complete Conflict Compendium is a "collection of things that will crash your Mac, or make it act strange." It tells you how to correct them. It covers all Mac operating systems, including the early ones, and includes a special section on the iMac. You can subscribe to a free weekly mailing list and stay on top of possible conflicts.

theiMac.com

www.theiMac.com

Robert Aldridge and George Cole are the brains behind theiMac.com. Robert is the Webmaster and George is the marketing guy. Robert has plenty of experience in printing and Web and graphic design, and George works for a major online retailer, so both know how to serve the public—and theiMac.com does just that.

You can find well-written features, daily news, columns, and tutorials. A weekly live chat on Tuesdays at 12 P.M. CST and Thursdays at 7 P.M. CST lets you ask questions, discuss pressing issues, and have fun.

Special beginners guides, upgrade tutorials, software updates, technical support, and a great deal more fill this site.

The Mac Conflict Solution Site

www.quillserv.com/www/c3/c3.html

Here is a site devoted to solving Mac conflicts, especially system extension problems. Each conflict is listed by software, symptoms, how to isolate it, and what to do to solve it. This includes problems with Mac's OS 8. A special Help Zone lets you ask questions about a possible conflict in applications, the System, or other Mac area. Links to tips, FAQs, and Web sites round out the site.

Version Tracker Online

www.versiontracker.com

Many conflicts with your Mac are caused by not having the proper, updated software. Visit this site often to make sure you know which is the latest version of software to use on your iMac. The updates are linked so you can download the software immediately. A special Update Highlights section informs you of recent important updates. Finally, a search engine lets you keyword search and sort updates. Updates are noted as beta, shareware, freeware, or commercial. If you are new to the Mac community, check out the top picks. A Sherlock plug-in searches for Version Tracker.

Buying Stuff

In Chapter 8, I gave you the rundown on which mail-order houses to use for purchasing goodies for your iMac. Unfortunately, the mail-order houses do not carry everything, and there are a lot of good used (now called preowned) equipment, parts, and peripherals out there to buy. Here are a few additional sites that let you purchase a wide range of Mac-related equipment, new and used, including the computer itself.

Remember that before you buy anything mail order, you should do some homework and make sure the company is not a fly-by-night outfit, one that will not deliver the goods. I often use C.O.D. if it's available. This way, you do receive a package before you pay. You can check a Better Business Bureau in the city where the company operates or the Attorney General of that state to check whether any complaints have been filed.

Absolute Mac

www.absolutemac.com

This is an excellent site for buying Macs and peripherals. One great feature lets you write the specs of what you want to buy so it can send them to more than 30 resellers.

Boston Computer Exchange

www.bocoex.com

The Boston Computer Exchange, founded in 1982, is one of the oldest wholesale and retail dealers in new, used, and refurbished PCs. It also performs warranty service on Apple computers.

Class Mac

www.classmac.com

This site allows you to place and read ads. A Feedback Forum lets you offer praise, recommendations, complaints, ideas, and suggestions.

Deal iMac

www.deal-mac.com

Deal Mac (and iMac) looks for special deals on Mac hardware, peripherals, and software and gives you the list with links to those deals when possible. This is a great site to visit to find prices when you want to add to your iMac.

Macintosh User Market (MUM)

www.maconcall.com/mum/index.shtml

Until the Web became really popular, the **comp.sys.mac.wanted** and the **misc.forsale** newsgroups on Usenet were the places to check for buying new and used Macs. This site was designed to fill the vacuum on the Web. Both new and used Macintosh products are offered from Mac resellers, value-added resellers (VARs), and the general public.

RAMWatch

www.macresource.pair.com/mrp/ramwatch.shtml

If you are looking to buy RAM and want to know the best price, check out this site. It keeps track of several companies and offers the lowest and average prices. I still personally recommend The Chip Merchant (**www.thechipmerchant.com**) for best overall prices and support.

SupportHelp.com

www.supporthelp.com

Looking for technical help from a software or hardware vendor? This Web site has hot links to the majority of newsgroups that provide tech support at the click of the mouse.

The United Index Of Used Microcomputer Prices

www.uce.com/index

Do you want to know the value of your iMac on the used market? Looking to buy some used iMacs? This site is a list of the average sale prices nationwide of used microcomputer equipment in the primary and secondary markets and specializes in Mac, although it does offer information on other platforms. It also includes information such as introduction dates, current retail prices, and various helpful statistics. The index is available as downloadable MacAppraiser software or Adobe Acrobat (PDF) files, or you can simply search its online database.

Finding A Local Help Line

Join a local Mac computer user group. A computer user group is like a Boy Scout troop. A group of excited people get together usually once a month and increase their knowledge base—in our case, about the Macintosh computer.

Apple user groups have been around since the founding of Apple Computer in the late 1970s. When the Macintosh made its appearance, it wasn't long after that Mac user groups started springing up everywhere. I started mine, Macintosh Enthusiasts Club of the Capital Area (MECCA) in Albany, New York, with eight other proud Mac owners in February of 1984. At its peak a few years ago, more than 2,500 user groups were registered with Apple Computer. With the popularity of the Net and the bad press about Apple during the last few years, the number of Mac user groups has dwindled to perhaps half that. Those that still exist are gold mines for help and information. You will find that many talented people belong to Mac user groups. Figure 9.3 shows my user group's logo, created by member Gil Irias.

User groups usually meet monthly. They might have a featured guest, raffle off some software or hardware, hand out a shareware disk of the month, and produce a newsletter. The most important part of the meeting is to share experiences with each other and to offer technical support and often moral support as well.

Figure 9.3
Logo for the Macintosh Enthusiasts Club of the Capital Area, Inc. (MECCA) in Albany, NY.

How can you find one in your city? The following Web sites will guide you.

Apple User Groups

www.apple.com/usergroups

This is Apple's official user group site, where you can type your location and find a user group near you. If you can't find one, resources here will help teach you how to start one.

HAC Ultimate Macintosh Users Group List

www.microserve.net/hac/ug/

Hershey Apple Corps user group listing is one of the most complete. This is a great place to start looking for an Apple user group in your area.

MacDirectory

www.macdirectory.com/pages/Usergroups.html

The MacDirectory has a searchable database where you type the user group code, name, or city and state, but I found this database somewhat lacking. It listed only seven user groups for all of New York state. (Apple's user group site listed 53.) It does have a submit form. Use this database with caution.

MUG News Service (MNS)

www.themesh.com/mesh8e.html

MUG News Service is a computer news service I started in 1987 to help editors of Mac user groups around the world. For years, we sent a monthly disk full of articles, reviews, shareware, tutorials, and offerings, which the editors delivered to their members. Each disk was sponsored by a third-party company and usually offered a special deal to members. Our first disk was sponsored by ACIUS, then headed by the legendary Guy Kawasaki.

MNS no longer sends the monthly disk, especially because the Net has replaced the need. MNS still sponsors the publishing of *The MESH—Inside Cyberspace*, a monthly Net magazine in hard copy and Web form (**www.themesh.com**), and *Inside The Net*, a weekly radio show about the Internet, broadcast on WROW 590AM in Albany, New York. The radio show is simulcast live through RealAudio Software (**www.wrow.com**).

The MNS portion of The MESH Web site has a list of Mac user groups.

10 Having Fun With Your iMac

Rittner's Computer Law: A formula for computing in the workplace: One third of the time is spent being productive. One third of the time is spent playing games. The remaining third of the time is spent trying not to get caught.

The Macintosh has come a long way from the days of Missile Command and Social Climber, two of the first software games for the Mac. Unfortunately, Apple never promoted the Mac as a computer that excelled in running games until the recent release of the iMac. The Mac has always been a superb graphics machine, and hundreds of commercial-quality games have been designed and released since the Mac first appeared on the computing scene in 1984.

When I wrote *MacArcade* (Ventana Press) in 1992, I reviewed the top-100 shareware games and featured the top 40 in the book. Many of these freeware and shareware games were commercial-quality products and were far superior to many of the PC games of the time. Many of them work on the iMac.

Today, there are many categories of games that you can play on your iMac. There are arcade, board, card-playing, Java-enabled role-playing and even multiplayer games, where you can shoot 'em up with people around the world while connected to the Net. Computer gaming has come a long way since the days of Pong. Hundreds, if not thousands, of computer games run on every brand of personal computer.

Even if you work hard, you still need to play. Even prehistoric times left evidence of playtime; it's part of being human. This chapter will show you how to use your iMac to get the latest information about games and entertainment online and where to download entertainment software, and a special section is dedicated to software games for kids.

Many of the games you play online are Java scripted, so you need a browser that is Java enabled. Both Netscape's and Microsoft's browsers that come with your iMac will work fine. Additionally, some games are based on MacroMedia's Shockwave multimedia plug-in. If you do not have that in your browser's plug-ins folder (it should be there already), you can download it from most game sites or **www.macromedia.com/shockwave/**, which is Macromedia's home page.

File Not Found

Sometimes, a Web page is moved or renamed, and you get the error message "File Not Found" when trying to connect. Delete the part of the address on the rightmost end of a Web address, and work your way back to the left one slash (/) at a time. You might find the moved page through that process.

Mac Game News And Updates

If your only interest in the iMac is playing games, you won't be disappointed. Hundreds of freeware, shareware, and commercial games show why the Mac is a superb graphics machine. The following Web sites will supply you with news and reviews, demos, and even download areas where you can grab the latest offerings.

Mac Gamers Ledge

www.macledge.com

This site features news, reviews, and downloads (commercial demos and shareware) for games on the Mac. It features a daily review special. Looking for a review on a particular game? Try the search engine, where you can conduct a keyword search.

The Mac Game Gate

www.macgate.torget.se/

Looking for information on the latest games, versions, and downloads? This site has that and more. Download the codebook and get Easter eggs (hidden presents), cheat sheets, and secrets about the games you play. Game utilities are available for downloading, but the best section is the library of games that you can download, all arranged in categories from 3D games to strategy and war. A weekly cool site (you can nominate one) and links to other game sites, developers, and game magazines makes this a great site to visit.

The Mac Game Resource Guide

http://cafe.ambrosiasw.com/csmg-faq/

Part of the Ambrosia Cafe, this site, maintained by Christina M. Schulman, lists in alphabetical and annotated order links to hundreds of game resources such as FAQs, game developers' Web sites, download archives, game lists, and more.

iMac FAQ

iMac Info (**http://imac.macguys.com**) and EveryMac.com (**www.everymac.com**) both have great FAQs on the iMac.

Marathon Central

www.marathon.org/

If you are a fan (or addict) of the game Marathon by Bungie Software, this site must be in your bookmarks. It contains almost every Marathon-related link, including links to network gamers. You'll get daily news about Marathon, several forums about making scenarios and maps, and plenty of Marathon-related downloads.

Vertigo

www.macvertigo.com

A relatively recent addition to the Net, Vertigo provides game news, features, editorials, interviews, and reviews. It has game release dates with links to the companies. Shareware, demos, and updates are available for downloading.

Online Game Supersites

You can play the following games online as an individual or with multiplayer capacity. Some of them require a download of a plug-in or program, but most allow you to play without one. Simply go to the site, read the rules, and begin playing.

Super Game Sites

These Web sites contain several online games ready for your enjoyment.

The Arcade Machine

http://arcade.from-the.net

You will spend a lot of time at this Java-based site. It has more than 500 games. Play classics such as Asteroids, Pac Man, Lunar Lander, and many more, including trivia games. You can spend hours playing old-time favorite games, in Java flavor, here at The Arcade Machine, as shown in Figure 10.1.

Pimpernal Online Games

www.pimpernel.com

Play these pure Java games: Casino Games, Twinning, Diceridoo, Safebreaker, Sokoban, Crossword, Mah-jongg, Spacebattle, Forinnarow, Spot 'em all, and Supertris.

Figure 10.1
The Arcade Machine.

Ezone

www.ezone.com

This site features more than 80 online games to play from arcade types to adventures.

Candystand

www.candystand.com/arcade/arcade.htm

Sponsored by Lifesavers, this Shockwave-enabled site has quite a few games, including pinball. (Don't try to put "English" on the ball.) Categories include Sports, Game Hall, Test Your Knowledge, Word Games, and more.

Riddler

www.riddler.com

Riddler has a variety of Java and non-Java games. If you want to play more games or if you want a chance of winning prizes, you must sign a small registration form and you must be at least 18 years old. This site is Java-based.

World Opponent Network

www.won.net/gameslist/

You can download and play a variety of games for free here, especially puzzles and trivia games such as You Don't Know Jack. If you own some of the commercial CD-ROMs, you can still play the games online.

Online Games

You play these games individually or sometimes against the computer.

Big Country Duck

www.mcny.com/duck.html

Shoot the ducks passing by on this Shockwave-enabled site.

Blackjack Java

http://javaboutique.internet.com/BlackJack/

This classic game of Blackjack works very fast at this Java-based site.

Excite Online Games

www.excite.com/games/online_games/

Excite, the search engine, lets you play online at this Java-based site. Find board games such as chess and checkers; word games such as crosswords, Jumble, sports crosswords, and word searches; and card games such as Euchre, Hearts, and Spades.

Faces

www.corynet.com/faces/

At this fun site, you can mix and match parts of your favorite celebrities' faces. It reminds me of Conan O'Brien's "What If" segment, where he considers what the offspring of pairs of famous people would look like.

Game-Land Shockwave

www.game-land.com/games/

You'll find games of chance, thought, and skill on this Shockwave-enabled site.

Jeopardy And *Wheel Of Fortune* Online

www.station.sony.com/jeopardy

This Shockwave-enabled site features the official Net versions of the popular TV game shows "*Jeopardy*" and "*Wheel of Fortune*." You have to sign in as a member, but it is free. Both games have multiplayer versions, as shown in Figure 10.2.

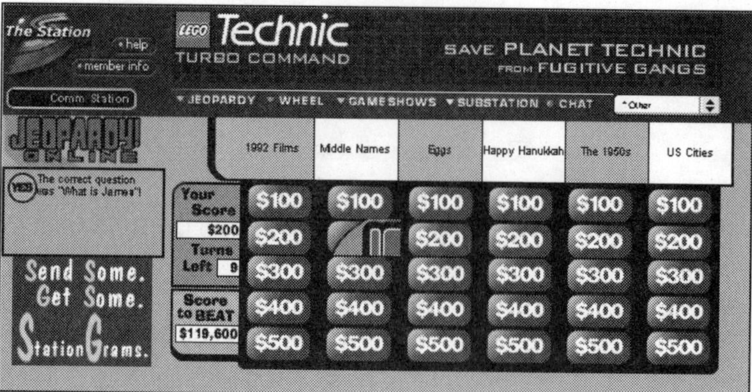

Figure 10.2

The Official Online Jeopardy Game for those who can't get enough of the TV version.

Mah-Jongg

www.cs.bu.edu/staff/ta/merryj/mah-jongg/index.html

The object of the game is to clear all the tiles from the board at this Java-based site.

Megabot

www.vr1.com/comics/megabot/games.html

If you like the Megabot comic book series, enjoy these five games: SIS (Signal Isolation System), Hyper Plasma Ball, X-3 Defender, Orn Patrol, and Orn Attack.

Missile Command

www.sdsu.edu/~boyns/java/mcii/

This Java-based site features the classic game Missile Command, one of the first shareware programs for the Mac from 1984-85, as shown in Figure 10.3. Missile Command is an old-time Mac user favorite.

Nights

www.sega.com/multimedia/games/nights/

Play an online version of Sega Saturn's NiGHTS. The site is Shockwave enabled.

Nimitz Class

www.nimitzclass.com

Fly an Apache attack helicopter and defend the Nimitz Class carrier from enemy attack at this Shockwave-enabled site.

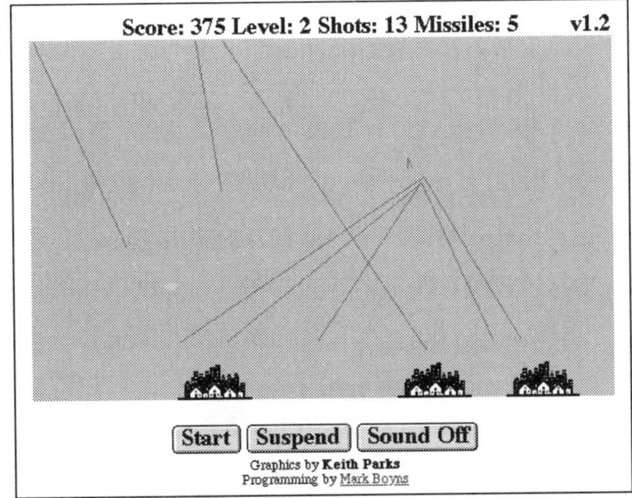

Figure 10.3
Missile Command—one of the first Mac games.

Pass The Pigs

www.ultranet.com/~gkramer/PassThePigs.shtml

The first player who rolls a total of 100 points wins in this dice-like game.

Put O.J. Simpson In Jail

www.geocities.com/SoHo/Lofts/3140/oj.html

I know; haven't we had enough of this? Click O.J. if you can, and put him behind bars at this Java-based site.

Rubik Unbound

www.tdb.uu.se/~karl/java/rubik.html

Play a classic game of Rubik's Cube online. This site is Java based.

The Blip

www.fringenet.com/blip/

Chess, Sumo, Spin-o-Matic, Space Weather, Luddite Games, Perambulator GP, and some games that you can beta-test are on this site, but you must have the Shockwave plug-in.

The Java Triangle Puzzle

http://imagiware.com/triangle/

Harder than it looks! Move balls around in a triangle by jumping over one at a time. This site is Java based.

The Virtual Arcade

www.thearcade.com

This Shockwave-enabled site offers many games in the arcade, strategy, role-playing, and board genre.

UFO Attack

http://204.96.11.210/kidz/ufogame/

Guide your missiles and shoot the aliens at this Java-based site.

Virtual Vegas

www.virtualvegas.com

You guessed it: You'll find a lot of casino-type games at this site, such as blackjack, slot machines, roulette, and more. This site is both Java and Shockwave enabled. Gamble without losing your house! Try out Virtual Vegas and play casino games, as shown in Figure 10.4.

Warriors Of Virtue

www.warriorsofvirtue.com/game.html

This game is MGM's online version of the movie. You (as Roo) must defend the "lifespring" from oncoming enemies.

Figure 10.4
Gambling Vegas style!

For Kids Only

The next time people tell you the Internet is not for kids, just give them a few of the following Web sites. Hundreds of great Web sites are geared for all age levels—from kindergarten through 12th grade.

The kids' sites listed here are free of violence, sex, or other issues that make parents shudder when they hear the word Internet. These sites are designed around theme-oriented activities from TV, movie, or cartoon characters or are education oriented in a fun way. Kids can find pictures to color, stories to read, activities to do, and parents can join in as well. A few of the sites need adult supervision (for example, NASA) so that the kids can find the appropriate age-level activities.

365 TV-Free Activities
http://family.starwave.com/funstuff/activity/tvtoc.html

Aesop's Fables
gopher://ftp.std.com:70/00/obi/book/Aesop/Fables.Z

A Bird Without A Song
www.marlo.com/wguy1.htm

Ah, Slither And Slide
www.marlo.com/all4kids.htm

A Tribute To Dr. Seuss
www.polar7.com/cc/9510/0003cxwd.html
If your kids like to do crossword puzzles, this is a good site, as shown in Figure 10.5.

Anagram Insanity
www.infobahn.com/pages/anagram.html

Art Serve (Parental Help Needed On This Address)
http://rubens.anu.edu.au/

Aunt Annie's Crafts
www.auntannie.com

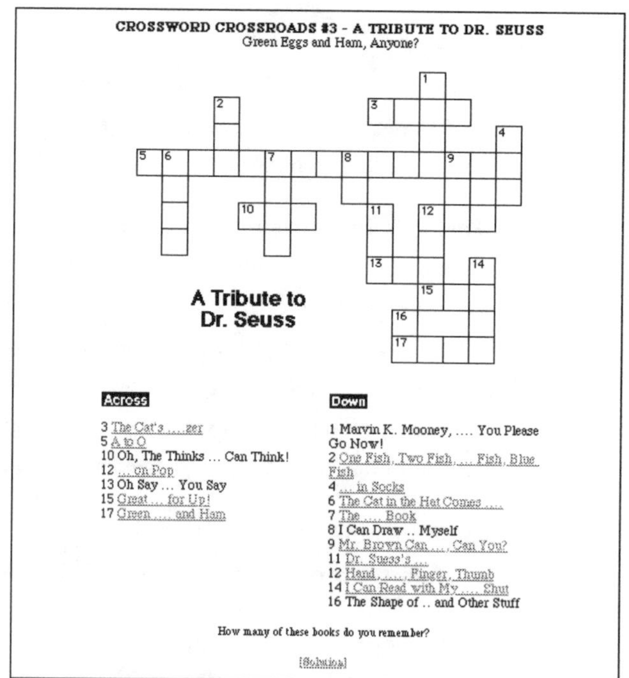

Figure 10.5
Dr. Seuss crossword puzzle.

BeanTime Stories
www.meddybemps.com/5.1.html

Bill Nye, The Science Guy
http://nyelabs.kcts.org/

Britannica Toys Through Time
http://toys.eb.com

Build An Egret
www.Friend.ly.Net/scoop/activity/airplact.htm

Candlelight Stories Home Page
www.CandlelightStories.com

Carlos's Coloring Book
www.ravenna.com/coloring

Children's Literature Web Guide
www.ucalgary.ca/~dkbrown/index.html

Children's Television Workshop
www.ctw.org/

Choose Your Own Adventure
http://hillside.coled.umn.edu/class1/Buzz/Story.html

Crayola
www.crayola.com

Curious George Rides The Bus
www.hmco.com/hmco/trade/hmi/george/game/index.html

Cyberkids
www.woodwind.com/cyberkids/index.html

Cyber Jacques's Treasure Hunt
www.cyberjacques.com

Dilophasaurus
www.ucmp.berkeley.edu/education/education.html

There are many sites that are not only fun to visit but are educational in nature, as shown in Figure 10.6.

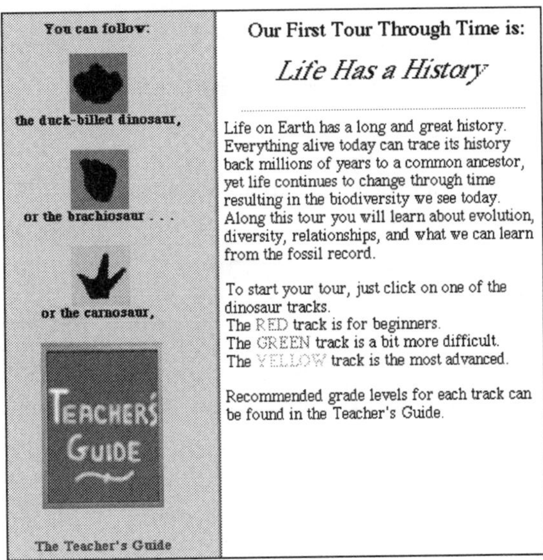

Figure 10.6
Tracking dinosaurs.

Disney
www.disney.com

DoDo Land In Cyberspace
www.swifty.com/azatlan/

Frog Prince
www.fln.vcu.edu/Grimm/frog.html

Fun Stuff At Gilbert House Children's Museum
www.acgilbert.org/mainhome.html

Global Show-N-Tell
http://emma.manymedia.com:80/show-n-tell/

Grimm's Fairy Tales
gopher://ftp.std.com:70/11/obi/book/Fairy.Tales/Grimm

How A Book Is Made
www.harperchildrens.com/index.htm

Interactive Frog
http://george.lbl.gov/ITG.hm.pg.docs/dissect/info.html

International Kids' Space
www.interport.net/kids-space

Internet For Kids
www.internet-for-kids.com

Internet Public Library—Youth Division
http://ipl.sils.umich.edu/youth/

Jason's Web Kite Site
www.latrobe.edu.au/Glenn/KiteSite/Kites.html

Joseph Wu's Origami Page
www.origami.vancouver.bc.ca/

Just For Kids
www.hmco.com/hmco/school/kids/index.html

Keys For Kids
www.gospelcom.net/cbh/kfk/kfk.shtml

Kids' Com
www.kidscom.com

Kids' Corner
http://kids.ot.com

Kids' Corner Personalized Story
http://kids.ot.com

Kids' Crambo
www.primenet.com/~hodges/kids_crambo.html

Kids On The Web
www.zen.org/~brendan/kids.html

Kidopedia
http://rdz.stjohns.edu:80/kidopedia/

KidPub
http://en-garde.com/kidpub/intro.html

Kids Web
www.npac.syr.edu/textbook/kidsweb/

Knock, Knock
www.marlo.com/knockjj.htm

Koala Trouble Series
www.scribbles.com.au/max/

Kody's Beary Scary Stories
www.usit.net/public/johncg/Kody/KodyPage.HTML

Lamb Chop's Play Along
www.pbs.org/charliehorse/kids/index.htm

Learn How To Make Pictures On Your Computer
www.sillybilly.com/draw95.html

Lego
www.lego.com

Lion King WWW Unofficial Archive
www.lionking.org/

MathMagic
http://forum.swarthmore.edu/mathmagic/

Mazes
www.wln.com/~deltapac/maze/mazepage.html

MCA Home Entertainment Kid's Playroom
www.mca.com/home/playroom/

Mike Is Hungry
http://mosaic.echonyc.com/~spingo/Matt/Mike.html

Mister Rogers' Neighborhood
www.pbs.org/rogers/

Mr. Bear's Birthday Book
http://pages.prodigy.com/U/S/A/USFY50A/party1.htm

Mr. Potato Head
http://winnie.acsu.buffalo.edu/potato

My Hero
http://myhero.com

Muppets
www.ncsa.uiuc.edu/VR/BS/Muppets/muppets.html

National Aeronautics And Space Administration (NASA)
www.nasa.gov/
Reach for the stars on this Web site, as shown in Figure 10.7.

Naughts And Crosses
www.bu.edu/Games/tictactoe

Figure 10.7
The official NASA Web site.

Nikolai's Web Site

www.nikolai.com

Parents And Children Together Online

www.indiana.edu/~eric_rec/fl/pcto/menu.html

Planet Yes

www.sillybilly.com/yestit.html

Platypus Family Playroom

www.platypus-share.com

Ponyshow's KidsNet

www.PonyShow.com/KidsNet/website.htm

Professor Bubbles' Official Bubble Home Page

http://bubbles.org

Sally On The Island

http://users.aol.com/cimal/candlelight/sallyone.htm

Sally Saves Christmas

http://users.aol.com/cimal/candlelight/page1.htm

Sharon, Lois, And Bram
www.destinyweb.com/elephant

Silly Billy's Books
www.sillybilly.com

Sports Illustrated For Kids Online
www.sikids.com/index.html

Stage Hand Puppets Activity Page
http://fox.nstn.ca/~puppets/activity.html

Star Wars
http://stwing.resnet.upenn.edu:8001/~jruspini/starwars.html

thekids.com
www.thekids.com

The Last Book
www.sillybilly.com/lasta.html

The Littlest Knight
www.pacificnet.net/~cmoore/lk/

The Nine Planets
http://seds.lpl.arizona.edu/nineplanets/nineplanets/nineplanets.html

The Simpsons
www.digimark.net/TheSimpsons/index.html

The Winning Game
www.marlo.com/t1.htm

Tic Tac Toe
www.bu.edu/Games/tictactoe

Tigger's Shareware Page
www.kidsdomain.com

Ultimate TV List

www.ultimatetv.com

Virtual Mr. Spud Head (Now Called Apple Corps)

http://apple-corps.westnet.com/apple_corps.html

Volcano World

http://volcano.und.nodak.edu

Wacky Web Tales

www.hmco.com:80/hmco/school/tales

Wooden Toys Exhibit

www.pd.astro.it/forms/mostra/mostra_i.html

Your kids can learn all about the history of wooden toys from this site, as shown in Figure 10.8.

Usenet Newsgroups Relating To Games

If you want to discuss the topic of games, you can subscribe to the following Usenet newsgroups using Outlook Express.

Figure 10.8

Wooden toys exhibit.

The Alt Hierarchy

alt.2600

The magazine or the game system.

alt.anagrams

Playing with words.

alt.flame.mud

To all the MUDs I've loved before.

alt.games.gb

The Galactic Bloodshed conquest game.

alt.galactic-guide

Hitchhiker's Guide to the Known Galaxy project.

alt.games.air-warrior

The Air Warrior combat computer game.

alt.games.apogee

A real high point in any gamer's day.

alt.games.cosmic-wimpout

A dice game popular in the computer crowd.

alt.games.doom

An extremely popular PC game.

alt.games.doom.announce

Announcements about the PC game Doom (moderated).

alt.games.doom.ii

Ladies and gentlemen, we are in hell. On Earth!

alt.games.doom.newplayers

Helping people who are new to this extremely popular PC game.

alt.games.frp.2300ad

The 2300 AD role-playing game.

alt.games.frp.dnd-util

Computer utilities for Dungeons And Dragons.

alt.games.frp.tekumel
Empire of the Petal Throne FRPG (Fantasy Role Playing Game) by M.A.R. Barker.

alt.games.gb
The Galactic Bloodshed conquest game.

alt.games.jyhad
Another trading card game like Magic, the Gathering.

alt.games.lynx
The Atari Lynx.

alt.games.mk
Struggling in Mortal Kombat!

alt.games.mornington.crescent
Discussion of the Crescent game.

alt.games.mtrek
Multi-Trek, a multiuser, *Star-Trek*–like game.

alt.games.netrek.paradise
Discussion of the Paradise version of Netrek.

alt.games.omega
The computer game Omega.

alt.games.quake
Natural disasters as sport.

alt.games.sf2
The video game Street Fighter 2.

alt.games.torg
Gateway for the TORG mailing list.

alt.games.ultima.dragons
Hints for Ultima games.

alt.games.vga-planets
Discussion of Tim Wisseman's VGA Planets.

alt.games.video.classic

Video games that originated before the mid-1980s.

alt.games.whitewolf

Discussion of WhiteWolf's line of gothic and horror RPGs.

alt.games.xpilot

Discussion of all aspects of the X11 game Xpilot.

alt.games.xtrek

All about a Star Trek game for X.

alt.mud

Like **rec.games.mud**, only different.

alt.pub.coffeehouse.amethyst

Realistic place to meet and chat with friends.

alt.pub.dragons-inn

Fantasy virtual-reality pub similar to **alt.callahans**.

alt.sega.genesis

Another addiction.

alt.super.nes

Like **rec.games.video.nintendo**, only different.

alt.toys.hi-tech

Optimus Prime is my hero.

alt.toys.transformers

From robots to vehicles and back again.

The Bit Hierarchy

bit.listserv.games-l

Computer games list.

The Rec Hierarchy

rec.games.abstract

Perfect information; pure strategy games.

rec.games.backgammon
Discussion of the game of backgammon.

rec.games.board
Discussion and hints on board games.

rec.games.board.ce
The Cosmic Encounter board game.

rec.games.board.marketplace
Trading and selling board games.

rec.games.bolo
The networked strategy war game Bolo.

rec.games.bridge
Hobbyists interested in bridge.

rec.games.chess
Chess and computer chess.

rec.games.chinese-chess
Discussion of the game of Chinese chess, Xiangqi.

rec.games.corewar
The Core War computer challenge.

rec.games.cyber
Discussions of cyberpunk-related games (moderated).

rec.games.deckmaster
The Deckmaster line of games.

rec.games.deckmaster.marketplace
Trading of Deckmaster paraphernalia.

rec.games.design
Discussion of game-design issues.

rec.games.diplomacy
The conquest game Diplomacy.

rec.games.empire

Discussion and hints about Empire.

rec.games.frp

Discussion about role-playing games.

rec.games.frp.advocacy

Flames and rebuttals about various role-playing systems.

rec.games.frp.announce

Announcements of happenings in the role-playing world (moderated).

rec.games.frp.archives

Archivable fantasy stories and other projects (moderated).

rec.games.frp.cyber

Discussions of cyberpunk-related role-playing games.

rec.games.frp.dnd

Fantasy role-playing with Dungeons And Dragons.

rec.games.frp.live-action

Live-action role-playing games.

rec.games.frp.marketplace

Role-playing game materials wanted and for sale.

rec.games.frp.misc

General discussions of role-playing games.

rec.games.go

Discussion about Go.

rec.games.hack

Discussion, hints, and so on about the Hack game.

rec.games.int-fiction

All aspects of interactive fiction games.

rec.games.mecha

Giant robot games.

rec.games.miniatures
Tabletop wargaming.

rec.games.misc
Games and computer games.

rec.games.moria
Comments, hints, and information about the Moria game.

rec.games.mud
Various aspects of multiuser computer games.

rec.games.mud.admin
Administrative issues for multiuser dungeons.

rec.games.mud.announce
Informational articles about multiuser dungeons (moderated).

rec.games.mud.diku
All about DikuMuds.

rec.games.mud.lp
Discussions of the LPMUD computer role-playing game.

rec.games.mud.misc
Various aspects of multiuser computer games.

rec.games.mud.tiny
Discussion about Tiny MUDs such as MUSH, MUSE, and MOO.

rec.games.netrek
Discussion of the X Window system game Netrek (XtrekII).

rec.games.pbm
Discussion about play-by-mail games.

rec.games.pinball
Discussions of pinball-related issues.

rec.games.programmer
Discussion of adventure-game programming.

rec.games.rogue
Discussion and hints about Rogue.

rec.games.roguelike.angband
The computer game Angband.

rec.games.roguelike.announce
Major information about Rogue-style games (moderated).

rec.games.roguelike.misc
Rogue-style dungeon.

rec.games.roguelike.moria
The computer game Moria.

rec.games.roguelike.nethack
The computer game Nethack.

rec.games.roguelike.rogue
The computer game Rogue.

rec.games.trivia
Discussion about trivia.

rec.games.video
Discussion about video games.

rec.games.video.3do
Discussion of 3DO video game systems.

rec.games.video.advocacy
Debate on merits of various video game systems.

rec.games.video.arcade
Discussions about coin-operated video games.

rec.games.video.arcade.collecting
Collecting, converting, and repairing video games.

rec.games.video.atari
Discussion of Atari's video game systems.

rec.games.video.cd32

Gaming talk, information, and help for the Amiga CD32.

rec.games.video.classic

Older home video entertainment systems.

rec.games.video.marketplace

Home video game stuff for sale or trade.

rec.games.video.misc

General discussion about home video games.

rec.games.video.nintendo

All Nintendo video game systems and software.

rec.games.video.sega

All Sega video game systems and software.

rec.games.xtank.play

Strategy and tactics for the distributed game Xtank.

rec.games.xtank.programmer

Coding the Xtank game and its robots.

rec.puzzles

Puzzles, problems, and quizzes.

rec.puzzles.crosswords

Making and playing grid word puzzles.

Other Entertainment-Related Web Links

Entertainment takes many forms, not only game playing. Keeping up with the news, sending friends postcards, keeping abreast of the latest music developments, TV shows, or movies, or gossiping about favorite stars also keeps one entertained.

Sports-Related

Although it may seem that sports and computing don't mix, many sports-related Web sites are in the computing world.

MacSports

www.suzerain.com/macsport/

Here is a site for those with a passion for sports. Dedicated to that field of Mac games, it covers not only the games, but also hardware, devices, and other peripherals that will make your sports playing worthwhile. Each game is grouped by sport, rated, and reviewed, and you'll see the system requirements, price, and the publisher's link if it has a Web site. You can follow a link to an online mall if you want to order online. Links to other sports-related sites that provide tips or product-specific information are included.

Music-Related

Yes, Web sites are devoted to music and your Mac, too. Many famous musicians took to the Mac early because of the easy-to-use graphical interface and easy connection to MIDI.

dotmusic

www.dotmusic.com

Looking for the new Beatles invasion? This site combines United Kingdom music publications. Check the charts, read reviews, and look for dance and music acts. You'll find a lot of information about the music scene across the ocean.

Macrocks.com

www.macrocks.com

This Web site is devoted to providing information on music and making music with your Mac. Ever wonder which musicians use Macs? Find that list here along with reviews, features, and even games.

Television Entertainment

Although it may seem ludicrous to use the computer for television, it is only a matter of time until you will be watching TV and movies online. WebTV certainly is trying to cross the gap. Currently, many Web sites will give you the lowdown on your favorite TV show or movie, gossip about the stars, and even the day and time of your favorite shows. Remember also that in Chapter 6, you learned you can even chat in realtime with others who are watching the same TV show at the same time.

TVGen

www.tvgen.com/tv/trivia/

This is the online version of *TV Guide*, complete with TV listings. Type your ZIP code and get the listings tailored for your home area, including cable or commercial. If you register—it's free—your tailored listings will remain for the next time you log on. You can read features and columns, keep track of the soaps, and even chat in realtime with TV stars.

Ultimate TV

www.ultimatetv.com

You can design your own TV grid for your viewing area, read the latest news or gossip about your favorite stars, participate in online chats, and even take a poll. Do a quick search for your favorite program. If you are bored with American TV, you can visit hundreds of other countries at the click of a mouse. (You'd better have a huge satellite dish, though.) Yup, even all you want to know about your favorite soaps is here. If you're a couch potato, this is a hot potato for you. Figure 10.9 shows how you can use Ultimate TV to keep track of your favorite TV stars and shows.

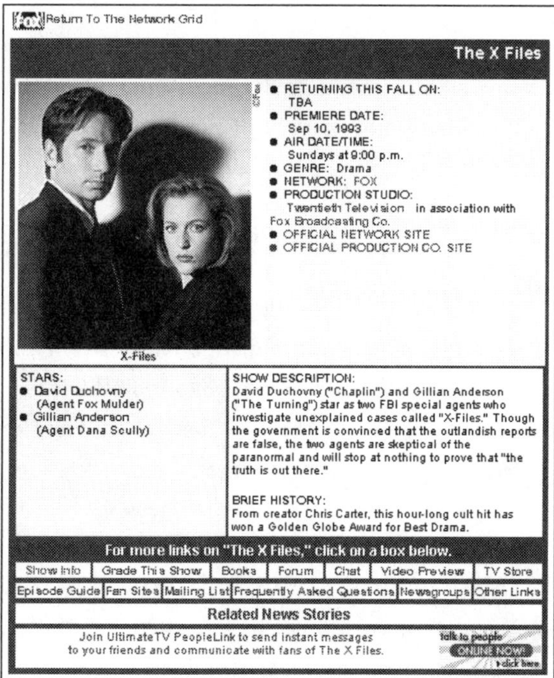

Figure 10.9
Ultimate TV.

Movies

What was the name of that movie star opposite Bogart in *Casablanca*? Finding this and other interesting movie trivia is easy.

The Hollywood Reporter

www.hollywoodreporter.com

If you cannot get enough news and rumors about the movie industry, check out the online edition of the famous *Hollywood Reporter*.

The Internet Movie Database

www.imdb.com

Read about reviews, previews, openings, recent box office ratings, and industry news. A searchable database lets you search on a variety of criteria such as title, cast, and character name. You can even add your own reviews. TV is covered as well. Very little about movies isn't covered here.

Mainstream News

Getting your fix of the daily news only a few years ago meant reading your morning paper or listening to TV or the radio. You didn't have much of a choice either. You were spoon-fed what the national or local media considered news. In some cities, where only one newspaper serves the community, you often read slanted conservative or liberal views, depending on the publisher.

More than 3,000 newspapers from around the world are online. There are hundreds more sources from alternative news services, wire services, and even freelance journalists. Thousands of ezines (electronic magazines) are available for free, not to mention mainstream magazines such as *Time, Newsweek, National Geographic,* and others. You can find the mainstream newspapers such as *The New York Times, Wall Street Journal,* and *Boston Globe* as well. In fact, you never have to buy a newspaper again; fire up your Web browser. The following news sites will fill your needs.

Daily National Mainstream Newspapers

There isn't a reason not to read the major national newspapers because many of them now feature online coverage.

Boston Globe

www.bostonglobe.com

No registration required: Just log on and start reading about Bean Town.

The New York Times

www.nytimes.com

The *New York Times* asks you to register for no charge. Here, you can read the top news and just about all the departments you can find in the print version. You can even get your news from media institutions like the *New York Times* online, as Figure 10.10 shows.

The Washington Post

www.washingtonpost.com

If you want to know what is going on in the nation's capital, read the online version of the paper that broke the Watergate scandal.

USA Today

www.usatoday.com

The paper that claims to be the nation's daily is here for you to read in living color.

DISCOVER BROKERAGE

CLICK HERE

The New York Times

ON THE WEB

NYC Weather 44° F

MONDAY, DECEMBER 14, 1998 | Site Updated 1:00 AM

QUICK NEWS
PAGE ONE PLUS
International
National/N.Y.
Politics
Business
Technology
Science
Sports
Weather
Opinion
Arts/Living
Automobiles
Books
Diversions
Job Market
Learning
Real Estate
Travel
SITE INDEX
FOR LISTINGS, VISIT

PRESIDENT. FACING VOTE, DENIES PERJURY AND SAYS HE WON'T QUIT

Unable to escape the constitutional crisis engulfing his Presidency, the President fielded questions about his own fate in Israel on Sunday. Go to Article

Many Republicans Don't See Political Fallout for 2000 Vote

Prominent Republicans, some of whom complained that their leaders badly mishandled the White House scandal all year long, now say the party's march toward impeachment would cause no lasting political damage. Go to Article

Carnegie Hall Expanding With Underground Space

Carnegie Hall is turning a subterranean recital hall from 1891 into a high-tech performance space for small operas and other productions. Go to Article

In Israel, President Clinton laid a Wye River stone on the grave of Yitzhak Rabin, the assasinated Prime Minister. Go to Article

TECHNOLOGY
Analysis: If Microsoft Loses Case, Remedies Are Thorny

SPORTS
Jets Beat Miami; Giants Upset

Figure 10.10
New York Times online.

National Magazines

Magazines give a different slant on the news because they usually have more time to research a story. Several of the leading magazines now provide free access to their major features, and a few will provide extra material for a subscription.

Consumer Reports

www.consumerreports.org/index.html

Here is the electronic version of this excellent consumer magazine. Find out ratings for almost anything you want to buy.

National Geographic

www.nationalgeographic.com/main.html

Read stories, participate in online forums, and more from this magazine that brings the world to you.

Time Magazine

www.pathfinder.com/time/

This weekly turned daily online gives you a great deal of analysis on the day's issues.

U.S. News & World Report (Online Version)

www.usnews.com/usnews/home.htm

This is another long-time news magazine with an online presence.

National Radio

You can listen to radio streamed live or archived.

ABC News

www.realaudio.com/contentp/abc.html

Using RealAudio, you can listen to the hourly news.

National Public Radio (NPR)

www.npr.org

National Public Radio has a great site here. News every hour and favorites such as All Things Considered, Morning Edition, and Talk of the Nation are available using RealAudio.

News Wire Services

Most breaking stories still come from the national wire services.

CNN Interactive

www.cnn.com

The number one trusted news agency, CNN offers this interactive Web site, which includes text and audio.

Reuters

www.reuters.com/index.html

One of the premier wire services offers this Web site, where you can read the latest news.

Worldwide News Sources

If you are a news junkie, the following site will link you to worldwide news sources.

Newslink

www.newslink.org/menu.html

This site lists thousands of news publications and media outlets from around the world, as well as original writings related to the media.

Send An Electronic Postcard

I find it pure fun to send friends a nice-looking electronic postcard of a rare butterfly or a colorful Monet.

Electronic Postcard

http://persona.www.media.mit.edu/Postcards/

Want to send a friend a postcard without postage? You can from this site. Choose from many categories of graphic postcards. Just fill out the postcards you choose and type the recipients' (email) addresses, and they will receive email about how to pick up their postcards.

Appendix
Worldwide Domains

Top-level domains from around the world are listed in Table 1. Now you can be sure of where a particular Web site or email is from. When in doubt, check this list.

Table 1 Worldwide top-level domains.

Domain	Country
AD	Andorra
AE	United Arab Emirates
AF	Afghanistan
AG	Antigua and Barbuda
AI	Anguilla
AL	Albania
AM	Armenia
AN	Netherlands Antilles
AO	Angola
AQ	Antarctica
AR	Argentina
AS	American Samoa
AT	Austria
AU	Australia
AW	Aruba
AZ	Azerbaijan
BA	Bosnia-Herzegovina
BB	Barbados
BD	Bangladesh

(continued)

Table 1 Worldwide top-level domains (continued).

Domain	Country
BE	Belgium
BF	Burkina Faso
BG	Bulgaria
BH	Bahrain
BI	Burundi
BJ	Benin
BM	Bermuda
BN	Brunei Darussalam
BO	Bolivia
BR	Brazil
BS	Bahamas
BT	Bhutan
BV	Bouvet Island
BW	Botswana
BY	Belarus
BZ	Belize
CA	Canada
CC	Cocos (Keeling) Islands
CF	Central African Republic
CG	Congo
CH	Switzerland
CI	Ivory Coast
CK	Cook Islands
CL	Chile
CM	Cameroon
CN	China
CO	Colombia
CR	Costa Rica
CS	Czechoslovakia
CU	Cuba
CV	Cape Verde
CX	Christmas Island

(continued)

Table 1 Worldwide top-level domains (continued).

Domain	Country
CY	Cyprus
CZ	Czech Republic
DE	Germany
DJ	Djibouti
DK	Denmark
DM	Dominica
DO	Dominican Republic
DZ	Algeria
EC	Ecuador
EE	Estonia
EG	Egypt
EH	Western Sahara
ES	Spain
ET	Ethiopia
FI	Finland
FJ	Fiji
FK	Falkland Islands (Malvinas)
FM	Micronesia
FO	Faroe Islands
FR	France
FX	France (European Territory)
GA	Gabon
GB	Great Britain (U.K.)
GD	Grenada
GE	Georgia
GH	Ghana
GI	Gibraltar
GL	Greenland
GP	Guadeloupe (French)
GQ	Equatorial Guinea
GF	Guyana (French)

(continued)

Table 1 Worldwide top-level domains (continued).

Domain	Country
GM	Gambia
GN	Guinea
GR	Greece
GT	Guatemala
GU	Guam (US)
GW	Guinea Bissau
GY	Guyana
HK	Hong Kong
HM	Heard and McDonald Islands
HN	Honduras
HR	Croatia
HT	Haiti
HU	Hungary
ID	Indonesia
IE	Ireland
IL	Israel
IN	India
IO	British Indian Ocean Territory
IQ	Iraq
IR	Iran
IS	Iceland
IT	Italy
JM	Jamaica
JO	Jordan
JP	Japan
KE	Kenya
KG	Kirgistan
KH	Cambodia
KI	Kiribati
KM	Comoros
KN	Saint Kitts Nevis Anguilla

(continued)

Table 1 Worldwide top-level domains (continued).

Domain	Country
KP	North Korea
KR	South Korea
KW	Kuwait
KY	Cayman Islands
KZ	Kazakhstan
LA	Laos
LB	Lebanon
LC	Saint Lucia
LI	Liechtenstein
LK	Sri Lanka
LR	Liberia
LS	Lesotho
LT	Lithuania
LU	Luxembourg
LV	Latvia
LY	Libya
MA	Morocco
MC	Monaco
MD	Moldavia
MG	Madagascar
MH	Marshall Islands
ML	Mali
MM	Myanmar
MN	Mongolia
MO	Macau
MP	Northern Mariana Islands
MQ	Martinique (French)
MR	Mauritania
MS	Montserrat
MT	Malta
MU	Mauritius

(continued)

Table 1 Worldwide top-level domains (continued).

Domain	Country
MV	Maldives
MW	Malawi
MX	Mexico
MY	Malaysia
MZ	Mozambique
NA	Namibia
NC	New Caledonia (French)
NE	Niger
NF	Norfolk Island
NG	Nigeria
NI	Nicaragua
NL	Netherlands
NO	Norway
NP	Nepal
NR	Nauru
NT	Neutral Zone
NU	Niue
NZ	New Zealand
OM	Oman
PA	Panama
PE	Peru
PF	Polynesia (French)
PG	Papua New
PH	Philippines
PK	Pakistan
PL	Poland
PM	Saint Pierre and Miquelon
PN	Pitcairn
PT	Portugal
PR	Puerto Rico (U.S.)
PW	Palau

(continued)

Table 1 Worldwide top-level domains (continued).

Domain	Country
PY	Paraguay
QA	Qatar
RE	Reunion (French)
RO	Romania
RU	Russian Federation
RW	Rwanda
SA	Saudi Arabia
SB	Solomon Islands
SC	Seychelles
SD	Sudan
SE	Sweden
SG	Singapore
SH	Saint Helena
SI	Slovenia
SJ	Svalbard and Jan Mayen Islands
SK	Slovak Republic
SL	Sierra Leone
SM	San Marino
SN	Senegal
SO	Somalia
SR	Suriname
ST	Saint Tome and Principe
SU	Former Soviet Union
SV	El Salvador
SY	Syria
SZ	Swaziland
TC	Turks and Caicos Islands
TD	Chad
TF	French Southern Territory
TG	Togo
TH	Thailand

(continued)

Table 1 Worldwide top-level domains (continued).

Domain	Country
TJ	Tajikistan
TK	Tokelau
TM	Turkmenistan
TN	Tunisia
TO	Tonga
TP	East Timor
TR	Turkey
TT	Trinidad and Tobago
TV	Tuvalu
TW	Taiwan
TZ	Tanzania
UA	Ukraine
UG	Uganda
UK	United Kingdom
UM	U.S. Minor Outlying Islands
US	United States of America
UY	Uruguay
UZ	Uzbekistan
VA	Vatican City State
VC	Saint Vincent and Grenadines
VE	Venezuela
VG	Virgin Islands (British)
VI	Virgin Islands (U.S.)
VN	Vietnam
VU	Vanuatu
WF	Wallis and Futuna Islands
WS	Samoa
YE	Yemen
YU	Yugoslavia
ZA	South Africa
ZM	Zambia
ZR	Zaire
ZW	Zimbabwe

New Domains?

Recently, seven new domains have been approved, although not implemented yet. They are called Generic Top-Level Domains (gTLDs). The term "generic" TLD is used by The International Ad Hoc Committee (IAHC), a consortium of international organizations that set technical standards for the Internet, to refer to a Top-Level Domain in which any entity from any country may register, whether or not it has an international character, without having to conform to any particular criteria.

The New Names?

.ARTS—for entities emphasizing cultural and entertainment activities

.FIRM—for businesses, or firms

.INFO—for entities providing information services

.NOM—for those wishing individual or personal nomenclature

.REC—for entities emphasizing recreation/entertainment activities

.SHOP—for businesses offering goods to purchase (initially introduced as .STORE)

.WEB—for entities emphasizing activities related to the World Wide Web

Glossary

Here are some terms you will read or hear about relating to computers, your iMac, and the Internet.

ADB (Apple Desktop Bus)—A port used by most Macs to communicate with peripheral devices such as a mouse, keyboards, and so on. This port has been replaced by USB on your iMac.

Alert box—A rectangular box that pops up on your monitor when the Mac needs to tell you something important, usually bad news.

Apple menu—The menu on the top-left corner of your iMac that contains desk accessories, the Chooser, and other useful mini-applications.

Applet—The name for an application written in the Java programming language that works on a Web page.

Application—Usually refers to a software program, not the files it creates. ClarisWorks is an application.

Archie—An early search tool for the Internet. Also, an early cartoon strip.

ARPANET (Advanced Research Projects Agency Internetwork)—
The genesis of the Internet. Developed in the late 1960s by the U.S. Department of Defense, at the beginning of the Cold War. The idea was that ARPANET would be a redundant communication network able to survive a nuclear war and allow politicians and the military to keep in contact. Good thing it wasn't tested.

ASCII (American Standard Code for Information Interchange)—The letters and numbers you type, which all computers worldwide recognize based on each letter or number consisting of 8 unique bits. There are 128 standard ASCII codes, each of which can be represented by a 7 digit binary number: 0000000 through 1111111.

Asymmetric Digital Subscriber Line (ADSL)—A new technology that will transmit communications over existing twisted-pair copper phone lines from 1.5 to 9 megabits-per-second. It means you will have very fast Internet access at home.

Backing up—Making copies of your software and data files off your hard drive onto floppies or other removable media and storing it in a safe place.

Bandwidth—The term used to explain how much data can be sent through a connection, measured in bits-per-second. Your iMac modem can send 56,000 bits-per-second to another modem. Think of bandwidth as a pipe. The larger the pipe, the more water that can flow through it at once.

Beta—The stage in software development that lets the widest number of people test it to work out software bugs.

Binhex (binary hexadecimal)—A method for your iMac to convert non-text files (non-ASCII, or binary) into ASCII, straight-text files. The Internet can only handle ASCII.

Bit—A binary 1 or 0, the smallest unit of data. Recycled electrons.

Bondi blue—Another word for teal.

Bookmark—A shortcut or favorite Web site stored on your Web browser.

Boolean—George Boole (1815-64), an English mathematician, founded symbolic logic that is used in database queries. AND, OR, and BUT used in conjunction with keywords will give a more refined search for the information you are seeking.

Booting up—Starting your computer. Rebooting is when you restart a computer after it is on.

BPS (bits per second)—How fast your data is moved from one place to another. See also *bandwidth*.

Browser—A special software program that lets you use the World Wide Web, the multimedia interface of the Internet.

Byte—8 bits.

Cam—Short for camera. A video camera that can be attached to your computer so you can see people and places on the Internet.

CD-ROM (Compact Disk Read Only Memory)—You use a CD-ROM to install your software onto your hard drive. You can take information off the CD, but you can't put information on it.

Chooser—A desk accessory that lets you select something on a network such as a printer, scanner, network device, fax modem, and so on.

Clipboard—The place in memory where things are stored when you perform a cut or copy action. It is temporary storage that holds only one item at a time.

Close box—See the small square in the upper-left corner of the window? Click it.

Compression software—Software such as StuffIt that shrinks a file, or files, into one smaller file. This reduces space needed for storage on a hard drive or reduces the amount of time needed to send a file over the Internet.

Control Panel—A small application file that lets you control a look or action on your iMac.

Cookie—A text file stored on your computer. A Web server can look at it for information such as the last time you visited a site, your password to a site, and other information. It is information sent by your browser to a Web server.

Cursor—The cursor looks like a capital "I". It blinks after you place it with a click of the mouse.

Cyberspace—The collective word for the Internet and everything associated with it. Author William Gibson in his novel *Neuromancer* created the term.

Daisy chain—Connecting more than one computer peripheral.

Database—A collection of information that can be searchable using keywords.

Desk accessory (DA)—A mini-application that appears on the Apple menu.

Domain Name Service (DNS) address—The name given to anyone registering his or her computer or network on the Internet; the type of Internet site. The domain belongs to a certain category (.com, .org, and so on). You can have many computers with the top-level part of the domain address, but each computer still must have its own unique address.

Downloading—Taking data from a remote computer and bringing it to your computer over the Internet.

DPI (dots per inch)—A measure of resolution on a printer or scanner. The more dots per inch, the more detailed and smooth the print. Laser writers usually have better resolution than ink jet printers.

Easter eggs—Hidden features placed by programmers in their software applications. Sometimes displayed as secret messages, cute graphics, and other interesting bits.

Email—Electronic mail over the Internet.

Emailer—A software program that lets you send and receive electronic mail. Outlook Express is the emailer that came with your iMac.

Emoticon—A special symbol created by characters on your keyboard that represents a feeling. You can read it by turning your head. **:)**

Ethernet—A fast networking technology that lets you connect other iMacs and send information between them at a rate of up to 100 megabits-per-second.

Extension—A file located in the extension folder in the system folder. Extensions modify the behavior of the Mac operating system and are usually small programs that let the iMac work with particular software or hardware. They also can cause a lot of conflicts. Extensions were once called inits.

FAQ (Frequently Asked Question)—A summary of questions and their answers put together for new users on Usenet newsgroups or the Internet.

File—A single unit of data that is either an application (such as a word processor) or the product of one (such as a document).

Flame—A derogatory comment or series of comments made between people on the Internet. When more than two people become involved, you get a flame war.

Floppy drive—A device you use to store data on called floppy disks. The iMac does not have one.

Folder—A digital place to hold digital files.

FTP—(File Transfer Protocol)—A process that allows you to access another computer, grab a file, and bring it back to your computer or to send a file to another computer.

GIF (Graphic Interchange Format)—The most common format for graphic files on the Internet. GIF images are not as good as JPEG images, the other common format.

Gigabits per second (Gbps)—1,073,741,824 bits per second.

Gigabyte (GB)—1,024 megabytes (MB).

Gopher—An early search tool that is menu driven for finding Internet resources on FTP sites.

GUI (graphical user interface)—The type of interface on your iMac operating system.

Hard drive—A storage device in your iMac that contains all your files. Your iMac has a 4 gigabyte hard drive.

Hit—The result of a search on the Internet. The links that a search engine returns are called hits.

Home page—Normally refers to the first Web page your browser displays when it starts.

Host machine—A computer on the Internet that serves as a machine for delivering Web pages, email, or Usenet news.

HTML (Hypertext Markup Language)—The formatting in a text file that lets a Web server display its content. Every Web page must be in HTML format.

HTTP (Hypertext Transport Protocol)—The language of the World Wide Web. It's how Web servers and Web documents interact.

Hub—A device that contains one or more USB ports so you can connect more peripherals to your iMac.

Hyperlink—Underlined words or phases on a Web page that, when clicked, will take you to another Web page. It's a jumping-off point.

IMAP (Internet Message Access Protocol)—A newer email protocol.

Init—A small file that loads into the memory of the iMac when it starts and adds features or hooks into other programs. Inits are now called extensions.

Initializing—Erasing the directory of a storage medium so that new data can be written over the old data. Do not initialize your hard drive by mistake.

Inside the Internet—An Internet radio program that airs every Saturday from 1:00 to 2:00 P.M. EST on **www.wrow.com**.

Internet—The global network of millions of computers and computer networks that speak the same language.

Internet domain—A group of computer networks that share a broad category, such as commercial companies sharing the .com domain, educational institutions sharing the .edu domain, and so on.

IP (Internet Protocol) address—The numeric version of your machine's Internet address. Every computer on the Internet must have its own IP address.

IRC (Internet Relay Chat)—The protocol for live realtime chat with other people on the Internet. Many IRC servers around the world are linked to each other. You can create a public or private channel to carry on a discussion with more than one person.

IrDA (Infrared Data Association) protocol—A protocol that lets you beam information to and from your iMac using the infrared sensor in the front of the computer.

ISP (Internet Service Provider)—Your online connection to the Internet. You usually pay a monthly fee for unlimited access.

Java—Computer language for the Internet that is computer platform independent.

JPEG (Joint Photographic Experts Group)—JPEG is the other common graphic file format on the Internet. It's good for displaying photographs.

Kilobyte (KB)—1,024 bits.

LDAP (Lightweight Directory Access Protocol)—Used to provide online directories over the Internet.

Listserv—A software program for creating and maintaining mailing lists or a slang term for a mailing list. Listserv is now used generally for all mailing list software. Listserv is actually a registered trademark of L-Soft International, Inc, makers of Listserv, the software.

MacBinary—A special format for storing Mac files on another computer.

Mailing list—A public discussion group on the Internet distributed by email.

Megabits per second (Mbps)—1,048,576 bits-per-second.

Megabyte (MB)—1,024 kilobytes.

Megahertz (MHz)—A measure of a computer microprocessor's clock speed.

MIDI (Musical Instrument Digital Interface)—Enables you to connect musical instruments to your computer.

MIME (Multipurpose Internet Mail Extensions)—The standard protocol for attaching binary files (graphics, spreadsheets, Word documents, sound files, and so on) to Internet mail messages.

Modem—Short for modulator/demodulator. An electronic device that translates digital information from your computer to sound and sends it over the phone to another modem, which performs the reverse process.

Mouse—An input device for moving within your iMac's interface.

Netiquette—Online etiquette. It's very important that you learn it.

Network—Two or more computers connected so they can share resources.

News—Slang for Usenet newsgroups.

Newsgroup—A public discussion group on Usenet.

Newsreader—A special software application that lets you join, read, and manage Usenet newsgroups. Outlook Express is a newsreader.

NNTP (Internetwork News Transport Protocol)—How Usenet newsgroups travel along the Internet.

OCR (Optical Character Reading)—Software that lets you scan a text document and make it a live document ready for editing.

Offline—Not online.

Pixel—Short for picture element. The dots that make up an image on your monitor. They are square, not round.

Plug-in—A piece of software that adds special features to a software program that the program normally does not offer. Plug-ins for Web browsers are common.

POP (Post Office Protocol or Point of Presence)—Post Office Protocol refers to the way your email software (Outlook Express, which came with your iMac) gets mail from the mail server. Point of Presence, the other POP, is a location where your ISP can connect, usually with dial-up phone lines.

Post—To submit an article on a newsgroup or to send email.

PPP (Point-to-Point Protocol)—The instructions that travel between your computer and your Internet service provider to make your computer think it's on the Internet.

PRAM (Parameter Random Access Memory)—A small amount of live memory kept alive by a battery that remembers the date and other Control Panel settings.

Preferences—Files created by most software applications, including the Finder, that store default settings.

Printer—A hardware device that gives you printed output from your computer, usually on paper.

Printer driver—A software program that interfaces your printer to your iMac so you can print.

Protocol—Special rules for computers to follow so they can communicate and share information.

RAM (Random Access Memory)—Volatile memory used by your iMac computer and video that provides temporary storage of information.

Reset switch—The hole in the right panel of your iMac between the modem and Ethernet ports that lets you restart your iMac.

Server—Another name for a computer that your ISP uses for connecting you to the Internet.

Signature—A few lines of text or artwork after your sign-off on an email message.

SLIP (Serial Line Internet Protocol)—An early protocol for using a regular telephone and a modem to connect to the Internet. SLIP is being replaced by PPP.

Smiley—See *emoticon*.

SMTP (Simple Mail Transfer Protocol)—The way email gets routed around the Internet.

Software—The programs you use on computer hardware.

Spamming—Sending the same post to many newsgroups at the same time. Also, sending the same message to more than a few email addresses. Spamming is something to avoid doing.

Superdisk—A replacement for the 1.4MB floppy drive that did not come with your iMac.

Surfing—Using your Web browser to visit more than one Web site on the Internet.

System folder—The "engine" of your iMac. The system folder contains the system, Finder, and other files that make your iMac work in harmony with the computer—and you.

TCP/IP (Transmission Control Protocol/Internet Protocol)—The language every computer on the Internet must use to communicate with each other.

Telnet—The ability to remotely log on to a computer terminal, anywhere in the world, as though you were sitting in front of it.

Terabyte (TB)—1,024 gigabytes.

The MESH—My Web site at **www.themesh.com**.

TIFF (Tagged Image File Format)—Another graphic format that is very large and contains the most amount of data, which means great resolution. However, TIFF files take a while to download on the Internet.

Tilde (Can you say till-da?)—That little squiggly mark (~) on some URLs. You can find it on the key next to the number one. It had to be put to use for something.

Unix—A computer operating system for techies. It's the most common operating system for servers on the Internet. Usenet started on Unix computers.

Uploading—Taking data from your iMac and putting it on a remote computer somewhere on the Internet for others to access it.

URL (Uniform Resource Locator)—The accepted way to give anyone an address of a destination on the Internet.

USB (Universal Serial Bus)—Apple's fast serial communications to connect peripherals to your iMac.

Usenet—A distributed news network older than the Internet. Discussions are sent as articles and are called newsgroups. You need a special newsreader to participate.

User ID—Your driver's license for the Internet. It is the name you will use to identify yourself to the millions of people on the Internet. Make it easy to remember.

Virtual memory—Using a piece of the hard drive to trick the computer into thinking it is RAM.

Virus—A nasty little program that can eat your data or destroy your hardware.

Virus checker—A software program that eats viruses.

VRAM (Video Random Access Memory)—Fast memory that your monitor uses for storing an image before it is displayed.

Web—The nickname for the World Wide Web, the multimedia interface for the Internet.

Web browser—A software application that lets you explore the World Wide Web. Netscape and Microsoft browsers come with your iMac.

Word processor—An application to let you write letters, books, or any other text creation. ClarisWorks has a built-in word processor.

World Wide Web (WWW)—The multimedia interface of the Internet. Allows the integration of text, video, graphics, audio, and animation into a hypertext environment.

Index

B

C

D

E

F

G

H

I

J

K

L

M

N

Q

R

S

T

U

V

W

X

Y

Z